GUIDEBOOK TO COMMUNITY CONSULTING

Guidebook to Community Consulting provides advice for people interested in starting or growing a career in community consulting. Drawing on the authors' years of experience as community consultants, it offers a wealth of practical guidance to anyone considering or establishing a successful career serving and empowering communities. It includes guidance about the personal qualities, values, and technical skills needed; how to start a consulting practice; how to collaborate with colleagues; and, most importantly, how to collaborate with communities. Practical advice and tips are motivated by core guiding principles and goals including an understanding of consulting as a partnership between consultants and communities; decoloniality; anti-racism; and equity. The text is animated with illustrative anecdotes and lessons gained from real-world experience.

Susan M. Wolfe, chief executive officer of Susan Wolfe and Associates, LLC, has been working with communities for over thirty-six years. Her award-winning work includes research, evaluation, coalition development, advocacy, needs assessments, and strategic planning. She has published her work in journals, books, and blogs, and regularly teaches workshops and gives presentations to professional audiences nationally and internationally.

Ann Webb Price, president of Community Evaluation Solutions, Inc., works with community coalitions, nonprofit organizations, and foundations that focus on systems change. She conducts workshops throughout the country on coalition development and evaluation. She has a podcast called *Community Possibilities* where she speaks to community leaders doing the hard work of community change.

Guidebook to Community Consulting

A COLLABORATIVE APPROACH

Susan M. Wolfe

Susan Wolfe and Associates, LLC

Ann Webb Price

Community Evaluation Solutions, Inc.

Shaftesbury Road, Cambridge CB2 8EA, United Kingdom

One Liberty Plaza, 20th Floor, New York, NY 10006, USA

477 Williamstown Road, Port Melbourne, VIC 3207, Australia

314–321, 3rd Floor, Plot 3, Splendor Forum, Jasola District Centre,
New Delhi – 110025, India

103 Penang Road, #05–06/07, Visioncrest Commercial, Singapore 238467

Cambridge University Press is part of Cambridge University Press & Assessment,
a department of the University of Cambridge.

We share the University's mission to contribute to society through the pursuit of
education, learning and research at the highest international levels of excellence.

www.cambridge.org
Information on this title: www.cambridge.org/9781009244336

DOI: 10.1017/9781009244329

First published 2023

A catalogue record for this publication is available from the British Library.

Library of Congress Cataloging-in-Publication Data
Names: Wolfe, Susan M., author. | Price, Ann Webb, author.
Title: Guidebook to community consulting : a collaborative approach /
Susan M. Wolfe, Ann Webb Price.
Description: Cambridge, United Kingdom ; New York, NY : Cambridge
University Press, 2023. | Includes bibliographical references and index.
Identifiers: LCCN 2022044514 | ISBN 9781009244336 (hardback) |
ISBN 9781009244329 (ebook)
Subjects: LCSH: Community psychology. | Community organization. |
Community development. | Consultants.
Classification: LCC RA790.55 .W65 2023 | DDC 362.2–dc23/eng/20221223
LC record available at https://lccn.loc.gov/2022044514

ISBN 978-1-009-24433-6 Hardback
ISBN 978-1-009-24430-5 Paperback

For my husband, Charles Hipkins. Because of his support and encouragement, I was able to open my consulting business and engage in the work that mattered to me in a way that is consistent with my values.

—SUSAN

For my husband, Dan Price, and the family we are building and for the family of choice I gathered along the way. Each in their own way, helped create the community I needed to feel safe and loved.

—ANN

Contents

Figures

Tables

Acknowledgments

We need to acknowledge all of those who supported us as we wrote this book.

Thank you to our publisher, Cambridge University Press. We are grateful to Stephen Acerra, the editor for psychology and neuroscience, for reaching out and initiating our relationship and for ushering us through the process from proposal to publication. Thanks also to Rowan Groat, editorial assistant, for the support and guidance she provided.

Thanks also go to the seven anonymous reviewers who read our original proposal and provided us with constructive feedback.

With gratitude, we thank our internal review team – Gabrielle Hawkins-Stewart, Akimi Smith, Kamaladevy Sivalingam, and Jessica Metcalfe. Each of our internal review team read every chapter and provided us with valuable edits and insights.

And finally, and most importantly, we acknowledge and thank all the community members, partners and collaborators, coalitions, and community-based organizations that have trusted us to collaborate with them. They have taught us the lessons we shared with you in this book. We hope you will benefit from the book and that the communities you serve will benefit as well.

1 Introduction

Let the tech firms and consulting firms build your skills, but be sure to ask
yourself, "Am I maximizing my impact?" "Am I living up to my values?"
—Wendy Kopp (McNamara, 2015)

*In Chapter 1, we define community, consulting, and other concepts that inform
and influence our work as community consultants. We explain how community
consulting is different from other types of consulting, describe the purpose of the
book, and provide guidance for readers in making the most use of the information provided.*

"I want to be a **consultant**." If we had a nickel for every time someone told
us that, we could retire to a tropical island. This statement is almost always
followed by "Can you give me any tips?" or "How do I get started?" or "How
do you get your clients?"

A few years ago, while attending the national conference of the American
Evaluation Association (AEA), we (Ann and Susan) were talking about how
often people asked us for advice about consulting and it suddenly occurred to
us that we could fill a whole book with the answer to that question! There are
already excellent books that talk about how to start and grow an evaluation
consulting business (see one of our favorites, Barrington, 2012). But we felt
a need to delve into the content of consulting, whether you are doing it as
a business or doing it as part of another type of job. There is so much more
involved in working with **communities** than setting up a business, and we believe
that many individuals whose job titles do not include the term consultant
also fulfill this role. We wrote *this* book for community psychologists, social
workers, public health professionals, applied sociologists and anthropologists,
other psychologists, evaluators, and individuals who want to consult in communities – either as an employee at an organization or independently within
their own business. Additionally, we believe an equity focus is required when
working in communities and is a core feature of community consulting.

We want to be clear about two things. First, the information we provide in this book comes partly from the literature on communities and consulting and partly from our own collective experience. Together we have over sixty years of experience consulting in communities. Second, we are both based in the United States, and so our examples and much of our guidance is most applicable to consultants working there. However, Susan has done some international work and found that many of the foundations that we describe and the guidance we share can often be applied to international work, especially in Westernized nations.

As community consultants there have been times when we feel as if we have conquered the world, and times when we look at events or a project and wonder what ever possessed us to engage in this work in the first place. Even the most seasoned consultants have occasions when things go terribly wrong, or projects that just do not work out the way we expected. In fact, our colleague Kylie Hutchinson published a whole book about failures that describes the mistakes made by some of the most prominent members in the field of evaluation (Hutchinson, 2019). Throughout this book, in addition to the informational content, we share our success stories and some stories of when we were not so successful. Our stories will highlight how the level of planning and thinking things through, difficulties with others, and resource limitations have affected our consulting and community work. Our success stories will highlight what worked well and what made these projects successful.

We start this chapter by sharing the purpose of this book and then explain how *we* define **community** and consulting. We then describe our academic background and how that is related to what we mean when we talk about community consulting. Next, we describe how we distinguish community consulting from more traditional forms of consulting. Finally, we finish this chapter with information about some ways you may use this book.

1.1 The Purpose of This Book

The purpose of this book is to provide professionals and students with a comprehensive source of information and guidance for consulting with communities. The skills and competencies described are applicable for individuals who want to set up their own consulting business, as well as those who serve in a community consulting role as an employee of an organization. The book will provide information about the foundations needed and what distinguishes community consulting from other types of consulting, such as program evaluation, strategic planning, and organizational development services. We also explain the range of employment settings where professionals apply the foundations we describe. Finally, we describe the soft skills such as personal qualities and hard skills such as coalition development, participatory research, or resource development.

1.2 How to Use This Book

Before we share ideas of how you might use this book, we would like to point out a few key features of each chapter. Each chapter begins by sharing a summary of the content. Then, at the end of each chapter you will find the key takeaway points. At the end of this book, we provide a glossary with definitions for words that have been **bolded** in the text, a reference list for all our sources, an appendix with a professional development planning tool specifically for community consulting, and an appendix with resources where you can find more information about selected topics.

You can use this book in a variety of ways. If you haven't done community-based work before, this book will provide guidance that will help you and the community that you partner with to have a more positive experience in your collaboration. We hope that it will help you avoid missteps.

If you teach classes that require community-based work such as evaluation courses, public health or social work interventions, or community psychology, you might find some chapters helpful as course readings for your students. This book is written for practitioners, avoiding academese language, so that students may find practical advice presented in an informative and accessible way.

You may find this book useful as a reference. Sometimes during community consultations situations arise where it can be helpful to have something to read that will spark a solution to a challenge. We present information that is useful across situations and contexts throughout this volume.

We often read books with content that we are familiar with, but we find that sometimes it helps to be reminded of or to expand how we think about the content of the reading. Our thinking about how we approach communities and work with them has shifted over the years as we have learned and embraced new perspectives introduced in academic literature, by our colleagues, at conferences, or through our own experience. It is our hope that this book will be a resource for you, expand your perspective, and help you think of your community work in a new way. If you haven't worked in a community, or maybe haven't done so in a while, we are hopeful that you will find some helpful information to remind or guide you.

1.3 What Is Community Practice?

1.3.1 Our Roots: Community Psychology

In the interest of full disclosure, we will admit up front that we are both community psychologists and much of this book is informed to a considerable extent by **community psychology** goals, approaches, and practice competencies (Dalton & Wolfe, 2012). At the start of this chapter, we presented a quote by Wendy Kopp about building your skills. Her quote is relevant in that it specifically guides students to go beyond approaching their work using only their technical skills. Kopp also stresses the need to incorporate values into their work.

This said, we will start by answering the question that is frequently asked of us when we tell people we are community psychologists, "What is community psychology?" The definition provided by Nelson and Prilleltensky (2010, p. 23) is "the sub discipline of psychology that is concerned with understanding people in context of their communities, the prevention of the problems of living, the celebration of human diversity, and the pursuit of social justice through social action." In plain English, it is the branch of psychology that focuses on preventing problems and promoting health and mental health by changing communities and **systems** instead of focusing on changing people. We change communities and systems by gathering information through research and **needs and resources assessments**, evaluating what we and others are doing, and by promoting **social justice**, **equity**, and social action through partnering with community members.

In 2006, the Society for Community Research and Action (SCRA) Practice Council, whose mission is to expand the visibility, reach, and impact of community psychology practice, articulated the first official definition of "**community psychology practice**." We are sharing this definition because it most accurately describes our approach to community practice and states that community psychology practice aims "to strengthen the capacity of communities to meet the needs of constituents and help them to realize their dreams in order to promote well-being, social justice, economic equity and self-determination through systems, organizational and/or individual change" (Julian, 2006, p. 68).

Many of the guidelines we provide are rooted in **critical community psychology** (CCP) and its stated principles (Angelique & Kyle, 2002). First, CCP advocates for full **collaboration** and **partnerships** with communities. When we talk about community practice, we really mean working "with" communities rather than working "on" them. While we may refer to them as "clients" at times (being consistent with the language of consulting), we view them as our collaborators and partners. This perspective leads us to take a **participatory approach** in our work. It also requires that we work with communities that we are invited into and respect community members' wishes if they want to uninvite us. Additionally, it means that we allow community members to guide our work and leave them with full decision-making authority.

Second, we promote methodological diversity. We recognize the need for and value of gathering numbers and we also believe that to really understand people and their communities we need to use **qualitative methods** as well. We will go into depth later about the need to decolonize our methods by honoring the wishes and traditions of communities while allowing communities to define the scope of inquiry and questions asked.

Third, we acknowledge the role that inequitable conditions – classism, racism, sexism, and ageism to name a few – play in communities. At the same time, we acknowledge our own positions and privileges as white, cisgender women.

1.3.2 SCRA and AEA: Our Professional Homes

We both have membership in two organizations that provide us with our underlying vision, goals, and practice principles. First is SCRA, which is our community psychology "home." We embrace SCRA's vision, and its principles underlie our approach to consulting in communities. We suggest that you check SCRA's websites at www.scra27.org and www.communitypsychology .com to learn more about their vision, principles, and community psychology as a field.

We have found that SCRA's vision and underlying principles are applicable to consulting in communities and have practical applications that have facilitated our success with our consulting practices. Our commitment to empowerment means that our goal is to build organizational and community capacity rather than creating dependency and reliance upon our continued engagement. We respect diversity and promote social justice and equity. Our work includes attention to context as we use a **systems approach**. A systems approach, often using an ecological model, is one that considers the multiple levels of influence on individual behavior and communities. We share our knowledge and skills with our clients and acknowledge and honor the knowledge and skills they bring. Many of the organizations and communities we consult with find this refreshing after years of contracting consultants who maintain their distance and keep their processes shrouded in mystery, a model that results in ongoing dependence on the consultant.

Because so much of our work is evaluation, our second professional home is with the AEA, a professional association of over 7,000 evaluators with diverse academic backgrounds and training. Our evaluation work is guided by the AEA principles of systematic inquiry, competence, integrity/honesty, respect for people, and responsibilities for general and public welfare. Detailed information about the AEA and their principles can be found on the AEA website (www.eval.org).

1.4 Our Definitions

Before we begin, we want to offer our definitions of two of the most relevant terms used in this book: community and consultant, as well as the combined term community consultant. In addition to "formal" definitions found in dictionaries and the literature, we will define what we mean when we use these terms and how they apply to our work.

1.4.1 Community

Merriam-Webster Dictionary (n.d.b) defines community as follows:

> A unified body of individuals, such as: (1) the people with common interests living in a particular area; (b) a group of people with common characteristic or interest living together within a larger society; (c) a body of persons of common and especially professional interests scattered through a larger society; (d) a body of persons or nations having a common history or common social, economic, and political interests; (e) a group linked by a common policy; (f) an interacting population of various kinds of individuals in a common location; or (g) a state, commonwealth.

When we refer to community throughout this book, we are using the term in a way consistent with this definition of community.

This definition captures the full range of what might constitute a community and describes what we consider to be community in our work. Sometimes the communities we work with are geographically defined, but other times they are comprised of individuals with a similar interest or issue or a common characteristic. Most often, we are working with nonprofits, coalitions, and foundations that serve people who are marginalized and vulnerable by virtue of their race, economic status, gender, disability, or other factors. In these cases, we acknowledge the privilege we and the funding agencies hold and the need to prioritize the desires, hopes, and priorities of community members.

1.4.2 Consultant

Carol Lukas (2001, p. 3) defines consultation as "a temporary relationship to provide assistance to a person, group, organization, or community wanting to build their capacity, accomplish a task, or achieve a goal." There are several key components to this definition that are important. The first is that consulting is a temporary relationship. **Consultants** work with their clients for a limited amount of time, although in some cases this may be ongoing for as long as an organization has a grant or need. Another key component is that consultants work with individuals, groups, organizations, and communities, and not necessarily a single individual client. It is not necessarily a one-on-one relationship, which is especially true for community consultants. And finally, the purpose of a consultant's activities is to build capacity or achieve a goal.

1.4.3 Community Consultant

When we put these definitions together, we arrive at the definition of a **community consultant** we will use for this book: Someone who enters a long- or short-term relationship with a group of individuals to share knowledge, skills, and tools to build the group's capacity to reach a goal.

1.5 Community Consulting Is Interdisciplinary

While we are community psychologists, we most often work collaboratively with other disciplines. Community psychology is not a large field, and we usually find ourselves working with professionals from disciplines such as **applied sociology**, **evaluation**, **public health**, **applied social psychology**, **social work**, **public administration**, education, nursing, health care, and **applied anthropology**. There is overlap between the values and principles of community psychology and those of other health and social sciences – in other words, there is a focus on helping others, social change, diversity, equity, and social and health disparities. Even though our orientation is grounded in community psychology, readers from a variety of disciplinary backgrounds will find this book relevant and relatable.

The foundations we describe in this book originally began with the community psychology practice foundations as defined by the field in 2012,[1] which we found to have a lot in common with foundations and skills defined by other fields, such as public health and social work. Since our field and practice rooted in equity and social justice has evolved since those foundations were defined, we have expanded on and updated the skills and foundations for community consulting practice. The overlap in foundations and skills across disciplines suggests that consulting in communities is not the domain of one single profession. In fact, community consulting can be approached from a variety of perspectives, draw upon a range of tools, and, in our experience, is often most successful when an interdisciplinary team is engaged.

1.6 What Distinguishes Community Consulting from Other Types of Consulting?

We distinguish community consulting from other types of consulting. First, and foremost, what sets it apart is perceived accountability. In our experience with organizations, many individuals who they engaged as consultants considered themselves primarily accountable to the organization that contracted them. Community consultants are accountable to the members of the community who are most affected by the intervention, program, service, or strategy being implemented. Of course, we make sure we report to our clients, meet our deliverables, and give our clients what they ask for and need. But underneath it all, we feel most responsible to the individuals experiencing a specific

---

[1] As we are writing this in 2022, plans are underway to revise the community psychology "competencies" (including what they are called) using antiracism and decoloniality lenses, to revise the definition of community psychology practice, and to add two new foundations – antiracism and decoloniality.

issue, who are members of the community, or who are served by a program or policy we are evaluating. We make this clear to the organizations we work with in our initial meetings, before we sign the papers so that they are informed and can decide if we are the type of consultants they want.

Second, community consultants may be working with a single organization, but we always consider processes and outcomes within the context of the larger systems they inhabit. For example, if we are evaluating a program for a community-based organization, we look at the processes and outcomes directly related to it, but we also incorporate aspects of community context into our work and ensure that program staff and other key stakeholders see how their program fits into this larger picture. We also look at how their program relates to others. Does it add to or subtract from existing work in the community?

Third, community consultants have the skills and experience to work with larger systems. For example, when we work with community coalitions, we consider their history and development, assess community needs and resources, and manage the politics and dynamics inherent in working with diverse individuals and groups. In other words, we attend to organizational level details and keep our eye on the larger community at the same time. We help coalition members to understand the difference between addressing community problems through individually focused programs and creating systems change through changes to policy or organizational structures and/or networks.

As an example, Susan has been the evaluator for a community coalition for several years. As part of her evaluation work, she has attended meetings, analyzed community data, produced reports for the coalition to use for planning, conducted surveys or interviews with coalition membership each year using standardized tools, and evaluated the coalition's activities and outcomes. For two years the coalition received funding from the state, which required the state contractors to conduct the evaluation instead of Susan. The evaluation team, located at a university, told Susan that they hadn't done a lot of evaluation work, but the state had approached and asked them to do this. Over the two-year period they did not require the coalition to have any specific outcomes, or to change anything. The evaluation measures included a social network analysis, a survey of the members, and reporting on the number of meetings and attendance. The evaluators never visited the community, nor did they attend a coalition meeting. As a result, they were not able to produce reports that were of use to the coalition and the community derived no benefits from the evaluation. Through her engagement over time with this coalition, Susan has been able to make actionable recommendations that help to strengthen the coalition and move it forward toward action.

It is our belief that changing problem behaviors or solving social problems does not necessarily require that we work to change individual people.

Smedley and Syme (2000) contended that it is unreasonable to expect people to change their behavior when the environment doesn't support change. So, behavior change on a larger scale is ultimately more likely to be successful when the context is changed. A good example is tobacco use. Over the last twenty years, the prevalence of smoking has declined not because myriad programs promoted the health risks of smoking, but through policy changes that increased prices, prohibited indoor smoking, and introduced restrictions on advertising that glamorized the behavior, thus changing social norms about tobacco use. The same was true for infant car seat use. Only 25 percent of parents used infant car seats before laws were passed requiring their use.

Most importantly, in our approach we do not come in as the "experts." Yes, we have expertise in some areas such as evaluation and facilitation. But these are simply tools that can be applied by communities to support the work they are doing. We believe our clients are the experts in their communities, and they have knowledge and skills that we lack. We always approach our work as a collaboration with our clients.

We cannot overemphasize the importance of using a collaborative approach with community members. Unless you are working in your own community and are a community member, it is always important to remember that you are a guest in someone else's community. They live there and may work there, while you are merely a temporary visitor. Ideally, you have been invited in to help with a specific need. Collaboration is the best way to ensure that what you do is the right thing to do, and that you are addressing the right need. There is rarely a "one size fits all" approach to addressing community needs given the complexities and uniqueness of each community. By using a collaborative approach there is a better chance that the work you do will address the right need, in the right way that specifically fits each unique community.

1.7 How This Book Is Organized

The chapters in this book are divided into sections. The first section (Chapters 2–5) includes chapters that describe foundations for community consulting. Chapter 2 describes the various work settings where community practitioners who are interested in consulting might seek employment and gain experience. As stated earlier, you don't necessarily have to hang a shingle start a consulting practice to engage in community consulting. You may find that there are plenty of other types of positions you can work in that will also allow you to serve in a community consulting role. This chapter will include a description of the types of community consulting experiences available in a variety of settings. One of the goals of this chapter is to demonstrate the benefits of gaining practical experience before striking out on your own.

Chapter 3 explains why community consulting may not be for everyone. We describe the "soft" skills or personal qualities required for engaging in community consulting, as well as the values and perspectives in which work by all community consultants should be grounded. This does not mean that someone who doesn't have *all* the personal qualities may never be successful as a consultant; however, in some instances, someone who does not have many of the qualities needed may not enjoy this work. The values and perspectives are required in order to engage in community consulting that is responsive and respectful to the community. This chapter is presented to provide those who are thinking of consulting in communities with specific things to consider before making a career move.

Chapter 4 covers foundational values and knowledge, including how they will help you work as a community consultant. We also share examples of how they look in practice. While they are mostly taken from the community psychology competencies (Dalton & Wolfe, 2012), they are also foundational for other professions including social work, evaluation, and public health. As we noted earlier, our work is grounded in principles of equity and social justice which are consistent with the values and knowledge we describe in this chapter.

Chapter 5 describes skills you may need, depending upon the type of work you are doing. Examples are provided from the authors' own work and work of their colleagues to give readers further insight into how the skills translate into community practice. This chapter includes guidance on how you can develop the skills. We derived the collection of skills and their descriptions from community psychology practice, social work, public health, public administration, and evaluation.

The second section in this book (Chapters 6–9) describes the business and work side of consulting. Chapter 6 provides guidance for setting up and maintaining a consulting practice. Information includes how to determine the business structure and location, how to market your business, and how to find work. Much of the content in this chapter is equally applicable to professionals who wish to consult as employees of other organizations; relevant information specific to that audience is also included. Chapter 6 includes tips for effective networking and professional development and marketing using social media.

Whether you consult with communities within a company or externally, you will need to collaborate with colleagues or other professionals. Chapter 7 provides information to consider when choosing colleagues or teammates, deciding whether to go it alone, to hire staff, or to subcontract some of the work. We also discuss how to be a good collaborator. We offer guidance for those who do not have the luxury of picking their workmates and find themselves faced with challenging work relationships. Building project teams requires a strategic approach and this chapter provides information that will be helpful for developing and accomplishing the work. It also requires additional self-reflection to determine whether *you* are someone that people will want on their team.

As a community consultant, you will not only be working with your team, but you will be collaborating with clients and community members. Chapter 8 provides insight into the types of situations that may be encountered such as resistance or hostility toward "consultants" or "outsiders." This chapter provides guidance for overcoming these challenges. You might be asking "what does this have to do with the business of consulting?" Building relationships with your clients and community members is how you build your reputation as a business and as a professional. One way to do this is to manage difficult interpersonal situations effectively and diplomatically. Also, when you are consulting from a collaborative model, if you are not able to build a solid relationship with community members and establish trust, you will not be effective in your work.

Responding to a request for proposals (RFP) to obtain funding can be time-consuming, and, if you work independently, it is time that is typically unpaid. If you work for a larger organization, it is "overhead." Chapter 9 provides guidelines about making a living as a community consultant. We provide guidelines to help you determine whether it is worth investing time in responding to an RFP and whether the RFP is a good fit for your organization. It also presents guidelines on how to develop a proposal, determine the budget, develop the scope of work, and how to write a good proposal. It also provides ideas for what consultants can do when they encounter slow times and there is less work available.

In Chapter 10, we close the book by providing insight into trends and other factors that may or may not bode well for a future in community consulting. It will present how changes at multiple levels may impact the future for community consultants.

1.8 How to Get the Most from This Book

To get the most out of reading this book you should recognize that *each* time you work with a community-based organization, a coalition, or a public entity you are likely engaging in some form of community consulting. For example, nonprofit organizations and grant funded projects rarely operate in isolation. They are accountable to board members, advisory committees, and the people from the communities that they serve. Even if your role is simply to conduct an evaluation of a single grant funded project, your findings will likely affect the program operations or funding which in turn affects the community. Therefore, other consulting engagements that impact the organization, such as strategic planning and organizational development activities, should be considered.

Engaging in self-exploration, self-awareness, and a willingness to be honest with yourself will help you to truly benefit from this book. For example, when you read about the soft skills required, if more than a few things really do not sound at all like you, then we suggest you think long and hard about whether community consulting is the right path for you. Being happy and successful in your career requires that you find something that really fits with not only what you would like to do, but with who you are and your assets and strongest skills. If you find that engaging in the deep dive to think about requisite qualities that you may lack is uncomfortable, then this may not be the right career choice.

Community consulting requires a great deal of self-reflection and self-awareness throughout your career. It occasionally requires that you take a long hard look at yourself, your behavior, an attitude, or another attribute that you may not like so much. This work is all about you in relation to others, so it requires that you learn to be comfortable with sometimes being uncomfortable. Sometimes community consultants must outwardly admit that they are not the best person to be engaging with certain individuals, organizations, or communities. Finally, to get the most from this book, we recommend that as you read you find ways to relate the information to your own work or life experiences. Success in community consulting requires continuous individual growth and professional growth.

1.9 Key Points

- Community consulting, as defined for this book, has roots primarily in community psychology, as well as in evaluation, social work, public health, and other disciplines.
- Community consulting is different from other, more traditional consulting models. Community consultants are accountable to the communities they serve, include considerations of context in all their work, and are able to work with larger systems.
- To benefit from this book requires self-exploration, self-awareness, and being honest with yourself.

2 Community Consulting: How to Prepare and Where You Might Work

All labor that uplifts humanity has dignity and importance and should be undertaken with painstaking excellence.

—Martin Luther King, Jr.
(The Martin Luther King, Jr. Center, 2021)

To build community requires vigilant awareness of the work we must continually do to undermine all the socialization that leads us to behave in ways that perpetuate domination.

—bell hooks (2003)

In Chapter 2, we describe the education and experiences that can be helpful to prepare for a community consulting career. It includes a description of the wide variety of employment opportunities for community consultants and the types of skill and education that can help to get you there. It also highlights the interdisciplinary nature of this type of work.

As we defined in Chapter 1, a community consultant is someone who enters a relationship with a group of individuals to share knowledge, skills, and tools to build the group's capacity to reach a goal. Our definition of community consulting includes sharing expertise with community members, members of community-based organizations, or members of your own workplace community. Community consulting may include facilitating coalition development, strategic planning, evaluation, program development or implementation, policy development or analysis, **advocacy**, grant writing, or something as simple as helping to identify appropriate evidence-based programs. Many professionals perform these services as part of their jobs without thinking of themselves as community consultants. This chapter will discuss how to get started in community consulting and describe the settings in which community consultants often work and the contributions made by community consultants.

2.1 How Do I Get Started?

Individuals begin working as community consultants either as a result of a purposeful career decision or by responding to opportunities that come their way. In any case, if you are going to engage in community consulting you need a combination of relevant education and experiences to gain the necessary expertise (Viola & McMahon, 2010). This section of the chapter will describe some of the ways that you can prepare for a career in community consulting.

2.2 What Type of Education Do You Need?

As we mentioned in Chapter 1, we have degrees in community psychology, which provide the range of practice foundations that are useful for community consulting. We describe the personal characteristics, foundations, and skills in Chapters 3–5, so we will not elaborate on them here. While we are admittedly somewhat biased toward community psychology training, we have found that many other disciplinary backgrounds also provide the necessary foundations and skills. Professionals interested in community consulting should ideally engage in some cross-disciplinary education, either during their formal educational process or through continuing education opportunities after graduation. Disciplines that provide relevant skills include social work, clinical psychology, public health, applied sociology, urban planning, program evaluation, public administration, applied anthropology, and most of the other social sciences. We recommend at least a master's degree in your chosen field. A PhD may or may not be required, depending upon your goals and the settings in which you plan to work. Though a PhD garners respect in many settings, in others it can be viewed less positively and may serve as an obstacle during a job search. In our experience, some potential employers view individuals with a PhD as overqualified people who do not understand the "real world," or as being too expensive. On one occasion, after Susan interviewed for a job, one of the individuals from the department where she interviewed confidentially shared that she was rejected for the job because she had a PhD and nobody else in the department had one. It made them uncomfortable.

If your formal education or life experience has not provided you with all the skills you need, you might supplement it by seeking out opportunities to attend workshops, certificate courses, or other professional development opportunities. Such opportunities are often offered through professional associations or community-based organizations. Another option is to explore distance learning and internet-based courses. Some organizations offer fellowships, internships, volunteering, or other development opportunities. For example, the American Psychological Association (APA) offers opportunities for graduate students, master's and doctoral level psychologists, and other professionals in social and behavioral disciplines to serve as Health Equity Ambassadors (American Psychological Association, 2016)[1] where the APA Health Equity Ambassador program provides training in a variety of topics relevant to community consulting. The AEA sponsors the Graduate Education Diversity Internship (GEDI) program (American Evaluation Association, 2022).[2]

Keep in mind that your work in communities is stronger when you include people with lived experience. The communities you serve will benefit and together you will create and more relevant strategies. For example, including team members of a marginalized gender or race for projects serving these populations or those with a disability for a project serving people with disabilities, or including those who grew up poor, experienced homelessness, abuse, or went through the foster care system will strengthen your ability to serve those communities. Including those with lived experience provides the knowledge that cannot be gained through formal education.

2.3 Why Experience Is Important

Regardless of the level of education or types of training you have, education alone will not be sufficient for you to effectively engage in community consulting. Coursework provides a solid foundation for work in the community, but, without experience, it's difficult to get a feel for how classroom learning translates into real settings. Community settings are always complex and messy, and experience is the only way to gain expertise and learn what really works across situations and settings. Experience provides newly graduated professionals with the opportunity to observe the politics and complexity of interorganizational relationships, and how power dynamics, racism, and other factors affect what gets done and how things get done within a community. Community politics and dynamics can potentially sink the most well-designed, empirically based initiatives and overwhelm even seasoned professionals.

Perhaps the best way to gain experience is to work as an apprentice with someone who already has experience working in communities. When seeking out a **mentor**, look for someone who is ethical and someone who shares your values and philosophy (Viola & McMahon, 2010). It may not be easy or even possible to find such a person within your geographic or professional area. If that is the case, you might look for a mentor willing to process your experiences to gain additional insights through email, telephone, or online conferencing conversations. Look for opportunities within your professional association and networks. For example, we are both members of the AEA

---

[1] See www.apa.org/pi/health-equity/ambassadors.
[2] See www.eval.org/gedi.

Independent Consulting Topical Interest Group (IC TIG), which has organized **mastermind groups**, informal weekly chats, and book clubs. Ann offers mentoring sessions for early career evaluators interested in consulting. There are likely to be many other opportunities for you to engage with others working in communities as well.

The earlier you begin to gain experience working in communities the better. Ideally, you should seek out opportunities for experience while you are still in school, if that is possible. Take advantage of **internships** and practicums, part-time jobs, and volunteering opportunities to get as much experience as you can. Participating in a broad range of opportunities will improve your skills and help you to build your résumé. Such experience will help you to be more competitive in the job market and expand the number of potential mentors and job references in your circle.

No matter where you are in your career, building capacity by working alongside individuals who have experience in areas where you lack experience is always valuable. We have found that even in those areas where we have experience, sometimes collaborating with others helps us to further develop our skills or find even better ways to do things. Expertise is not something you get and then just add to your résumé and move on. It requires an ongoing commitment to lifelong **professional development**. No matter how good you are at something, there is always room to continually improve. We also encourage you to be willing to learn from those with less experience and training. Some of our younger and less experienced colleagues are a good source of new information or insights for us.

2.4 What Type of Experience Is Needed?

The type of experience you need depends on your interests and goals. The logical first place to start is in positions and settings that are the entry level for your chosen profession. Look for a position that will give you broader, rather than narrower, experience. For example, if you plan to work as an evaluator, focusing only on evaluation experiences will not give you the range of expertise needed. Gaining experience in areas like program planning and implementation, strategic planning, and coalition development is useful. Having good evaluation skills is essential but being able to help organizations use data and results for planning and to understand what went wrong during implementation, or being able to determine what types of evaluative information will be useful for coalition members are also important.

We recommend that, if you have an interest in gaining experience in respect to a *specific* community consulting focus, you learn from those with experience in these specific areas. Identify individuals who are doing the work that interests you; read their résumés or bios to see what types of experience and training they have engaged in relating to the work they are doing. Look for commonalities across their experiences, but also look at the differences. Keep in mind that there is most likely more than one way to get where you want to go.

We also recommend **informational interviewing**. Informational interviews, unlike job interviews, involve speaking with people about their current job and career trajectory. The focus is on learning about the knowledge, skills, and experiences they have that have contributed to their own professional journey. If the individual agrees to an informational interview, be sure to schedule only half an hour and never take more than an hour of their time. When you meet, have questions prepared and remain on topic. If the interviewee decides that they would like to talk longer or take the conversation in other directions, then go along with this but remain respectful of their time. Be sure to maintain a professional appearance and demeanor as well. Keep in mind that this is an expert in your field who may be able to influence your career in the future. You want to make a good impression.

2.5 Roles and Settings

Community consultants may be internal to an organization or working as external consultants. In this section of the chapter, we discuss the roles of internal and external consultants and present the variety of options available for working in community consulting, including positions that do not carry a "consultant" title.

Consulting opportunities can be found inside organizations as an employee or from outside the organization as a contracted consultant. As a contracted consultant, you may be a sole proprietor, or work at a small, medium, or large firm. Sometimes **external consultants** are hired as **subcontractors** by larger firms.

Internal consultant opportunities may be found in evaluation or research departments, training or human resources, or other setting-specific departments, such as population medicine at a medical center or parent engagement in a school district. There are benefits and drawbacks to working as a consultant whether you are working internally or externally to the organization.

Perhaps the greatest benefit of being an internal consultant is that as an insider you can really get to know the organization and the individuals who work there and have an inside view of the organizational culture. You will likely have a better idea of the resources that are available for initiatives and be able to assess the likelihood of the initiatives being accepted at various levels of the organization. You will also have opportunities to see the application of your results and possibly even participate in implementing your recommendations.

There is also a downside to being internal to the organization. If you find you must take an unpopular stance, report something negative, or disagree with a co-worker it can be risky for your career. While you still work there the individual whose toes you stepped on may block promotions. If you leave you may not be able to use this job as a reference. An internal role may offer fewer opportunities for community engagement with community serving more often as context rather than the focus of the work. When internal organization members have an interest in maintaining the status quo, even if it is contrary to the best interests of the community, they may become defensive if you try to change their status and power dynamics.

Susan once experienced very negative backlash from recommendations she made in an internal evaluation report. She managed a rape crisis center that served a community and someone in a senior position decided to change a crisis hotline so that calls were routed to a new department. After the change, callers in crisis, some of them suicidal, were being put on hold for as long as fifteen minutes. She became concerned about the potential negative outcomes that could come from such a move and decided to draw on her evaluative skills to look more deeply into the matter. Susan gathered data from the telecommunications department, which documented the hold times and hang-ups. She then informed individuals at the top of the organization of the change, shared the results of her data-gathering, and described the potential consequences of the change. She did not cite the names of those responsible. The crisis line was then outsourced to an organization that specialized in such hotlines, thus better serving individuals experiencing sexual assault in the community. The backlash came later when Susan started a new job with the federal government. The individual who had initially made the change to the crisis hotline received the request for information for Susan's security clearance and recommended that it not be granted. She claimed that Susan "did not provide a united front with management." Fortunately, Susan had informed her new supervisor of the tensions and her prior actions, and she received her security clearance.

Working to avoid negative consequences within an organization may require compromises that you are not comfortable making. What if Susan had not spoken up and the delayed response on the crisis line had led to someone's death? Community consulting often requires bringing uncomfortable conversations to the forefront. As an internal employee you risk becoming unpopular, gaining a reputation as someone who makes people feel uneasy or as a whistle blower. You may even get fired. Early in 2004, Ann was hired to head the Office of Child and Youth Protection for the Archdiocese of Atlanta. It was at the height of a child sex abuse crisis. Ann was tasked with finding a prevention course suitable for all volunteers and staff in the archdiocese, conducting prevention training, and supporting victims of abuse. From the beginning, she faced roadblocks from the highest levels within the chancery. The story is too complicated to explain here but suffice it to say that once the auditors who were charged with assessing whether the archdiocese was meeting the promises made by the bishops gave the archdiocese a successful rating (United States Conference on Catholic Bishops, 2002),[3] Ann was isolated from the supervisor that hired her. She was unsuccessful in her attempts to have the archbishop's advisory board review prevention materials and was told it was "too shocking" for church members. A member of the advisory board made a formal complaint to the National Office of Child and Youth Protection regarding a violation of the charter. Ann had knowledge of the call and felt that the advisory board member was within her rights and obligations to make the complaint. But because Ann did not report the call ahead of time to the archbishop's office, and for many other reasons, Ann was fired. So, what do you do when you have been fired? Start your own consulting business of course!

On the other hand, we have talked with many aspiring consultants who describe the position of an outside consultant in somewhat glamorous terms. It is often anything but that. While being an outside consultant has its benefits, there are also drawbacks and challenges. One of the benefits is that for some reason, people seem to think that if someone comes from outside the organization, they might know more than the people who work there. We have seen many instances where organizations have even sought consultants from other cities or states rather than local consultants because there is a perception that they bring more expertise to the work. Thus, if you are the outsider, especially from another city or state, the organization may be more likely to comply with your recommendations. While this has not been documented formally, consultants often talk about this phenomenon among themselves.

Another benefit of being an outsider, especially if you are consulting across organizations, is that you encounter a wider range of opportunities to engage in a range of work. In our work, as outside consultants, we have had opportunities to engage with a variety of organizations that include government, foundations, and nonprofits. We have opportunities to engage with very knowledgeable and interesting individuals who are doing amazing and important community work. Sometimes engagements are short-term, and our time and efforts are limited, and at other times we work with community organizations over several years.

Despite the wonderful opportunities that we have enjoyed, there are challenges and less than desirable moments. There are times you may deliver news to an organization that they do not want to hear. For example, when you deliver evaluation results, rather than accept the findings, they might prefer to shoot the messenger and blame you and your methods, even going so far as to discredit your name rather than admit that they need to make some changes.

---

[3] See www.usccb.org/issues-and-action/child-and-youth-protection/charter.cfm.

They may even find another consultant who is willing to support their beliefs, adding credence to their claims. Another example would be when an organization asks you to come in to assist with developing a strategic plan and those who are engaging you tell you as an aside what their real agenda is. Your reputation as a consultant is tied to your earning potential, and such situations can either hurt your pocketbook directly through loss of business or take up billable time as you work to correct such situations.

As an outside consultant, after you share your final **deliverables**, you are often done with the project. The organization may put your products on the shelf and choose to ignore them, or they may decide to make changes in a way that is not consistent with your guidance, or even act contrary to your recommendations. We have experienced frustration when the community organizations with which we work fail to implement recommended changes or simply choose not to act. Some get stuck and you are left wondering why you were engaged in the first place. Ann once had a situation in which someone got fired after a project was complete. This was certainly not her intent, and she always starts consultancies with the clarification that she does not do personnel evaluation. But in some cases, a chief executive officer may decide a change is needed. Both of us have been on projects where the final report was buried because the organization did not like the results. These situations are very frustrating, especially when you see your findings and recommendations misapplied in ways that are not in the best interests of community members. It is at these times that you need to remind yourself that ultimately the community should be calling the shots, and you are there to advise, not control the situation.

2.6 A Description of Settings

As we mentioned earlier in this chapter, community consulting can be done within a variety of settings. In this section, we will describe a range of settings where community consultants may work. We have tried to be inclusive of all possibilities, but there are likely to be many more potential settings than the ones we describe here.

2.6.1 Forming Your Own Company

Starting your own consulting company is probably the first thing that comes to mind. Both of us have done this, and it worked for each of us. Ann owns Community Evaluation Solutions, a consulting firm that has grown over the last seventeen years. For the past several years, she had full-time employees but has now moved to using a small group of highly skilled contractors. Susan decided she did not want to grow her consultancy because she is in a later stage of her career and chose to work solo. We discuss these choices in greater depth later in this book. Forming your own company is a viable option if you have the right circumstances and experience. While some consultants started their companies very early in their careers, we have noted that the most successful consultants usually gain experience in at least a few jobs that provided relevant experience.

There are pluses and minuses associated with **independent consulting** in your own company. Solarz (2013) described independent consulting as a job with no benefits, no paid vacation, in which you pay for your own office supplies and computer and have no job security. That said, many independent consultants will say that the benefits far outweigh the pitfalls. The benefits of independent consulting include independence and flexibility, opportunities to pursue all kinds of interesting projects, and you can use a wide range of skills, as well as have control over your assignments and products (Solarz, 2013). However, along with this wonderful independence and control comes a great deal of responsibility. While we would like to think that as independent business owners we have a great deal of control, there are limitations because of the availability of work. For example, as a solo consultant Susan found it challenging to be able to work on the types of projects she liked because they sometimes required a team. There are times when you can assemble a team of independent consultants to bid on a project. This strategy can be effective, but such proposals are not always as competitive as organizations with teams that work together on site regularly and can demonstrate a proven track record.

The perception that having your own consulting business will give you the flexibility to allow for the easy scheduling of personal appointments and life events can often prove to be just that – a perception. Often consultants do not have as much control over their time and activities as they would like or as others would think. For example, when there is an overlap in projects (one ending, one starting) it often requires working longer than desired hours. We sometimes find that we end up working more hours than we would like, and at times we would prefer to be off. Finishing a report by the deadline can mean having to give up a Saturday or Sunday, or the entire weekend. Sometimes events related to a specific project can conflict with personal plans. For example, Susan planned a vacation only to find that her client felt that they really needed her to facilitate a coalition meeting on the day she was leaving. Fortunately, her flight left later in the afternoon, and she was able to accommodate the client's request, but it changed her plans for her first day of vacation.

If you decide to work on projects that are not local, you may end up traveling. At first, the travel can feel fun and new. You can use it to accumulate airline miles and hotel points and see places you have never been. However, after some time, when you miss family gatherings or other events because you are out of town, or your children get sick while you are across the country somewhere, it can become wearisome. When you are on site working, there is usually little time to experience the cities you visit. When Susan worked on a contract in Cairo, Egypt she only had three and a half days there. The client, a university, was funding the trip and put her in university housing. She was traveling alone shortly after the revolution took place, so it was not a good time to venture out alone or extend her trip to a vacation. The clients were kind enough to arrange time for her to visit the pyramids and see the square where the revolution had taken place, but most of her brief time in the country was spent working.

Another option if you start your own consulting company is to hire employees or subcontract consultants. This will allow you to take on larger and more interesting projects. Some community consultants have very successful organizations that have grown over the years to employ large numbers of staff and consultants. Ann's company, Community Evaluation Solutions, has grown over time and thus she has needed to hire employees and consultants over the years.

You might consider forming collaboratives with other consultants or seeking out opportunities to serve as a subcontractor. For example, Susan subcontracts with universities and other consulting firms. Sometimes large consulting companies seek out medium-sized and small consultancies to subcontract on projects. If you are classified as a Historically Underutilized Business (HUB), Women-Owned Small Business (WOSB), or Women's Business Enterprise (WBE) and listed with your state, larger companies may reach out to you to fulfill subcontracting requirements on large projects.

2.6.2 Working for a Consulting Firm

Community consultants whose specific job is to work directly as consultants work across a variety of consulting settings. Some work for large nonprofit research and evaluation organizations (Tanyu, 2017). In this role, they and their teams may work collaboratively with community programs, health care organizations, and educational institutions to collect program evaluation data. Others work in small evaluation firms where they may spend a lot of time meeting with clients to ensure that they have the information necessary to do their work (Bloodworth, 2017). Many people who provide consulting services to nonprofit organizations do so after gaining experience in other settings or upon retirement (Goldstein & Daviau, 2017; Wolfe, 2017).

If you are interested in pursuing a career and opening your own business as a consultant, we highly recommend you first spend some time working as an employee in a consulting firm. You will gain good exposure and learn about the business of consulting. For example, you will learn about balancing billable hours with time spent on unbillable tasks, **branding**, creating products, and other lessons that can be helpful if you decide to open your own business. **Billable hours** refer to those hours where you are doing work that is directly related to a contract versus unbillable hours such as administrative tasks or engaging in professional development. If you are working in a firm that does mostly local business, it is likely that you will be required to sign a non-compete clause, so think this through carefully before you sign. A non-compete agreement will limit the work you can do for at least the first year after you leave employment. If you also plan to serve the local community, it may bar you from engaging with many key organizations for a certain period.

Working for a company also gives you exposure to different consultants. You can learn from them and thereby expand your skills and expertise under their guidance. You may have the opportunity to learn how to do things like develop and conduct training programs for community-based organizations, facilitate strategic planning sessions and board retreats, and learn more about local funding sources and the strategies required to engage with them. Communities are multi-layered systems comprised of people and organizations with varying agendas and a mishmash of intertwining subcultures. Navigating them with experienced consultants is helpful for avoiding missteps that can follow you for years.

You should be aware that there are differences in working in **for-profit** and **nonprofit** consulting firms. In her role in a for-profit consulting firm, Martin (2017) describes generating income and pleasing clients as the primary focus of her work. While the opportunity was valuable in providing incredible insights into the business development process (which is important for survival as a consultant) and promoting professional development of technical skills, such settings can be less community-focused than someone interested in community consulting may prefer. Martin recommended that applicants ask about the types of projects the organization does during the interview process.

In 2015, Susan transitioned from independent consulting to working for a nonprofit consulting firm. She enjoyed many benefits, but the transition was not without some challenges. She benefited from the support of a collaborative team of co-workers and daily social contact. Support staff did a lot of the things she did not like doing (for example, invoicing clients and preparing training materials) and there were other tangible benefits, such as a regular paycheck and paid vacations and holidays. Susan enjoyed more opportunities to work on diverse projects because she joined an organization that is well-known in the community.

The change also had negatives. Unlike working at home, Susan had to jump out of bed at the sound of the alarm clock, dress professionally each day, and commute to work. The organization had specific, set work hours and a dress code. She no longer had complete control over her schedule or which projects she was assigned. Sometimes she worked to develop a relationship with a client, only to have that client re-assigned to another consultant. She had fewer opportunities to indulge in her "introverted moments," and too frequently was required to attend departmental and organizational level meetings. She had much less flexibility in her schedule and was required to record what she did during time entered as "unbillable" into the timekeeping system. The time she spent on projects was carefully monitored and she had to get permission to work more than the originally proposed number of hours if she found the nonprofit she was working with needed more consulting time than initially estimated. All her work was local and she missed the travel (and air miles and hotel points).

Perhaps the biggest con was the mismatch in priorities between Susan and her supervisor, the executive director. Susan's focus was on the needs of the organizations and ensuring that she was meeting their needs. That is why she chose to work in a mission-focused nonprofit. However, over time, she realized that her supervisor was operating the organization as if it were a for-profit and was pushing staff to sell products (data visualization services – even to nonprofits that did not have a solid evaluation in place) and increase their billable hours. Whenever Susan and her colleagues went over the projected hours on a project, she pressured them to cut services or ask for additional money. For Susan, the perceived pros outweighed the cons initially, but then over time the cons (reality) added up and, after two years, Susan returned to her own consulting company.

2.6.3 Education

Researchers, evaluators, and other employees of educational institutions or school districts often find themselves in consulting roles. Many school districts have departments focused on parent engagement or community relations or have specially funded grants in these areas. Working in these contexts often requires some level of community consulting. For example, if you are managing a grant for unhoused students, it might require going out to schools to provide consultations on specific issues to support these students. You may have to visit with community-based organizations to develop stronger support systems for students and their families.

Most school districts have data or evaluation departments. If you work as an internal evaluator in a school district, you will analyze student and district level data, deliver findings, and explain their implications to diverse audiences. For example, you may be called on to explain findings to teachers, principals, school officials, or parent groups. Such situations are sometimes sensitive or politically charged and may require extreme diplomacy. You may also train staff about evaluation, data collection, and how to use evaluation results. One of Susan's former co-workers came from an evaluation department in a large school district where she spent a considerable amount of time consulting with personnel at schools or working on grant-funded initiatives to assist them with designing and implementing evaluations.

Other educational settings include private and charter schools, community colleges, and other higher education settings. Community colleges and universities often have offices that engage in reporting and analytics that provide data and evaluation services to the school. They sometimes have programs designed to support special student populations or individuals in the surrounding community. There are many jobs within these settings that involve some community consulting skills, either for the internal or external community. One example is Majer's (2017) description of his faculty role at a community college where his work engages community consulting skills such as coalition building as department chair, community organizing by forming a psychology club for students, and advocating for systems changes.

If you are interested in pursuing a career that involves doing evaluation or consulting with educational institutions, experience working within such a setting is essential. If you did not receive your training specifically from an education-focused graduate program or did not engage in education-related work during graduate school, it is even more important. If you eventually decide to start an independent consulting practice this is an area ripe with opportunities, but it is also competitive. Typically requests for proposals require experience specifically with educational institutions or programs. If your experience does not include working with or in an educational institution, you will likely not be successful pursuing consulting work in this area.

2.6.4 Medical and Public Health

Medical centers are increasingly focusing on **population medicine**, **health equity**, and other community-focused **prevention** and **intervention** solutions. There are many jobs in these settings that involve community consulting. They include developing **coalitions** or **community collaboratives**, facilitating community needs assessments, **community engagement**, and outreach services. Some medical centers support grant-funded programs and other intervention services that provide community consultation services in areas like domestic violence, childhood obesity, HIV/AIDS, and maternal and infant health. If you are interested in health-related topics or institutions, working for a medical center is good experience. In addition to the community consulting related experience, you may also have opportunities for program development or management, research, and evaluation, or gain other skills and competencies that will be valuable to you as a community consultant.

Susan once worked for a large medical center managing community-based and grant-funded programs. She gained experience writing grants, evaluating programs, managing budgets and staff, and navigating internal and external politics. Some of our colleagues work in population medicine departments or coalition development roles and are heavily engaged with their surrounding communities, serving in consultative roles. William Neigher (Neigher, Lounsbury, & Lee, 2010) directed strategic planning for Atlantic Health, a multi-provider health care system where his responsibilities included strategic planning, program development, and community needs assessment. He worked internally in a consulting role with individuals at all levels of the organization, and externally with community agencies.

A related arena is working at a state or local public health department. Depending on the setting, you may have similar opportunities to those offered by medical centers. Dr. Kyrah Brown created a two-year postdoctoral program at the health department in Wichita, Kansas, where her duties included agency-wide consultation and providing research and evaluation capacity building for staff (Levin, 2017). When her post-doc finished, she had ample experience for her next job as a community consultant. You may also have opportunities to engage in policy development or advocacy, community organizing work, outreach and education, or grants, programs, and direct services management. Health departments often employ **epidemiologists**. If you did not receive your training in a public health program, working in this field presents an opportunity to expand your analytic knowledge. In such settings, and likely others that we mention, there may be opportunities to share data and findings with community-based organizations and community members and expand your data management and visualization skill sets.

2.6.5 Nonprofits, Nongovernmental Organizations, and Community-Based Organizations

There are a variety of jobs in nonprofits, **nongovernmental organizations (NGOs)**, and **community-based organizations (CBOs)** that provide opportunities for community consulting. Some positions that come to mind include program manager or director, executive director, program analyst, or analyst or advocate positions in advocacy organizations. Working in nonprofits that implement programs and services provides opportunities to engage in program development, advocacy, community development, fundraising, grant writing, program implementation, evaluation, and reporting. Individuals in those positions are often engaged with coalitions related to the topic area and have opportunities to work on collaborative programming with other organizations. In any of these positions you will find a need to draw on community consulting skills on occasion, and build your own skill set at the same time.

There is no one degree that is particularly appropriate for this type of work. Program development may require a degree in psychology, social work, public health, nursing, education, or another field depending upon the content and requirements of the programs. For example, if it is an education-focused nonprofit a degree in education may be most beneficial. A nonprofit working on mental health related issues will require a psychology or social work degree. Advocacy organizations will require a knowledge of policy, advocacy skills, and understanding of the issue at hand; therefore, a policy-related degree may be advantageous. If you are seeking an administrative or development position, a degree in business, public administration, or communications might be preferable. Experience is also relevant, and those interested in working in this sector should explore jobs that are of interest and talk to individuals in them to strategize a career path.

Nonprofits in international settings are referred to as NGOs. Their operations will vary widely, depending on the setting and problem area. Experience and expertise with U.S.-based nonprofits will not be sufficient. If you are interested in working in an international arena, you should get experience by working for U.S. AID, the Peace Corps, the United Nations, or a **global initiative**. Another strategy is to attend international conferences or work with local organizations that work internationally (Harvey & Mihaylov, 2017). To find out how to gain entry to, and the skills needed for, international work, network with individuals through professional associations and listservs. For example, the American Evaluation Association has an International and Cross-Cultural Topical Interest Group and the American Public Health Association has an International Health Section.

2.6.6 Government

Government options for working in the community include local (city, county), state, and federal government positions. **Local government** positions will likely provide opportunities to work more directly in one specific community. Each city and county are structured differently and identifying appropriate employment positions requires doing homework on your local government entities. As an alternative, you might consider running for an elected office. Debi Starnes, a community psychology practitioner, served on Atlanta's city council for several years. Norma Martinez-Ruben, an evaluator, served on her city council and as mayor of the Californian city where she resides.

At state governments, community psychologists described duties that included working on initiatives with local health departments and working with community members to achieve legislation and policy changes, as well as collaborations with other state agencies (Garate, 2017). State government positions can range from statewide work to regional work. Statewide work provides better opportunities to have an impact on policies and practices, and regional work is more likely to provide opportunities for local engagement. As with local government, each state is structured differently. Depending upon your area of interest, you might look for departments of education, health, human services, disability, or aging services. Within each department there will likely be divisions of interest. Work at the state level will generally require that you reside in or near the state capital; however, regional positions may be located around the state in the regional centers.

At the federal level, there are opportunities to work with community-based recipients of federal grants to provide technical assistance for program implementation and evaluation at the Centers for Disease Control and Prevention (CDC) (Armstead, 2017). Staff at the National Institute on Drug Abuse (NIDA) provide technical assistance to grant applicants and collaborate internally with other National Institutes of Health (NIH) institutes (Jenkins, 2017). The Department of Health and Human Services (HHS) has regional offices around the United States, and staff working in these offices engage directly with the community to provide resources and technical assistance as well.

If you are interested in federal employment, you may want to reside in or near Washington DC, Atlanta, GA, or one of the other major cities with regional offices. The federal government has regional offices in Boston, New York, Philadelphia, Atlanta, Chicago, Dallas, Denver, Kansas City, San Francisco, and Seattle and some offices in other localities as well, depending upon the agency. For example, the CDC is in Atlanta. Many of the larger agencies, such as Health and Human Services, the Department of Education, and the Department of Labor have offices in the regional centers. In some cases, individuals employed in the regional offices work on a national basis, in others the work is localized to the region. There are ample opportunities within the federal government itself or in working for a government contractor.

If you are interested in consulting with communities from a government position you should explore the various levels of government, search their websites to learn more about the potential positions, and read job postings to learn more about the types of jobs that are available and the required education, knowledge, skills, and abilities. One example is the federal USAJOBS.gov website that lists federal jobs for all agencies. Each state, county, and city has its own website with a link to employment opportunities. You might network with government workers to learn more about their jobs and the career path to get to them. If you are interested in a federal government position in a regional office, it is best to start early in your career and find your niche and career path. Susan and her colleagues found that once you reach the level where positions are above entry level, unless you can relocate to Washington DC, it is much more difficult to move around across agencies or departments because of limited opportunities and inside competition.

2.6.7 Criminal Justice

There are opportunities in criminal justice organizations to engage in community consulting. Police departments are increasingly concerned with community relations, family violence, juvenile crime, and other psycho-social related issues that cross into law enforcement issues. Community consultants with knowledge and understanding of the criminal justice field can help to create bridges between the two domains. For example, for her master's thesis Susan conducted a needs assessment with a police department to gather information regarding how to better handle domestic violence calls.

Juvenile and adult justice systems are two areas in the criminal justice field that can benefit from community consulting skills. Skills in prevention can be employed to develop solutions with community organizations to prevent juveniles from entering the system. These diversion programs help to prevent juveniles and adults from descending further into the criminal justice system. Juvenile diversion, prostitution diversion, and other such programs have demonstrated success in changing lives and provide rich opportunities for community consultants to have impact. For those leaving juvenile detention or prison, skilled individuals are needed to develop, implement, and evaluate re-entry programs that will facilitate a smooth transition from incarceration to community life. Those interested in engaging in work in the criminal justice field should seek out internships while still in school, take criminal justice courses, and explore local police departments and other criminal justice organizations to learn about the types of positions that may be available. Research the needs and then determine how your skill set will help to fill them.

2.6.8 Foundations and Corporate Philanthropy

Foundations and corporate **philanthropy** provide a large share of the money that funds nonprofits and community initiatives. In addition to providing funding, foundations and corporations often develop their own initiatives and set priorities for where organizations will focus their efforts. Examples of the responsibilities of foundation staff include developing initiatives, monitoring grantee progress, coordinating communication across grantees, coordinating capacity building at multiple levels, and providing technical assistance to grantees (Meyer, 2017).

For a job in philanthropy, it is helpful to enter the field early in your career. We have observed that it is often much easier to get a foot in the door via an entry level position. Networking and learning about the types of foundations and how they work is important. There are many different types of foundations with varying missions and structures. Family foundations, corporate foundations, and community foundations all work very differently from one another.

It is important to understand those differences to find your best fit and the type of positions that will allow you to engage in community consulting activities.

2.6.9 Entrepreneurship, Business, Technology

While much of community consulting occurs within medical, educational, and other organizations whose missions are to help people or somehow contribute to their growth or well-being, community consulting can also be done from settings that would seem unlikely, such as businesses or technology settings. You might even decide to engage in **social entrepreneurship**. Martin and Osberg (2007) defined "social entrepreneurship" as having three components. First is identifying a group that is excluded, marginalized, or suffering without the financial or political means to address this. Second is finding the opportunity, developing a solution, and bringing it forth to challenge the current status quo. Third is the solution becoming the new status quo, which alleviates the target group's suffering, exclusion, or marginalization. Social entrepreneurship requires entrepreneurial skills – recognizing an opportunity, having a creative solution and the determination to follow through, even in the face of adversity – coupled with values such as social justice and racial equity. Social entrepreneurs share the characteristics of entrepreneurs in general but their focus and mission is to alleviate suffering rather than profit from their solutions.

There is room for community consulting within the corporate sector. Most adults spend most of their waking hours at work. Work settings are in their own way communities, and they can benefit from the same skills and interventions as the larger community in which they are located. Training in organizational, health, or clinical psychology, working with organizational consultants, and gaining experience with business consulting firms are all strategies to gain employment in the business or for-profit sector. Corporations are increasingly focusing on wellness among their employees and focusing on ways to improve mental and physical health.

Community-based and other organizations working on behalf of the public good frequently seek technology solutions. There are opportunities to serve them by working in technology-based organizations. For example, the SAS Corporation employs social scientists to develop and facilitate data analysis and visualization solutions for government, education, and other organizations. There are companies that develop software for client management, reporting, fundraising, and other technology solutions for the nonprofit sectors. These include companies such as Social Solutions which offers the widely used ETO and Apricot technology for case management programs, and Salesforce, which is used by nonprofits to track their customer relations, marketing, and increasingly used to manage client data. Individuals working for these types of technology solutions may find themselves assisting community-based organizations with selection, implementation, and use of technology to work more efficiently and effectively. For example, ETO can be programmed to produce reports to support the work of the organization and evaluation efforts. Having knowledge of data analysis and reporting, how data can be used for quality improvement efforts, and data management can help the nonprofit to take full advantage of the technology solution and ensure that it meets their needs.

Some corporations have community outreach positions. For example, health insurance companies employ individuals who do outreach in communities by sharing health insurance related information with community-based medical centers and clinics and by engaging with coalitions and other community-based groups to co-develop solutions for uninsured individuals.

2.7 Deciding Where to Work

The previous section of this chapter pointed out options for employment that can be entirely focused on community consulting or may incorporate community consulting as a portion of the job duties. Many of these jobs offer opportunities to gain needed experience as part of a path to becoming a full-time community consultant. Deciding where to go among them will depend on current and future career interests.

When making your decision, think carefully and honestly about your needs and interests, but also spend time reflecting upon the type of organization in which you are most comfortable. One important factor for developing experience for consulting is the extent to which the organization and the position allow for professional growth and support professional development. Another is whether your work style and values are consistent with the organizational culture. Consider how closely policies such as dress codes and work hours or locations match your needs and preferences. Also pay attention to the information you hear through informal networks, including information related to management issues, high turnover, community reputation, and financial problems.

2.8 What Do Community Consultants Contribute?

This section of the chapter will discuss some of the areas where community consultants can make substantial contributions, regardless of their chosen work setting. We will describe the various skills and methods community consultants use to help communities and community-based organizations. While reading the descriptions of skills and methods, keep in mind that solving complex community problems often requires some combination of these skills.

They are seldom used in such a singular and siloed manner. Chapters 4 and 5 will provide information about the more specific values, foundations, skills, and knowledge needed and how you can acquire them.

2.8.1 Evaluation

Evaluation is one of the most common sets of skills and expertise used in community consulting. Education, government, and community-based organizations all have a need to measure and report on their processes and outcomes. Evaluation is useful for planning and decision-making. Grant-funded programs and organizations usually have some evaluation requirement for their funding. Community coalitions and collaboratives use evaluation to gain feedback about their internal processes, measure the impact of their activities, and to help them to plan and learn more about their focal issue or community. There is a wide range of potential to use evaluation and evaluation methods and tools in community consultation and provide valuable feedback to help build an organization or community's capacity to fulfill a mission or tackle a problem.

2.8.2 Community Needs and Resources Assessment

Many communities and community-based organizations require community needs and resources assessments. Many hospitals conduct a community health needs assessment and adopt an implementation strategy. Every four years the Susan G. Komen foundation requires its affiliates to prepare a Community Profile. The Ryan White CARE Act also requires community needs assessments for planning on how to use resources and fill care gaps every three years. These are just a few examples of the types of needs assessments that must be done in communities across the country. Communities also use needs and resource assessments to learn more about the extent and scope of problems, such as health disparities, domestic violence, or crime prevention. The information is essential for developing the needs statement in funding proposals and planning solutions.

2.8.3 Coalition Building and Community Organizing

Many community consultants choose coalition building or **community organizing** as the cornerstone of their work. Consultants such as Tom Wolff, Fran Butterfoss, ourselves and others spend much of their time working with health care or other community-based organizations to develop and maintain coalitions and other collaborative initiatives. Many community coalitions are made up of professionals interested in the same problem area who meet month after month to share information and network. There is a need for individuals who can facilitate coalition development that is action-oriented, community inclusive and empowering and harnesses the power of bringing people together to create lasting systems change.

2.8.4 Policy Review and Development and Advocacy

Community-based organizations and coalitions sometimes engage in **policy** and advocacy related work. Such organizations are typically dedicated to a specific area such as education, mental health, or health care. Their work often includes conducting research, developing reports and information briefs, educating legislators with such materials, and providing information to others who are interested in the topic area. They may need assistance with such tasks, with understanding the implications of laws, regulations, and policies, or with how to navigate the legislative process.

2.8.5 Organizational and Community Capacity Building and Development

Community-based organizations often need training in leadership and management skills development, change facilitation, and board development, just to name a few. For example, many leaders of community-based organizations and coalitions have backgrounds in the helping professions or as grassroots folk whose life circumstances turned them into advocates, such as cancer victims or neighborhood association leaders. As many of them move up the ladder, they sometimes find they need to develop their management and leadership skills.

It is not unusual for individuals to join or be appointed to the board of directors for a community-based organization without understanding the role of a board member. Consequences of this lack of understanding can include board members interfering with day-to-day operations, engaging in activities that represent a conflict of interest, disengaging because of conflict or ennui, or pushing an organization in directions that are not consistent with its mission. Understanding the role of the board of directors and effective board practices is another useful organizational development need that can be filled by community consultants. Many community-based organizations hold board retreats on an annual or biannual basis to ensure that new board members are properly trained and socialized to act in the best interests of their organization. Community consultants can serve a useful role as a trainer, facilitator, or even as a board member to support nonprofits and their boards of directors.

These examples illustrate just a few opportunities for community consultants to build the capacity of community organizations. **Capacity building** means partnering with organizations and communities to transfer skills and knowledge rather than keeping it and creating dependence. As a community consultant, you can use your skills and knowledge to strengthen an organization while reducing their dependence on outside help. Strategies for organizational capacity building might include providing technical assistance and organizational consulting such as training, coaching, and peer networking. Community capacity building strategies include leadership development, community organizing, and strengthening organizational collaboration and networks (Evans, Raymond, & Perkins, 2015).

Many of Ann and Susan's jobs involve building the capacity of nonprofit organizations and coalitions to engage in effective evaluation. Both of us provide one-on-one consulting and conduct workshops. Susan engaged in a project that involved developing data visualization portals to present the results of analysis of nonprofits' data for them. Building their knowledge and skills and analyzing their data prevented them from needing to contract with a third-party or outside evaluator. Ann provides training and technical assistance to build coalitions' evaluation capacity.

Capacity building and **organizational development** activities such as **facilitation**, **conflict resolution**, strategy development, **strategic planning**, leadership development, and resource development can be accomplished through consulting engagements, providing training and workshops, providing mentoring opportunities, or facilitating development of other resources.

2.8.6 Facilitation

Community leaders often need facilitation skills to engage their **stakeholders** and motivate them to do the work or to gather or share information and receive feedback. Good facilitation starts with creating energy from the moment people walk into the room. Make sure people feel welcomed and introduce new members to more experienced members. Ensure that the time spent *in* the meeting focuses on collaboration, perhaps using time for workgroups or breakouts to focus on assigned topics or tasks. Good facilitation skills also require being able to attend to all individuals in the room and ensure that all have an opportunity to participate at the same time, monitoring the conversation to ensure one individual or group does not dominate. Ultimately, the goal of facilitation is to ensure maximum participation and engagement throughout the meeting or event.

2.8.7 Conflict Resolution

In any community group, conflict is inevitable. Providing the community organization with some basic knowledge of group dynamics and conflict resolution strategies will go a long way in creating the capacity to manage the conflict that will inevitably happen. This can include a set of agreements that community members reach consensus on, like addressing disagreements immediately with the person or persons experiencing conflict. It also might include guidelines for engaging in conflictual discussions, including maintaining civil discourse, refraining from name calling, prohibiting sidebar conversations, building alliances, and fully listening to the opposing individual or group's perspective and argument. It might even include a formal process to resolve disputes among members or groups of members.

2.8.8 Strategy Development and Strategic Planning

Effective community change strategy includes not just simple programs and services but a comprehensive strategy that involves community members in activities that will lead to real change. Community strategies are most effective when they focus on the root causes of social and public health challenges using activities that address the policy, systems, and environmental change to achieve a change in the desired outcomes. Community consultants can help the group by using **root cause analysis** (the 5 Whys, the Fishbone technique, and so on) to identify the community strategy based on the identification of the root causes rather than simply generating quick fix, frequently used but ineffective remedies to problems (Ishikawa, 1990).

Strategic planning helps community organizations or groups focus on the work they need to do based on the outcomes they feel most strongly about. A good strategic plan identifies the areas the group will focus on and specifies the measurement used to define whether the desired outcomes were achieved. The work should then be assigned to the groups and committees aligned to the work. Meeting agendas can be structured so as to offer touchpoints on the status of the work. Developing a strategic plan can include conducting a Strengths-Weaknesses-Opportunities-Threats (SWOT) or Strengths-Opportunities-Aspirations-Results (SOAR) analysis, interviewing organization or community members, and gathering existing data to identify areas of need and determine group priorities. The timeline for a strategic plan should typically not exceed 18 months since most organizations and problems exist within dynamic environments. The progress toward implementing the plan should be monitored at least quarterly, and ideally bi-monthly to ensure focus on the priorities and convey the importance of fully implementing the plan. Additionally, if activities are not yielding results within specified timelines or if there are unintended consequences, frequent enough monitoring will allow the group to change direction more quickly.

2.8.9 Leadership Development

Many community organizations emerge from the grassroots level with community members who have little experience leading initiatives or collaboratives.

Therefore, leaders may need some training and development or just some support and mentoring. There is a well-developed body of literature on the characteristics of good leaders, so we won't go through them all here. But we will say that an ineffective community leader can kill even the worthiest of community change efforts. A leader that fails to be inclusive, respectful, and organized, or who is overly controlling, will not be effective in inspiring others and growing the community. Community consultants may offer training to support grassroots leaders. Leadership training may include tips on ideal personal qualities and behaviors, or it may focus on the nuts and bolts and technicalities of navigating systems or setting up a coalition. The type of leadership development provided will depend on the expressed needs of the community change leadership.

2.8.10 Resource Development

Communities and community-based organizations need financial, human, intellectual, and technology resources. Community consultants can play an important role in helping them to secure such resources. Financial resource development might include writing grants or helping with fundraising through events and donor engagement. Human resource development is often accomplished through training or may involve helping to develop job descriptions. Consultants can help with technology resources by assisting with database development or helping to identify resources to support technology acquisition or develop individuals' capacity to use technology. Susan worked with the Network of the National Library of Medicine where outreach librarians helped to develop intellectual resources by building public libraries and community-based organizations' knowledge and skills to support community members' health information needs. Community consultants might also help by providing linkages to intellectual resources or assisting with reviews of technical and academic literature. They might also help to identify evidence or research-based programs or assist with web searches for resources.

2.9 Summary of Contributions

This chapter described the range of contributions that can be made by community consultants, depending upon their education, experience, their role (internal or external consultant), and the setting in which they work. Community consultants need to build their toolbox to fully meet the needs of communities and community-based organizations. Community groups may need one or more of the many skills you possess from evaluation to the many ways to build the capacity of community organizations. Community consultants are uniquely qualified to help organizations reach their social change or public health goals.

2.10 Key Points

- Community consultants may be based internally to an organization in a staff position, or as an external consultant either as the owner of their own firm or an employee of a nonprofit or for-profit firm. Sometimes, larger firms subcontract work to smaller size consulting firms. In either case, there are a variety of settings that you may work in.
- Community consulting is not always done from a "consulting" office or with the title of "consultant." There are opportunities to engage in community consulting work through jobs in a wide variety of sectors.
- If you are interested in engaging in community consulting through employment in a non-consulting job, it is important to explore the options available by looking at organizations' websites, reading job postings, and talking with individuals in jobs that may be of interest.
- Even if you do not have opportunities to be a "consultant," you can find a satisfying career path that will allow you to use the same skills and do some of the same types of work.
- Community consultants work across a variety of domains that include independent consulting, consulting within a company, education, medical settings, public health, nonprofits, nongovernmental organizations, community-based organizations, government, criminal justice, foundations, corporate philanthropy entrepreneurship, business, technology, and even some unlikely settings not covered here such as in the arts and libraries.
- Services community consultants may provide include evaluation, community needs and resources assessments, strategic planning, coalition development and maintenance, advocacy and policy, community organizing, program development and implementation, organizational and community capacity building, facilitation, leadership development, and resource development.

3 Do You Have the Personal Qualities to Be a Community Consultant?

Nothing endures but personal qualities.

—Walt Whitman (1860)

Community consulting may not be for everyone. Chapter 3 presents a description of the personal qualities that are helpful to have if you wish to pursue community consulting. While it is not necessary that one individual possess all these personal qualities, if you possess only a few of them, you may not enjoy a career as a community consultant.

Ann often employs summer interns. At the end of their internship, she always sits down with them to discuss their experience. A few years ago, during one of these reviews, she asked her intern, "What have you learned through your internship?" She answered flatly, "I've learned that I don't want to do evaluation!" The data they worked with, she said, was just too messy. Without a doubt, program or strategy development, coalition building, policy work, or evaluation, especially within the context of the community, all require a high level of tolerance of **ambiguity**. If, like Ann's intern, you prefer your work to be unambiguous, we strongly advise you to *not choose* to work in community practice. *Do not* facilitate coalition development, and certainly *do not* work within communities or the field of evaluation. Naturally, individuals see the cause of problems differently. Community consultants generally approach things within a systems framework. By this we mean that a systems lens considers the external community-level factors that influence social problems. If you believe that social problems have singular causes occurring at the individual (person) level, you might prefer working in a university lab, conducting randomized control trials, or doing more traditional social science research. Even in these more "controlled" settings, we would argue, social scientists merely have the illusion of control. But that is an argument for another book.

So, do you have what it takes to work in the community? This chapter will explore some of the personal qualities or "soft skills" that community practitioners need.

3.1 Personal Characteristics of Community Practitioners

When you are considering whether you should pursue a career in community consulting practice, it is important to ask yourself some honest questions to determine whether you have the right personal characteristics and capabilities. This section will present some of the questions you should ask yourself (although we are sure there are more).

3.1.1 How Well Do You Tolerate Ambiguity and Uncertainty?

Community consulting is fraught with ambiguity and uncertainty. Each day is different and, often, unpredictable. Projects and funding come and go. Clients and community partners are engaged and then disengage. Social problems are complex, and solutions are not always clear. It is likely that you will have to compete for projects. Each time you submit a proposal, even if you are certain that your submission is stellar, you can never be sure that yours will be selected over other proposals. There are stated criteria, but there are also unstated factors that go into such decisions. To complicate matters, you may be rolling along on a project making wonderful progress when the funding is suddenly discontinued. For example, Susan worked with a federally funded project. Their funding application was successful, but two months later they received notification that funding of their five-year project would be reduced halfway through the project and the funding cycle end date was moved earlier by several months.

Community organizations and coalitions frequently change directions, priorities, members, and sometimes even their missions. One of Susan's clients submitted a continuation grant application only to have the client's parent organization pull the application before the funding decisions were made and notify the project staff that they would be shutting down. In truth, the only thing you can be certain of when you work with community organizations is that there will be a high degree of ambiguity and uncertainty.

3.1.2 Do You Appreciate Complexity or Like Things Simple?

If you said to yourself, "Yes! Simple!", then if you are working on a project this might be your idea of the perfect **theory of change** (see Figure 3.1).

Figure 3.1 Simplified theory of change

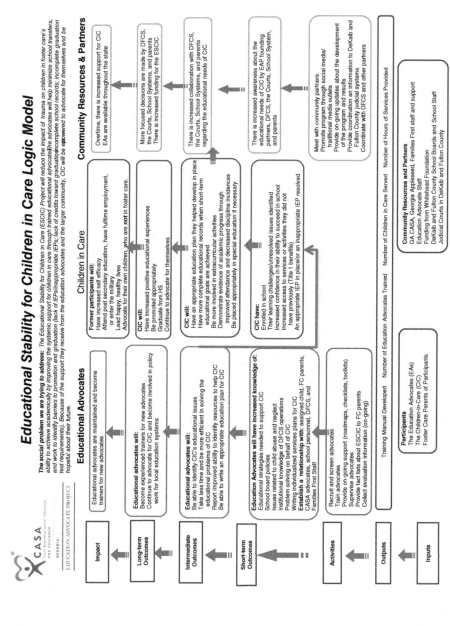

Figure 3.2 Systems change logic model

As mentioned earlier, there are layers of influence inherent in any social problem you may be addressing and, at the very least, these layers must be considered when you develop any program, policy, or evaluation plan. In reality social problems are quite complex and, therefore, the way we visualize our understanding of those social problems, and our solutions, should reflect that complexity. When we work with community intervention and evaluation projects, we often use **logic models** to clearly articulate a program and reflect their complexity. Some evaluators have stopped using logic models for really complex issues involving systems change, preferring to use **systems maps** or other tools instead. Figure 3.2 shows an example of a complex logic model that Ann did for the Education Advocate Project in Georgia.

When you see diagrams of systems like this, do you get tingly or nauseous? If nausea is your first reaction, or even a tinge of anxiety, you may prefer working in another area that is more straightforward.

3.1.3 How Patient Are You?

Patience is a virtue, and it will be tested continuously when you work with communities and community-based organizations. You need to have an overabundance of patience. Working with people and organizations in the community takes lots and lots of patience. We cannot emphasize this enough. Moreover, community practitioners work with myriad social issues that are complex and seemingly intractable. Social change is often slow, much slower than we would like, and certainly much slower than funders and politicians like. **Systems-level changes**, such as those driven by community coalitions, happen slowly. Community members may resist implementing the program, systems changes, or evaluation that you and they have worked so painstakingly to design. Your advice may not always be taken. Things just never seem to go as planned and you will need patience throughout the community process.

Sometimes, even *making the decision* to begin a community change process is daunting. We have both had the experience where we have met with someone who said they were interested in working with us, but they didn't follow through until much later. When we don't hear back in a short time, we may be quick to assume the organization is just not interested in engaging us. Often, the community leader who approached us was working behind the scenes in their organization, garnering support and resources for the organizational project or evaluation. You will need to be patient as community organizations ready themselves to fully engage in the project. It is much better for the community to move thoughtfully than to begin the community change process prematurely. For example, Susan submitted a proposal to do a project in response to a request for proposals and never heard anything back. She assumed they had selected someone else or decided not to pursue the project. Two years later, she got a call telling her that they were ready to start the project, had selected her proposal, and asked her when she could start. By this time Susan had forgotten she had submitted the proposal! The organization explained that they were distracted with other priorities until they realized that this project needed to be completed before funding expired. This is another example of how patience is required when you are working in communities.

3.1.4 Can You Talk to Just About Anybody?

In addition to patience, community practitioners need to be **sociable** in a variety of settings with many types of people. This does not mean that you need to be extroverted or the life of the party, but you do need to be sociable. Many people in the community and particularly leaders in community-based organizations may be fearful of evaluation or consulting. They may be wary of outsiders working with them. Therefore, the ability to put people at ease is critical. Before you discuss contract details, you must connect with your potential client in a personal way. We do not mean in a superficial or insincere way at all. We do not mean that you must become best friends or otherwise socialize outside of the consulting situation. We simply mean that you need to establish a comfortable rapport, perhaps by finding something you have in common. Later, if there are difficult conversations, this rapport and connection will help you and your client keep the relationship central. If for some reason you cannot connect with the person you will be working with, you might want to reexamine whether this is the client for you and consider making a referral to a colleague.

3.1.5 Are You Able to Exercise Tactfulness, Sensitivity, and Professionalism?

Working in communities requires that you relate to others with a sense of **tact** which Merriam-Webster (n.d.e) defines as "a keen sense of what to do or say in order to maintain good relations with others or avoid offense." You need to be sensitive to people and their emotions and maintain your professionalism, even in difficult circumstances. Once you connect with your client, you need to find out if they have been involved in a similar project before and if they have experience working with a community consultant. It is helpful to know if they have had a bad experience with either and what made their experience uncomfortable. For example, you will need to identify what worked well with past consultations, and what did not work as well and why. It is important to remain professional; you would never want to bash another consultant when you see bad work, just simply state that you have a different approach.

Knowing where people are coming from can help community practitioners relate to their clients and put their fears to rest. Getting staff to talk about their experiences with community consultants helps them to come to terms with their experiences and feel ready to move forward. For example, a previous bad evaluation experience may affect how they feel about evaluation and evaluators in general and can be a serious roadblock to their relationship with you. The same holds true of community consultants who specialize in strategic planning. Often, a potential client tells a story that goes like this:

> *We just did not feel listened to.*
> *We did not have the capacity to collect the data that the consultant told us we had to collect.*
> *We got a beautiful strategic plan that we did not know how to implement.*
> *The consultant was more interested in their questions than the questions our program needed answered.*
> *We felt excluded from the whole process.*
> *The design was not realistic or applicable to our community.*

We often start initial conversations with potential clients by asking them to tell us about their previous experiences: the good, the bad, and the ugly. A client's past negative experience can taint the work you are trying to do. We suggest that at the very first potential client meeting, you work to understand their history and address their concerns and fears.

There may be occasions on which clients will share the work of past consultants with you and ask for your feedback or comments on them. Susan once had a client who shared reports from the past evaluator. The reports contained grievous errors. These included using the name of other projects in the report where the client's name should have been, incorrect use of graphs, and graphs that did not match the numbers in the body of the report. Luckily, Susan can use phrases such as "I would have done this differently" with a straight face.

This illustrates another aspect of professionalism – the ability to maintain a neutral face no matter what is said. If you are someone whose expressions always let everyone know what is on your mind, you will need to be aware of this habit and consciously modulate your expressions. Conveying negative emotions on your face can become detrimental to developing good relationships, or at the very least make others feel judged.

And finally, professionalism also means being careful who you talk with about your clients. This is especially important in regard to sharing problems you are having or negative experiences. Clients may prefer that you not share their good news with others as well. So be sure and ask before sharing their findings in a new proposal, on your website, or on social media. Maintaining confidentiality is as important in a community consulting role as it is for professionals who work with individuals. Divulging organization or community information can have unforeseen consequences for those who are involved and may include loss of funding, individuals being fired, or disrupted community relations. It is also unethical practice.

3.1.6 How Well Do You Understand Organizational and Community Context?

Understanding your client's organization (for example, organizational politics, community and organizational constraints, and stakeholders) will help *you* to understand the nature of the organization and staff attitudes about working with a consultant. This understanding will help you as you guide them through the project. Some basic questions to consider include:

- Is the <u>entire</u> organization supportive of this project or do they tolerate it because funders or the board require it?
- Are frontline workers engaged and do they see the value of their participation?
- Are the top leaders supportive of the project?
- Has the organization dedicated the necessary resources and staff to the project?

We have both experienced several engagements where as soon as the contract was signed, the executives in charge of the project disengaged. This can send a signal, maybe not even intended, that this work is unimportant. When this happens, progress is slow or is halted altogether. Therefore, it is critical that leaders stay engaged throughout all phases of the project. Alternatively, we have both been on projects where frontline staff were not consulted and the project was slowed when information was not shared, or data were not collected.

Whether you are working with a community collaborative or a single organization, understanding the community context is important. Community contextual features include the community's history, demographics and demographic shifts, relationships among community members and groups, politics, norms and cultures, power structure, economics, geography, relationships with surrounding communities, and many other factors. For example, if your client is developing or implementing a new program that will rely upon referrals from other organizations, it will be helpful to understand the relationships among organizations in the community. Are relationships among the organizations involved collaborative or competitive? Do they even know one another? Have they worked together in the past, and if so, was the relationship positive or were there problems?

If you are working with an entire community, then it is especially critical to understand as much of the context as possible from the beginning. Susan and Ann worked together on a project that was building inclusive county-wide collaboratives. They encountered numerous contextual factors that would potentially impact the project success if not attended to at the outset. Some examples we witnessed included towns within the same county that had a history of conflict, a culture of racism, illegal activities supported by or at least ignored by the officials, and exploitation of the impoverished populations within the community. These issues were in addition to economic devastation, lack of resources, and other more typical problems often experienced within communities.

3.1.7 Can You Handle the Truth?

Typically, people who work to improve their communities are not the shy, retiring type. On the contrary, they are usually strong-willed people with equally strong opinions. The same might be said of some community consultants. In any case, the community consultant needs to be able to deal with the strong personalities of community activists and others. When you work with community organizations, you need to understand that community members and organizations do not always agree. In fact, they are almost always very passionate people who may not be tolerant of others who disagree with them. If you are working with community coalitions and collaboratives, you should expect that from time to time, community members will clash.

3.1.8 How Comfortable Are You with Strong Emotions?

At times, your community client may share strong emotions. You need to be comfortable if they become somewhat agitated or even angry. When this happens, be sure they feel they have been heard, and then bring them back into focus to move forward toward a positive and productive conversation.

You may find yourself in situations where two groups or individuals are arguing with one another, and you need to diffuse the situation to move forward. Sometimes the consultant may need to sit quietly and allow anger and other negative emotions to be expressed without displaying extreme discomfort as the disputing parties work through their differences. There may come times when you need to suggest a cooling-off period with some individuals or groups and walk away for some time.

As a consultant, you should model respect for the different viewpoints of community members. Working in communities requires comfort with people who express their emotions and the ability to bring them back into focus to move forward toward a positive and productive conversation if necessary. You need to be able to remain calm as tensions rise so that the situation does not escalate. Conflict resolution is a skill you will need throughout your life as a consultant. Reflective listening skills are useful and help facilitate a participatory approach.

If dealing with strong emotions makes you feel uncomfortable, you may need training in conflict management to develop these skills.

3.1.9 Can You Handle Norming, Forming, and Most Definitely Storming?

Working in and *across* community organizations can be challenging. Community change often happens through the work of community coalitions and collaboratives, organizations of community partners that come together for a common purpose. For simplicity's sake, we will just use the term coalition here. To be successful, coalition members must set aside the agenda of the organization they represent, or their own personal agenda. Clear and honest communication is needed to ensure that they achieve their strategic goals. When communication among leaders is not honest and open, parking lot conversations may become the norm. Gossiping and back biting may ensue and trust among members erodes. It is hard to remember to put the good of the community at the forefront. When you are consulting with a community, no matter how you feel about the individuals or organizations involved, you must do your best to remain as neutral as possible.

Several years ago, a newly formed community coalition with which Ann worked struggled to get going. Most members were community leaders who wanted to get to work on the focal problem immediately. Yet the community coalition lacked the foundational structures (that is, by-laws and workgroups) to be successful. Members expected the coalition coordinator to do all the work. The coalition could not reach an agreement on how to go about implementing community prevention strategies. Personalities did not mix well. A few community agencies pushed their own agendas. Things got personal. Some leaders quit the coalition.

What will your reaction be when the organization or group you are working with goes through a "storming" phase? What should you do when conflict occurs within the community organization: try to guide their discussions, arbitrate a solution to their conflict, or simply watch from the sidelines to see who wins the battle? It is important for the community consultant to maintain as neutral a stance as possible while guiding the parties toward their common goal(s) as an organization. This is where your knowledge of group dynamics and training in program development are needed. You need to recognize that conflict is a normal and perhaps even necessary part of the development of a community coalition. Help your client realize this too. Then help them focus on the structure they need to build to be successful. Use tools such as a logic model (a graphic representation of your program) or a theory of change (a big picture of the context and causal pathways) to help community participants to stay focused on the work and, when it gets personal, bring them back there to help them defuse contentious situations. Helping the group to develop a clear mission, vision, and values statement can also refocus members.

As we have discussed, and you may have experienced, community members have strong opinions and perspectives. It is likely that you will not always agree with them, but the community consultant must respect the different perspectives held by community leaders. Sometimes your client may choose to implement an intervention that you do not believe will be effective. They may want to measure their intervention in a way that you do not believe will be ideal. For example, clients may resist your advice to shorten a measure because they cannot bear the thought of losing information, or they may want to shorten a measure in a way that might threaten its reliability or validity.

You may not always agree with your clients' choices but as one supervisor once told Ann, "People absolutely have the right to their wrong opinion." Community members know their communities' needs better than you do. At the same time, you bring planning, evaluation, measurement, facilitation, and other expertise to the table. Be honest but be humble; express your best professional opinion but respect their choice to go in a different direction.

3.1.10 Are You a Politician?

Another important skill is the ability to manage politics and competing agendas. As former Speaker of the House, Tip O'Neill, was fond of saying, "All politics is local." Truer words were never spoken. Politics can occur at multiple levels, however. The community organization with which you are working is held within a state, for example. That state might be a red state or a blue state and this reality likely influences the beliefs of constituents and practical matters such as what gets funded. What is defined as legal is also influenced by political beliefs (for example, gay marriage or the legalization of marijuana). At the more micro-level, communities and neighborhoods within those communities have their own politics as well.

A wise community consultant begins by learning about state and local politics, identifies key community players, and understands how they and their interests relate to each other. For example, Ann had a client who was trying to pass a local social host ordinance (an ordinance that prohibits adults supplying alcohol to minors). Community coalition leaders took the correct first step: they identified the community stakeholders they should reach out to first. But they failed to appreciate the differing opinions of a powerful county commissioner and a local mayor. An innocent conversation with the mayor of one of the cities in that county nearly derailed the passing of the local ordinance. The county commissioner was irate to learn that the mayor was brought into the conversation. Failure to begin with the *right* key stakeholder might result in similar mishap. The same is true of any other systems change initiative such as a policy change, state legislation, or a community intervention. Know the politicians in the community that need to be consulted and be aware of whom should be involved and when.

Community members, organizations, and government agencies all have different and often competing agendas. While one person or group of people may see an issue as critically important, another group might have another priority. Take a community substance abuse coalition organized to prevent underage use as an example. Some community leaders may believe that youth alcohol prevention is the most important issue that the coalition should address. There is strong evidence (data) to support that alcohol is the substance most commonly used by teens in the United States. At the same time, other community leaders believe that another substance, say heroin for example, is more important than worrying about a more socially acceptable substance such as alcohol.

3.2 Additional Considerations If You Are Going Solo

3.2.1 How Much Do You Like to Be Alone?

If you thrive in a setting where you have a high level of interaction, then solo community consulting may not suit you. Many contracts are small to medium size ($5,000 to $20,000) and will not support other practitioners. If you prefer having colleagues read your reports or proposals before they are submitted, that may not always be available at this smaller level of engagement.

3.2.2 Do You Have a High Level of Self-Motivation and Self-Discipline?

Related to solo work, you will also need a high degree of self-motivation. There will be no boss (other than your client) to report to. You will likely develop deliverables and due dates, but you will need to motivate yourself to get them done. As a solo community consultant, you will mainly work alone, without the pay incentives and rewards systems of larger companies. You need to ask yourself if the work and any compensation will be motivating enough for you. Many times, your motivation will have to be enough to keep you *and* your client going, so pick work you enjoy.

Closely linked to self-motivation is the practice of self-discipline. You will have to discipline yourself to do the work. If you work at home, you may be tempted to stay in your pajamas or get distracted by household tasks. Nobody is around to witness you checking social media or working in front of the television. Emails can also be a distraction. Self-discipline is required to organize tasks and then work toward their completion. While a big plus of working in a solo practice is the flexibility to set your own schedule and choose your work, the work still must get done. Your reputation as a dependable partner is essential to your survival as a business. Even though we work at home, both of us adhere to regular routines of getting up, getting dressed, and going to the office as we would for any other job.

So, you are self-motivated and have great self-discipline – you are ready to set up your practice. How do you explain your practice to your friends and relatives? They may assume you will now have lots of time on your hands. For example, when Susan started her consulting practice, the first thing her tennis friends said was "Now you'll be free to play on daytime leagues." It took some time for her to convince them that although she works for herself and from home, it was important to treat each day as a workday. You are still a professional who goes to the office, even if you are not commuting. Sure, you can be a little more flexible and occasionally take time out for personal errands or tend to family needs, but it is important to keep your consulting practice in the forefront as your "job" and not treat it as a sideline activity.

3.2.3 Are You Highly Organized or a Train Wreck?

Working solo means you must be especially good at organizing your office and your time. There may be times when you will be juggling multiple clients. Keeping client documents and electronic files organized and easily accessible will really pay off. Clients frequently call or email with questions or needs and having systems in place that allow you to lay your hands on documents and information very quickly is essential. Having things in random piles on your desk or similarly disorganized electronic files will make you miserable and inefficient.

The same is true for being able to manage your time effectively and efficiently. Being chronically late is rude and not good business practice. Forgetting a meeting altogether is inexcusable when people are paying you for a service. The same is true for missing deadlines and submitting reports and other needed documents late. Dependability is really important as a community consultant in order to foster trust and confidence in your work.

3.2.4 Do You Have a Dedicated Space to Work and the Necessary Equipment and Infrastructure?

If you choose to work at home, you may not be able to set aside a room as an office, but you need to be able to set aside at least a corner of space for files, a work surface and equipment. If you plan to use the dining room table, that will likely only work out if you have another place for yourself or your family to eat. Showing up for meetings with papers stuck together with jelly or coffee stains will probably not promote your professional image. It is very helpful to have an "office" to go to each day, even if it is simply a small space set aside in your living room. We will provide more information about your space and equipment needs in Chapter 6 when we talk about locating and setting up an office.

3.2.5 Can You Afford to Quit Your Day Job, and Are You Good at Financial Management?

If you are the primary (or only) breadwinner or contribute substantially to your household budget, then this is a really important question to answer honestly. It takes time to start a consulting practice and even after you are rolling along, sometimes years later, there will be dips in your income. If you are the sole provider then you need to make sure you have enough funds saved to cover at least six months of expenses, preferably a year. Even if you are starting out with a large contract, sometimes things happen. You never want to be in a position where you must grab any work you can get because that will take up time that could be better spent finding projects that best suit your skills and interests. There are some consultants who contend that this isn't necessary. If you are hungry enough, you will find a way to make this happen. We advocate for a more cautious stance that will allow you to be more purposeful in your approach. You will also want to make sure that you have the support of your spouse, partner, or significant other if you have one, and that they too are prepared for the financial and emotional struggles of community consulting.

Having good financial management skills and being financially literate are also important. Even if you hire an accountant, you need to understand the financial side of your business so you will know if your accountant is honest and looking out for your best interests. If you do not hire an accountant, you will need to understand how to make quarterly tax payments and how much to pay, which type of retirement account you should open, and even how to determine how much money you should charge for your services. You also need financial discipline. It may be tempting to take that well-deserved vacation when you receive a large lump sum payment. But you have to consider taxes and other business expenses and remember to put something aside for unexpected events or expenses, like when your computer crashes or you unexpectedly lose a contract.

3.3 Some Considerations If You Work for an Organization

The considerations listed here are some things to think about when you work for an organization that is not your own, either as an internal consultant, or if you are looking for a job that will allow you to engage in community consulting work.

3.3.1 What Is Your Organization's Perspective on Community Consulting?

Hopefully, the organization you work for supports a collaborative approach to community consulting, meaning that they value and engage community members. A collaborative approach means that community members are present and active throughout the project. The community members are decision-makers throughout the process and are in charge, as opposed to you as the internal consultant. If your organization is not comfortable with this approach and would prefer that you stay in the "expert" role and maintain control, then you will not be able to employ a community consulting approach.

The mission of serving the community, rather than a focus on billable hours, should be your primary focus. If you are working for a consulting organization that is more concerned with bringing in business, focuses more on billable hours than community outcomes, and is not respectful of the community, then it is business- rather than mission-focused. If the organization expects you to support its interests at the expense of the community, then you have a decision to make. Of course, there must be some focus on the business side of consulting, but not at the sacrifice of the community's needs.

3.3.2 Is Your Organization's Approach Rooted in Colonialism?

Many nonprofits provide services, or initiate actions in communities or neighborhoods where none of their organizational members reside or have any true interest in the community. It is not unusual for a nonprofit to see a request for proposals as an opportunity to expand its services into neighborhoods where it does not have a presence. It does not work directly with community members, does not open an office in the neighborhood, and does not hire staff from the communities. The organization sends its staff in to do the work at existing nonprofits or other sites and stops services to that community when the funding ends.

Consequently, the project plan with activities and outcomes may be predetermined by the funding agency or the organization that receives the funding with little or no input from the community members. Often, if there is any input, it is in the form of a survey or some focus groups where the question design, analysis, and interpretations are all done by someone external to the community. The funding may require some community advisory team or collaboration, but this is often performative, and the community members rarely have real power to determine what is done or measured.

If you are consulting from such a position, then it is important to recognize that you and your organization's approach is rooted in **colonialism**. Your organization is getting the funding, and you are getting your job funded, but what is the community really getting? A program they probably did not ask for, that they likely had little or no input in designing, and one that will be gone when the funding ends, leaving the community as it was before – unchanged and not helped in a substantive manner.

3.3.3 What Is the Organization's Reputation in the Community?

You need to honestly appraise your organization's position and reputation within the community where you want to work. If the organization has a reputation as a "bully" or is for some reason untrustworthy you will likely not be successful as a consultant representing it. The same is true if the organization has a history of unsuccessful endeavors, negative community relationships, or is viewed as serving the needs of a specific group at the expense of others.

3.4 If We Haven't Scared You Off …

We don't present these personal qualities with the purpose of scaring you away from consulting, but to ensure that if you move forward to engage in community consulting, you have an idea of how much it will truly fit with your personality and life. We do want to say that we find community consulting to be personally rewarding in many ways. It allows unlimited opportunities for professional development. The work allows for flexibility not only in terms of scheduling but also in choosing the types of issues and clients with whom you work. We get to work on the social issues that mean the most to us, such as maternal and child health, substance abuse prevention, child abuse and families involved in the foster care system. There are other benefits as well and we will discuss those in later chapters.

3.5 Key Points

- Appreciate and be comfortable with complexity and ambiguity. Community work is not easy because social problems are complex.
- "Soft" skills are important for successful practicing in the community.
- Pack patience. Community work is hard and often progress is made slowly. The community will not always take your advice or move as quickly as you would like. DO respect that while you bring a certain expertise, community members are experts in their community.
- Those who fail to appreciate the past are doomed to repeat it. Before you get started, seek to understand the community or organization's history with community consultants, practitioners, and evaluators. The results of a bad experience may linger for some time and may influence your chances of being successful with a community.
- Understand the lay of the land. Along with history, you need to understand something about the organizational culture and how it supports community charge efforts and evaluation. Are the key leaders supportive or merely offering lip-service to the project? Have frontline staff been engaged so that they buy in to the project?
- Unlike chemistry, people do not always combine in predictable ways. How do you react when people feel strongly about an issue or even get irritable or angry? You will need to stay calm and as neutral as possible among competing emotions and opinions.
- Be aware of the power and influence of local politics. Your community client ideally will have key politicians at the table, but at the very least, you must take their perspective and concerns into account. Ignore them at your own peril.
- Are you ready to go solo? Working in the community can be ironically a lonely endeavor. This is truer still if you operate a solo community consulting practice. You will need to be self-motivated and self-disciplined to accomplish your deliverables and manage the many tasks involved in managing multiple community clients. You will need to be financially stable and have support from the significant people in your life.
- Choose your clients wisely. Not every relationship is meant to be.

4 Community Consulting Values and Knowledge

Grant that I may not so much seek to be understood as to understand.
—St. Francis (n.d.)

The diversity in the human family should be the cause of love and harmony, as it is in music where many different notes blend together in the making of a perfect chord.
—'Abdu'l-Baha (Effendi, 1938)

In Chapter 4 we describe how values and knowledge will help you work as a community consultant and share examples of how they look in practice.

In the last chapter, we described some of the "soft skills" or personal attributes needed for community consulting. The objectives of this chapter are to describe the necessary underlying values and knowledge for effective community engagement. The values are primarily grounded in our discipline, community psychology (Dalton & Wolfe, 2012), but are also foundational for other disciplines. Competencies from other disciplines such as public health (The Council on Linkages Between Academia and Public Health Practice, 2021), evaluation (American Evaluation Association, 2018), and social work (National Association of Social Workers, 2015) share the values we describe in this chapter.

4.1 Values and Knowledge for Community Consultants

The knowledge that you need to understand and apply when you are a community consultant is rooted in **values**. This includes cultural humility, anti-racism, social justice, equity, decoloniality, ecological frameworks, community inclusiveness, empowerment, ethical and reflective practice, and commitment to ongoing personal and professional development.

4.1.1 Cultural Humility

We reviewed competencies from multiple disciplines (that is, social work, public health, evaluation), and they all included sociocultural and cross-cultural competence and, more recently, **cultural humility**. For example, social workers are required to understand culture and its functions in human behavior and society, recognizing the strengths that exist in all cultures; have a knowledge base of the clients' cultures and be able to demonstrate competence in the provision of services that are sensitive to clients' cultures and to differences among people and cultural groups; and to obtain education about and seek to understand the nature of social diversity and oppression with respect to race, ethnicity, national origin, color, sex, sexual orientation, gender identity or expression, age, marital status, political belief, religion, immigration status, and mental or physical disability (National Association of Social Workers, 2015). Public health professionals must incorporate strategies for interacting with individuals from diverse backgrounds and ensuring the public health organizations with whom they work are culturally competent (The Council on Linkages Between Academia and Public Health Practice, 2021). In 2011, the American Evaluation Association published a set of guidelines for cultural competence (American Evaluation Association, 2011). Public administrators are required to communicate and interact productively with a diverse and changing workforce and citizenry (Network of Schools of Public Policy, Affairs, and Administration, n.d.).

For a long time, **cultural competence** was the focus for most professionals engaged with communities. Being culturally competent for effective community consulting requires learning skills and gaining knowledge and self-insight through books, workshops and classes, self-discovery, reflection of personal biases, feedback from peers or community members, and most importantly, experience in communities. Kien Lee (2015, p. 117) describes the following three key components to cross-cultural competency development: "1. Understanding the definition of 'culture'; 2. Navigating the effects of social identities; 3. Addressing privilege and power." Lee further defines cross-cultural competency as "the ability to interact, function, and work effectively among people who may not share your demographic attributes, language, beliefs, history, and experiences."

While it is helpful to know about a specific group's culture if you will be working with the group, it is also important not to assume that because individuals belong to a specific racial, ethnic, religious, or another group that they also share the same culture. There is diversity *within* groups, and similarities across groups of people and communities (Lee, 2015). For example, we have seen a tendency for many people to talk about individuals from Africa as though it is a single nation rather than a continent comprised of many different countries, languages, and cultures. The same is true when people describe all Asians as though they are a single group and ignore the differences between Chinese, Japanese, Vietnamese, Korean, and other Asian cultures. It is equally important to not assume that individuals from cultures other than your own interpret words and phrases similarly to you or one another. It is also not safe to assume that organizations such as churches, government, or the police serve the same functions or are experienced in the same way by other cultures or communities.

An important aspect of cultural competence is understanding the history and politics of a community and appreciating how privilege and power have impacted different groups within the community. Keeping abreast of current events in the community and getting to know the community through the eyes of community members is helpful to effectively partner with community members. Be careful not to interpret what you hear from your perceptions that are rooted in your experiences. A community's history and its experience of privilege and power are likely to impact the community members' ability to trust you, organizations, institutions, programs, or other entities. It may take time to build relationships and gain community members' confidence that you are legitimately there to work in partnership and do not have a hidden agenda.

As we mentioned earlier, "cultural competence" was the focus for most community-based professionals and social scientists, however, in practice this was not enough. Over the past several years there has been a shift from cultural competence to cultural humility. Hook, Davis, Owen, Worthington, and Utsey (2013) conceptualize cultural humility as the "ability to maintain an interpersonal stance that is other-oriented (or open to the other) in relation to aspects of cultural identity that are most important to the [person]" (p. 354). Tervalon and Murray-García (1998) describe cultural humility as a process, not an outcome. It requires a lifelong commitment to self-evaluation and self-reflective practice. Their point, and we agree, is that you will never get to a point where you are done learning. You must be humble and be willing to look at yourself critically. Cultural humility requires that you have a desire to fix power imbalances where none ought to exist. As community consultants, it means that we default to participatory methods when we are collaborating with communities. We recognize the value of each person, their opinions, their needs, and their desires for their community. Finally, cultural humility requires that we aspire to develop partnerships with people and groups who advocate for others (Tervalon & Murray-García, 1998) and obliges us to advocate within the larger organizations in which we participate.

Another important skill, **cultural responsiveness**, moves beyond competence and cultural humility. It challenges us, the "professionals," to recognize our personal and professional biases. We must be aware of how we tend to default when there is a question of power, especially when there is conflict. It means being aware of our own power and privilege to dialog with communities to work to address their needs. Cultural responsiveness, like cultural humility, "is an introspective, lifelong commitment to understanding unique cultural strengths, challenges, and their impact on community engagement" (Clark, 2019).

In summary, as a community consultant, developing cultural competence, cultural humility, and cultural responsiveness is an ongoing process and goes beyond the communities with whom you work. We must be able to let go of our own worldview while we are working in a community that is different from our own and engage with the community members based on *their* reality. Competence in this area requires keeping up with local, state, national, and world events and learning what those events mean for those who are affected from their perspective.

Take an honest, in-depth look at your own life experiences, position in society, and social and cultural identities and how they intersect with one another. How do they interact with your engagement with and understanding of others? For example, did you grow up and go to school in a racially and culturally diverse environment, or did everyone look like you? Have you ever been truly poor, such as not knowing where your next meal would come from for long stretches of time and not having anyone who could help? Check yourself and your reactions to daily events. For example, if you are white, if you walk down the street and see two young Black men walking toward you, pay attention to your physiological reaction. Do you tend to put extra space between yourself and them as you pass by? Do you feel a little fearful? Once you begin to recognize your biases, which likely developed somewhere in your childhood, you can begin to address them within yourself.

Self-reflection should also include reflecting on your privilege, especially "**white privilege**" if it applies. This is a concept that, when mentioned, elicits pushback and creates discomfort for some people. First, white people are not used to being described by their race. And second, especially for people from less advantaged backgrounds, it suggests they have not struggled, though many have (Collins, 2018). To be clear, white privilege is not a suggestion that white people have never struggled. It also does not mean that white people did not earn what they have accomplished. What it does refer to is the ability to move through the world without thinking about your race. As a result, you will more often than not be granted the benefit of the doubt, you more often see people who look like you in the media (unless they are showing examples of crime), and it means having greater access to power and resources than people of color.

Exercising cultural humility and becoming more culturally responsive requires learning about, and exposure to, cultures other than your own. Reading literature by authors from other races, ethnicities, and cultures is an excellent way to learn more about other cultures and perspectives. Through literature, authors describe the world through their eyes. If you read enough of them, you begin to see the commonalities within groups of people, but also the diversity of ideas, experiences, and cultures. Reading biographies and nonfiction accounts of events can help you to see the world and events from the perspective of those who were affected. As you read, keep in mind that authors from other races, ethnicities, and cultures who reach the level of success to become published are often from an elite class within communities of color.

Spend real time socializing with individuals from other backgrounds. This does not mean occasionally having lunch at work with the Black woman in your office, although that may be a start for some people. Attending a few festivals to sample the food is also nice, but also insufficient. It means to spend meaningful time with people who are different than you. For example, accept invitations to church when they are offered, do not shy away from discussions of differences and similarities with others, and broaden your network of friends. Finally, we suggest you listen. We mean *really* listen without letting your own defenses and filters get in the way. When you make a mistake, when your biases reveal themselves, own it, make amends, and resolve to do better. Exercising cultural humility and becoming culturally competent are processes and growth that continue throughout a lifetime. We are never 100 percent there.

If you have privilege in some form – are white, have an education, are heterosexual, live in a safe neighborhood, have easy access to food – then be sure when you do interact with others who lack such privileges that you acknowledge your privilege and understand your own positionality. It is equally important that you never claim to "know what that is like" if you have never shared the experience or characteristics of a community or individual. As much as we want to empathize, we know, as white women, that we will never *really know* what it is like to be Black. No matter who you are or where you come from, you will likely interact with communities and individuals whose experiences, histories, and backgrounds are different than your own, and you may find it helpful to always take a step back and reflect upon how this may impact your viewpoints, impressions, and interactions.

4.1.2 Anti-Racism

We have likely all heard someone say "I'm not racist" with the assumption that being "not racist" somehow absolves them of in any way supporting white supremacy. According to Ibram X. Kendi (2019), being "not racist" is a neutral position; it is not the opposite of **racist**. The opposite of racist is **anti-racist**, which Kendi defines as "One who is supporting an antiracist policy through their actions or expressing an antiracist idea" (Kendi, 2019, p. 13).

White supremacy is not limited to extreme groups and actions such as the Ku Klux Klan or the attempted annihilation of the Jews by the Nazis.

It permeates society. The Anti-Defamation League characterizes it as belief systems such as that whites should have dominance over people of other backgrounds; white people have their own "culture" that is superior to others; and that white people are genetically superior to others. Understanding white supremacy culture is important. In their *Dismantling Racism: Workbook for Social Change Groups*, Jones and Okun (2001) describe the characteristics of white supremacy culture which show up in our organizations. We have included a link to this free, online workbook in Appendix 2 at the end of this book. It contains a wealth of rich information and includes antidotes for each characteristic and we highly recommend that you take some time to check it out.

Asare (2021) describes four myths about white supremacy that can deepen our own understanding of our role in upholding it. The first myth is that white supremacy is always intentional. Many of us uphold white supremacy in ways that we don't even realize. For example, our notion of professionalism is often seen through a white lens. We may have standards of beauty that come from this lens. The second myth is that only white people uphold white supremacy. Black, Indigenous, and People of Color (BIPOC) may also unintentionally propagate white supremacist views and ideologies by distancing themselves from their ethnic or racial identity to gain access to opportunities or engage in **colorism**.

The third myth Asare describes is that white supremacy is not common. It is. White supremacists are not all extremists and domestic terrorists. Some of them are our neighbors, our colleagues, and members of our own communities. They are young and old. The fourth myth is that white supremacy disappears when there is new leadership. Unless the new leadership completely overhauls our laws, policies, systems, and social mores, white supremacy continues to exist.

So, what does this mean for community consultants? It means it is important to deepen your understanding of what white supremacy means, and what it looks like in policy and practice. Becoming anti-racist requires that community consultants become comfortable having those difficult conversations about race and racism. And it also means developing a level of comfort with expressing anti-racist viewpoints, pointing out when systems are demonstrating policies and practices that uphold white supremacy, and that even the most "woke" community consultant consistently engages in a personal deep dive regarding their own actions and viewpoints.

Kendi (2019) posits that anti-racism is not a destination, it is a journey that takes deliberate and consistent work. Everyone has grown up and been socialized with a set of beliefs, expressions, and behaviors, some of which may be racist. Many common phrases which some of us may have unknowingly used have racist origins, such as "peanut gallery," "sold down the river," "uppity," "no can do," and "long time no see." Gaining awareness and then erasing these phrases from our vocabulary takes learning, time, and effort on our part.

Another important concept to understand is "**white fragility**," a term coined by Robin DiAngelo (2011), who defined it as "a state in which even a minimum amount of racial stress becomes intolerable, triggering a range of defensive moves" which function to reinstate white racial equilibrium. Situations that might trigger white people might include people of color talking directly about their racial perspectives, receiving feedback that one's behavior had a racist impact, and people of color not being willing to tell their stories or answer questions about their racial experiences. Chances are you will encounter one of these or other triggers. As a community consultant, if you are white and work in communities of color, you will need to develop a level of comfort with being confronted or having your motives questioned. If you find that you have work to do in these areas and/or there are some communities where you would prefer to work, that is OK. What is most important is that you do the deep dive and come to those realizations before you do any harm.

4.1.3 Confronting Colonialism

When someone talks about colonization or calls someone a "colonizer" in modern-day society, it usually refers to the practice of centering the European or Western ways as the "right way."[1] **Decoloniality** means different things to different groups. For the purposes of our work, it describes meaningful and active resistance to forces of colonialism that perpetuate the subjugation and exploitation of minds. It means we must resist white supremacy ideologies, methods, and approaches while we resist supporting them in our work with communities, nonprofits, government, and funding organizations.

Linda Tuhiwai Smith's book, *Decolonizing Methodologies* (2021), describes the process by which Western knowledge was positioned as superior. Smith notes that researchers have historically gone into indigenous communities, done their studies, and published the results "describing" the community members through the eyes of the researchers. This is but one example of a colonizing practice.

How often do university professors, nonprofit leaders, and foundations use data about communities they have never spent any real time in for research, planning, and to support grant proposals to fund projects they decided to do? This is a regular practice. Recently Susan was reading a local health needs assessment. It started by proclaiming they used community-based participatory research methods. What they had done was conducted a survey and

---

[1] It should be noted that there is actually a much deeper meaning to the term "colonization," but we are using the term here as it is more generally applied.

facilitated a few focus groups. The needs assessment team took the data back to their offices and interpreted and reported it – through their eyes, from their perspective, and ensured there was nothing controversial. Susan was a participant in the listening sessions on which the needs assessment report was done. She knew participants had discussed at length about the role that racism played regarding access and poor health outcomes. But this discussion was not reflected in the needs assessment report.

This is not an isolated instance. Too often the voices of community members are absent. If their voices are included, it is after they have been filtered. Community members are seldom at the table when planning initiatives occur within their own communities. The desired outcomes are determined by the funders or program proposers, evaluation protocols designed to assess these outcomes with little input from the community other than to treat them as "subjects," and most of the programs are designed to somehow change the community members rather than the systems that are the root of the problem. Kivel (2007) describes this as providing social service (addressing the needs of individuals impacted by systems of exploitation and violence) rather than engaging in social change (challenging the root causes of exploitation and violence). Kivel uses as an example the proliferation of shelters and services for domestic violence survivors with no large-scale movement to end the violence.

Community consultants need to be willing and able to recognize colonization of communities by outsiders and to potentially confront it. For example, discussing with funding agencies, nonprofit organizations, and governmental entities how they can engage with communities in a manner that allows community members to decide what is needed and how money will be spent. It can also mean telling funders or service providers something they do not wish to hear. Each community consultant must determine their own optimal course of action. Only you can determine if you are willing to act in a way that is most respectful of and empowering for the focal community.

4.1.4 Racial and Social Justice, Equity, and Liberation

Community consulting work is most effective when it is done with an active commitment to improving public welfare, social justice, and **racial justice**. Having the skills to work to those ends is important for all who are engaging with communities. Working from this perspective incorporates advocacy, systems thinking, and similar skills. Cultural humility and an anti-racist stance is essential. We are always explicit with our clients that our work is grounded in this perspective. Ultimately, even though community consulting often requires working directly with community leaders and representatives from community-based organizations, in practice you are a guest of the focal community and must maintain a commitment to do your work in a manner that is for their benefit while serving as a resource to support their advocacy and their agenda.

Skills for work focusing on racial and social justice, equity, and **liberation** are explicit among several disciplinary fields. Social work competencies require social workers to advocate for human rights and social justice. This includes understanding oppression and discrimination and engaging in practices to advance social and economic justice. Advanced social work practitioners are required to demonstrate skills to change social institutions to be more humane and responsive and identify systemic weaknesses in systems and develop and propose policies to promote social justice (National Association of Social Workers, 2015). The Network of Schools of Public Policy, Affairs, and Administration (n.d.) mandates their programs train students to articulate and apply a public service perspective and demonstrate commitment to improving social welfare and justice. The American Evaluation Association draft competencies (2018) include contributing to public welfare through evaluation practice.

Acquiring these skills requires doing some research to understand social justice and **racial equity** issues and doing some introspection to determine the extent to which you can advocate on their behalf. There may be issues you are unable to embrace or advocate for, or issues of which you lack a deep understanding. In these cases, you should decline the consultation or work under someone who has this specific expertise. Be aware that taking a stand for social or racial justice sometimes requires taking positions or speaking out in ways that may make others uncomfortable. They may challenge you and require you to develop a thick skin.

Developing a commitment to social justice and racial equity requires that you and your work do not promote or support oppression or discrimination and other inequitable practices. It also requires that you recognize and explicitly address the role that the "isms" (for example, racism, sexism, **ableism**, **ageism**) play in creating disparities and inequities. It is not enough to feel the commitment internally, but you must demonstrate it through actions by the way you do your work.

It helps to research the roots, causes, and effects of racial inequity and develop a deeper understanding of how policies and practices contributed to current disparities and social conditions. For example, look at the history of housing policies in the United States, and then look at the history in your own community, or the communities in which you work. Learn about the forms of racism – interpersonal, internalized, institutional, and structural – and how to recognize and address them. *The Community Tool Box Collaborating for Equity and Justice Toolkit* provides a wealth of resources for explicitly addressing issues of social and economic injustice and structural racism. Seek out training opportunities, find and talk with local historians in the communities where you work, and engage in open and honest dialogue with others who share a commitment to social justice and racial equity. Spend time with professionals who are advocating for social justice and racial, economic, gender, and other types of equity. Learn what works for them, and what has not worked.

Additionally, cultural responsiveness requires that we become active advocates in this space. An example of this would be to mobilize people who look like us in our communities. As white women, we have found we can serve as allies working to address racism by having those difficult conversations with other white people and bearing the burden of their responses that are rooted in white fragility. We can use our power and privilege to elevate the voices of our colleagues of color and break through defensiveness and other behaviors that cause them harm. We can pave the way and open the door so they can engage in work to address racism and oppression without enduring such a high level of harm. As a result of our engagement with this work and through conversations with colleagues and active advocacy with them we have both grown, and we recognize that we must continue to grow.

4.1.5 A Trauma-Informed Approach

When you work in communities, it is common to work with individuals or communities that have encountered trauma. It may be as a victim of violence or sexual assault, or it may be the experience of racialized **trauma**. On an individual level, trauma can result in intrusive memories, shame, self-hatred, panic attacks, headaches, little or no memories, depression, irritability, and a whole host of other physical, behavioral, and mental health symptoms. When you are working with traumatized individuals, it is important that you don't do anything to trigger a traumatic response. It means thinking about trauma and shame when you design questions or conduct focus groups or interviews (Brown, 2020).

Many communities have experienced **intergenerational trauma** because of their race, economic circumstances, ethnicity, or other characteristics. This is a collective, complex trauma whereby the community has experienced a legacy of traumatic events over generations. Examples include Black communities that experienced structural and institutional racism and migrant communities of people who have experienced trauma prior to their arrival followed by family separations and fear of deportation.

According to Denise Long (Wolfe, Long, & Brown, 2020), a **trauma-informed approach** requires that community consultants take precautions to ensure they approach sensitive topics with care. First, when you obtain **informed consent**, you should be explicit about the content you will cover and the potential effects. Every member should be assured they can decline or "tap out" (leave the conversation) if they feel overwhelmed or stressed during the process. Second, community consultants should monitor the racial literacy of any focus group to ensure no members will speak in a manner that might retraumatize other members. Third, methods and instruments should be developed with community members who have lived experience with the focal issue. Fourth, the community consultant and others you work with should be trained on trauma and trauma responses.

Long also maintains that principles of trauma-informed care should be incorporated. They are:

- Choice – community members should have a voice and choices in whatever work you are doing with them.
- Collaboration – you should work with community members throughout the entire process.
- Cultural humility/equity – this includes allowing community members to control the narratives about their community and highlighting structural racism rather than individual or community needs.
- Empowerment – ensure community members have the power to determine the direction of any evaluation or initiative, have control over how funds and other resources are used, and own the process and outcomes.
- Safety – steps must be taken to ensure community members are not retraumatized or exposed to microaggressions and self-care and mental health should be part of the narrative.
- Trustworthiness – all evaluation results and other key documents should be shared and processed with community members. Communications, agendas, and strategic plans should represent anti-racism and structural change.

4.1.6 Ecological or Systems Perspectives

Individuals live in communities that are embedded within, and connected to, numerous organizations and systems. Having an **ecological perspective** is essential for understanding social problems within a community and is "the ability to articulate and apply multiple ecological perspectives and levels of analysis in community practice" (Dalton & Wolfe, 2012, p. 10). To facilitate change requires an understanding of how various elements within a community affect each other and how change in one will promote or hinder change in another.

Many professions include a focus on ecological or systems perspectives. For example, evaluation requires competence in the broader context in which a program operates. Social workers are required to be competent to engage, assess, intervene, and evaluate across multiple domains, including individuals, families, groups, organizations, and communities. Public health describes community dimensions of practice that include evaluating linkages among community entities. All these professions recognize the complexity of communities and the need for those who are working with communities to consider and address the complexity.

Two well-known and influential ecological theorists are Urie Bronfenbrenner (1974) and James Kelly (1966). Public health practitioners often use the Social Determinants of Health (SDoH) ecological model to demonstrate that where people live, learn, work, and play can all affect health and quality of life. Each of these models offers something useful in terms of a framework by which to analyze and address systems.

Bronfenbrenner's (1974) developmental framework, which includes the microsystem, mesosystem, macrosystem, exosystem, and chronosystem, illustrates the multiple layers in which individuals develop and the interplay between the systems. For example, there are interconnections between families (microsystem) and schools (exosystem) whereby changes to school policies may impact the family. To promote family engagement, some schools require parents to volunteer for a certain number of days each year. Working parents often use vacation time to meet this requirement, leaving them less time off work to spend leisure time with their children during summer or other school breaks. Taking time off for such activities may be viewed negatively by some employers, thus affecting opportunities for promotion and pay rises. This is another example of how the development of a strategy focusing on one positive set of actions (parents engaging more with the schools) can end up having negative consequences for the children and families in other ways.

Kelly's (1966) ecological approach draws on biological principles and has been influential in the field of community psychology. His four ecological principles are interdependence, cycling of resources, adaptation, and succession. Interdependence points to the interrelationships between parts of a system whereby change to one component affects or leads to change in another. Cycling of resources refers to the use, distribution, conservation, and transformation of resources in the system. Adaptation refers to the need for individuals and their environments to adapt to one another. We often expect and work to help individuals adapt to their environments, but it would likely be equally or more effective to think about how environments could be changed to better adapt to the needs of their residents. For example, in the fight against obesity, we often educate people to exercise and eat healthy foods. Implementing those behavior changes is challenging when people live in "food deserts" where the primary food available is at fast food chains and corner stores that primarily sell expensive, unhealthy foods and healthy groceries are limited or far away.

The principle of succession speaks to the changes over time that may be more or less favorable, and the need for communities to continually adapt. Community consultants need to consider the impact of their work across time, as well as understand the history of a community while anticipating future needs and resources. Consider the needs of a community with affordable homes and sufficient incomes where there is a stay-at-home parent. When their children start school, many of these parents may choose to volunteer at the school, engage in fundraising to support their children's activities, and enjoy having opportunities to socialize with other stay-at-home parents. Over time, as housing prices rise throughout the city and within their neighborhood, both parents in the family may need to work outside of the home. The schools and activities will experience a decline in the number of parents available to volunteer and spearhead fundraising, and there may be a greater need for afterschool programming rather than social activities for the stay-at-home parents. The needs and resources of this community will shift, along with the adaptive strategies needed to support the residents.

The SDoH model posits that one's health is determined by more factors than individual behaviors alone. Successful interventions may need to address socioeconomic status, geographic location, policies at all levels, and other sources of inequity and inequality. The five key areas of influence defined in the SDoH model are economic stability, education, social and community context, health and health care, and neighborhood and built environment. It is important for community consultants to see, describe, and advocate for interventions that target all levels. In much of our work, when a problem is identified and defined, we see organizations and collaboratives immediately choose individual-level interventions that target changing people rather than the systems that lead to the social problem. For example, there is a preponderance of activities focusing on obesity prevention to teach people better eating and exercise habits, while ignoring the need to address food deserts, school lunch quality, crime rates, lack of sidewalks and parks, and other deterrents to physical activity.

Nearly all human problems require coordinated interventions at multiple levels, which requires expertise in ecological perspectives. A neighborhood group organized by a project that Susan worked with was developing strategies to improve women's health. Their first project, which was chosen by the community residents, was to do something about the loose dogs that roamed the neighborhoods. The women in that area knew they needed to get more exercise for their health, but the dogs made it unsafe to walk in their neighborhood. The neighborhood group collaborated with animal control and activists to teach people responsible dog ownership and sponsored a spay/neuter campaign.

We have presented examples of ecological theories and perspectives here; however, there are others to draw upon when conceptualizing community consulting work. Regardless of which you favor (and at one time or another we have favored all of them) and no matter what type of work you do, community consulting requires an ecological and systems approach. Systemic thinking not only helps to understand the community, but also ensures that when you and your client consider solutions, you will focus on the broader context of organizations and communities, reducing the likelihood of unintended consequences.

The best way to learn more about ecological and systems theories is to read, develop a deep knowledge of the various theories and perspectives, and continuously observe the world around you with these theories in mind until this becomes the way you process events and situations, and interpret individual behaviors. Study the various systems layers and components in the communities in which you work and learn about how these layers and components interact with each other. Watch how changes in one part of the system impact other parts of the system.

How can we be most effective in supporting communities? To help, not harm, communities we can use strategies that are grounded in empowerment and participatory techniques.

4.1.7 Empowerment

Skills to promote **empowerment** are "the ability to articulate and apply a collective empowerment perspective, to support communities that have been marginalized in their efforts to gain access to resources and to participate in community decision-making" (Dalton & Wolfe, 2012, p. 10). This includes promoting the exercise of greater power for communities that have been marginalized; articulating and promoting collective empowerment among individuals to achieve shared goals; assisting community members to identify personal strengths and shared social and structural resources; working in genuine, inclusive partnerships with community members and organizations; and supporting diverse, contextual forms of collective empowerment. Perhaps key in these definitions is that a community consultant working from an empowerment perspective is a resource, providing support and expertise. The consultant is not necessarily the "expert." Rather, a competent community consultant maintains the position that individuals are experts in their communities.

This means that as a community consultant, you should be willing to step back while community members determine their priorities and identify the communities' strengths and resources. It also means making sure you are invited and welcomed to be in the community.

Your support will be dependent on their agenda and priorities. It could mean lending expertise; providing leadership or advocacy training to community members and leaders; writing a grant proposal; or facilitating a needs assessment process. It means sharing your skills to accomplish the tasks the community leaders and members decided must be done to accomplish their goals. In summary, an empowerment approach requires acting outside of the typical "professional" expert role whereby the expert knows best.

To develop the skills to support community empowerment be attentive to the role you are playing in the community. Seek feedback from others, including the critical friend who will call you out when your language is inconsistent with an empowerment perspective. Engage in reflective practice. Study your experiences to understand how you work and where you might improve. Explore all the work you do, analyze and be attentive to the ways you and others may be disempowering community members. If you feel that you are "empowering" communities, then you still need to continue to develop your knowledge of what the concept truly means. In other words, YOU cannot empower a community. You can contribute to community empowerment by sharing skills, tools, knowledge, or other resources with community members that will facilitate their empowerment. The idea that you are somehow granting them power (by decisions you are making) suggests disempowerment as you are still in the power position.

4.1.8 Community Partnership

While **community partnership** would seem to be easy to accomplish, it can actually be difficult to achieve. On more than one occasion we have heard community members complain about how professionals come into their communities promising change, they do research and gather data from community members, and then go away when the money is gone, leaving the community as it was before they came. Over time, community members have learned not to trust professionals and not to believe that things will ever change. To implement real community inclusion requires patience and the ability to gain the community members' trust.

When you are facilitating community partnerships, you are often working with professionals from community-based organizations. At times professionals are reluctant to hold meetings in the communities they are serving, preferring to meet in parts of town that are closer to their offices. They also schedule meetings and events according to their Monday through Friday, nine-to-five schedule. As a result, they are only engaging in activities within the scope of their job and when they are being paid for their time. Community residents are invited to participate on their own, unpaid time. If meetings are held during the workday, it often requires that they take time off from their jobs, and they may lose money. It can be challenging to convince professionals that to engage in true community partnerships requires that they meet in the communities at times and locations most convenient for the community members.

Community partnership is a two-way street. You should not expect community members to come to your organizations or groups unless you are willing to go to theirs. Sometimes it is more expedient to join an existing community organization or group (if they invite you, of course) than to try to convince them that they should join yours. Too often we have seen professionals develop a coalition. Once the structure is in place and the goals are established, they realize that maybe they should invite some community members. The professionals remain in their comfort zone because they have set the stage, while expecting community members to come in and just accept goals that have been established for their community by outsiders. That is not true inclusion or partnership. Susan's favorite tool when she is working with existing community groups is Sherry Arnstein's Ladder of Participation (Arnstein, 1969).

Arnstein's Ladder includes multiple rungs that range from non-participation (manipulation, therapy) to tokenism (informing, consultation, placation) to citizen power (partnership, delegated power, citizen control). The higher one climbs up the ladder, the greater the citizen empowerment. This conceptualization is an oldie, but a goodie for illustrating the difference between token participation and full inclusion. Susan shows it to collaboratives she is working with, describes each rung in more detail, and asks members where they are standing on this ladder, and where they think they should be. This forms the basis and framework for planning to create a more inclusive collaboration.

A skill associated with community inclusion and partnership is being explicitly open about positions of power and privilege, including your own. Not only your possible "white privilege" as discussed earlier (if that applies), but the privilege you enjoy as a professional. This skill will be especially important when you work with community groups, coalitions, and collaborations. It requires openness not only when addressing community members and professionals. We have worked with many groups of professionals who are unwilling to abdicate their position of power and approach communities with the "we are professionals, so we know best what you need" approach. Being explicitly open about power and privilege can lead to some challenging and sensitive conversations.

Gaining skills in community inclusion and partnership requires developing cultural humility and negotiation skills. Spending time in communities of interest, talking with people, REALLY listening to them without becoming defensive (leave your white fragility at home), and learning about their perspectives of the history and issues is one way to develop such skills. Spending time with individuals who are trusted and skilled at partnering with communities is another recommended strategy. It is important that you are comfortable in the communities in which you plan to work. Spend time eating at restaurants, going to events, and shopping in the grocery stores in the focal community.

4.1.9 Ethical, Reflective Practice

Across all the disciplines we reviewed, each included a set of guidelines, or at the very least a mandate, for **ethical practice**. Public health professionals are required to be able to describe and advise on the laws and regulations for ethical research conduct. Evaluator competencies include demonstrating integrity through ethical and culturally competent practice. Social workers are required to apply ethical principles in practice by recognizing and managing personal values to allow professional values to guide practice and making ethical decisions by applying the National Association of Social Workers' Code of Ethics. Public administrators are mandated to ethically contribute to decision-making by using evidence that recognizes stakeholders' competing values.

Ethical, reflective practice is "a process of continual ethical improvement" (Dalton & Wolfe, 2012, p. 11). This includes being able to identify ethical issues in your own practice and responsibly addressing them. Reflective practice requires articulating how your own values, assumptions, and life experiences influence your work and the strengths and limitations of your perspective.

Engagement in ethical, reflective practice is enhanced by developing and maintaining professional networks for ethical consultation and support. If something feels uncomfortable to you, or you are unsure, it is important that you have people you can call to process your situation with. Your network members should be people who are willing to examine the situation in depth and give you honest feedback even when they know it is not what you want to hear.

Ethical, reflective practice in community consulting requires consistently examining the actions you take and recommendations you make and determining the core of your motivation. It means sometimes recommending actions that are in the best interests of the community but that may not serve your own interests. For example, if you are an independent consultant or even working as a consultant for a larger firm, there may come a time when you need to recommend that a community uses a different consultant who is better able to meet the community's needs or pass on bidding on a project that looks very lucrative because you know you do not really have the qualifications to do the best job. One of the American Evaluation Association's guiding principles is that of competence. This includes ensuring that an evaluation team possesses the competencies necessary to work in the cultural context of the evaluation. It also means that they have the education, abilities, skills, and experiences required to complete the evaluation competently. This principle applies beyond evaluation to any consultation services provided.

Another example might be if an organization performs services that are inconsistent with your own belief system, and you feel that you cannot work with them without your personal beliefs influencing the recommendations you make or the way you approach work with them. Then you should be forth-coming and decline the work. Community consultants sometimes partner with other consultants or organizations. If you realize the organization has business practices that are not in the best interests of those whom they serve, then you might want to sever the partnership.

From time to time, we each turned down work when we felt like we were not the best consultant for the organization. Ann completed a project for a client but conflict between the board was so severe that she chose not to bid on the next phase of work even though the chief executive officer was pleased with the quality and results from the first phase. She felt strongly that they needed a consultant with more expertise in board development. The organiza-tion was able to identify another consultant with the exact experience needed and Ann continues to have a good relationship with her former client. You never know when a client may need you again. Even if they don't ever hire you again, you will have done the right thing by referring them to someone else.

Engaging in ethical practice requires looking at your own values and your profession's values and guidelines and monitoring your actions to ensure con-sistency. It requires that you do not allow personal needs and values to influ-ence your work if they are not in the best interests of the communities you serve. It is important that you uphold professional standards, engage in intro-spection regarding your own values, and process your experience with situa-tions that require ethical decisions and exercising integrity.

4.1.10 Dedication to Continuous Personal and Professional Development

As a community consultant, you should always seek to improve your knowl-edge and skills. To ensure that you are giving communities the best possible service, you must monitor your own and subordinates' personal and profes-sional development needs and identify appropriate resources to meet them. Some professions such as social work require members to obtain continuing education units to maintain licensure. As individuals move through the phases of life and career, their personal developmental needs evolve. For example, personal developmental needs differ between early career, mid-career, and late career phases. The same is true for both men and women during the differ-ent phases of family life (for example, having children, children leaving home, caring for aging parents). To be an effective community consultant requires being cognizant of and tending to your personal developmental needs and cir-cumstances and how they might relate to your work throughout your career.

Early in our careers we remember trying to balance demonstrating our strengths and gaining experience with more experienced professionals. Community consultants also need to extend their knowledge and skills to the extent they have them, while being comfortable with and openly acknowledging their limitations. Now that we are more advanced in our careers, competence requires that we share our expertise while still acknowledging that there are things we do not know. Whereas early in our careers we found the need to consult more experienced professionals, at this time in our careers, ironically, we sometimes find the need to consult less experienced professionals who may know more about technologies and new methods or have different viewpoints or training.

To truly benefit from professional development experience, you need to periodically conduct an honest assessment of your professional skills, identify areas that you want or need to develop, and identify appropriate resources to meet the need. You need to be willing to expend the time and resources on your development. That may require resourcefulness on your part. As an independent consultant, Susan often does small jobs and then puts aside the money earned from them specifically for conference attendance or some type of certification. Initially, this allowed her to attend the American Evaluation Association conference each year to network, learn new skills, and keep up with new ways of practicing. Now that her business is established, it allows her to reach further and attend international conferences, or extra national meetings. For some years we have been fortunate to be able to present at the American Evaluation Association Summer Institute and attend workshops at no cost.

As a community consultant, it is important that you budget funds to support conference attendance and other continuing education opportunities, as well as setting aside time to read and reflect. If your skills do not stay current and sharp, you ultimately short-change the organizations and communities that you are working to assist. If you do not keep up with current practices, in time someone will notice that you are stale and that your work is outdated, and you will lose opportunities and money. Your practice will become irrelevant as the field continually evolves. We have witnessed first-hand what happens when professionals do not take steps to continually engage in education, training, or supervised practice to learn new concepts, techniques, skills, and services. We have on more than one occasion been hired to work on projects where the former consultant just was not effective. This was often because it appeared that they failed to develop professionally, since their methods were outdated and no longer relevant to current issues and practices. In our practices, we have also found that continuous professional development has allowed our work to evolve while making us more effective and the work more fun.

If you work for an organization, negotiate for professional development support with your superiors. If they cannot budget money, at least convince them that attending training and conferences are a valid use of work time, rather than having to use your vacation time. You can help your supervisors see the value of their investment if you share the conference programs and offer to attend specific sessions and bring back the information to share with your colleagues. If your employer is unwilling to support your professional development, save your own money and use vacation time if you must. Do not let an unsupportive work environment be the reason that you do not continue to nurture your professional development.

4.2 Key Points

- Community consulting is both values- and knowledge-based. You can do a disservice to a community if you do not embrace social justice, equity, anti-racism, and decoloniality values and partner with the community in an inclusive manner.
- Cultural humility and cultural responsiveness are helpful to promote positive and respectful interactions with community members. They require continuous and ongoing self-reflection, a commitment to partnering with others to advocate and support groups who are marginalized, and a desire to confront power imbalances where none should exist.
- Communities are complex and best understood and served by a full knowledge and understanding of ecological models and systems perspectives.
- Developing values and knowledge for community consulting is an ongoing process. It begins with the knowledge you learn through formal education, and develops through self-reflection, feedback, reading, continuing education, and experience.
- Community consulting requires continuous learning as knowledge, approaches, and methods continue to evolve. As far along as we are in our careers, we continue to learn new skills, seek new certifications, and build our expertise. The knowledge, skills, tools, and methods associated with the work we do is constantly evolving and if we are not current, we do our clients a disservice.

5 Community Consulting Skills You *Might* Need or Want

What clients are really interested in is honesty, plus a baseline of competence.
— Patrick Lencioni (SUCCESS staff, 2011)

In addition to the personal characteristics, values, and knowledge, there are additional technical skills community consultants may want or need to develop, depending upon the type of work they are doing. Chapter 5 describes those additional skills and provides information about how community consultants can develop them.

In the last chapter, we described the foundational values and knowledge that all community consultants should develop. In this chapter, we describe technical skills that are optional, depending upon the type of work you choose to do. We identified these skills using the same sources as the foundational values and knowledge. In this chapter we will describe each skill and discuss why and when it is important for community consulting, how the skills may be applied, and some tips on how you might develop them. Before we describe the various skills, we discuss the decision of whether to become a practitioner who specializes in a specific topic area or a **generalist**.

5.1 Specialist or Generalist?

There are consultants who have built their entire practices and careers around a specialty area and have done quite well. A specialty area could be a focus on a specific topic (for example, mental health, maternal and child health, and so on) or a very specific skill area. Two of our favorite coalition experts, Tom Wolff and Fran Butterfoss, are good examples of this type of specialty. Of course, working with coalitions requires a combination of related skills, but by developing strong expertise in coalitions, they have built international reputations. Through their individual practices, Tom and Fran have helped many public health and other coalitions work through challenges to improve their communities and produce positive outcomes.

To become a **specialist** requires intense immersion and focus in a specific area, while continuing to develop all the skills that are related to the focal area as well as your business skills. Consider focusing on a single area if you find one aspect of consulting practice that you enjoy most, are able and willing to invest in developing the requisite expertise, and if there are opportunities to obtain enough work or a job that allows for this singular focus. If you choose this option, it is important that you remain constantly abreast of developments in your area and never let your skills or focus become obsolete or "old school." It is especially important to remain relevant and knowledgeable about trends and developments.

Many community consultants focus specifically on evaluation. Engaging primarily in evaluation still allows for the development and application of additional areas of expertise beyond evaluation. For example, while Ann's company focuses on evaluation, she does a lot of work with community coalitions and organizations focused on substance abuse prevention and public health. Susan is more generalized and works with coalitions and organizations as an evaluator, but also assists nonprofits and individual organizations with grant writing, strategic planning, and coalition development.

We should also point out that you could be a specialist in a specific skill, like data analysis for example. Examples are Ann Emery who specializes in data visualization and David Keyes who is an expert in using the statistical tool, R. The decision to be a specialist or a generalist depends upon several factors. If there is an area that is a special interest and strength, then you may want to focus your specialty in that area. Also, if a specific area is more lucrative or offers the most opportunities for consulting work or employment in your geographic area, it might make sense to specialize. If you enjoy engaging in a variety of different types of projects, then you may find that a more general practice works best for you. Also, if you live or work in a geographic area that has fewer community consultants and there is a shortage of skills (grant writers, evaluators, coalition builders, community organizers) or you do not wish to travel, then it would make more sense to be a generalist.

The decision to be a specialist or a generalist isn't strictly an either-or question. It is a decision you can revisit based on your evolving interests, client base, and skill set. For example, someone could start out as a generalist and narrow the topics they focus on as opportunities increase and their interests are refined. Some people start with a focus on one area (for example, strategic planning), but expand their services based on client needs and their own interests (for example, engaging in more grant writing). As an independent consultant, you have the flexibility and agency to revisit this question as new opportunities arise, and as your interests, skills, and needs evolve. Ultimately, which way you go will depend on your interest and strengths, needs and opportunities. Be forewarned, though, that neither presents a greater likelihood of career or business success.

5.2 Determining Which Skills You Need

Before you expend a lot of time, effort, and resources developing a particular set of skills, it is important to determine just which skills you will need, and what depth of knowledge is appropriate for the work you will do. How much you will want to invest in gaining a particular skill will be related to how much you will use it and how you will use it. For example, if you will be working on a team where you contribute to reports but producing the finished product and sharing it with the client isn't your role, then you need some understanding of good report design and data visualization, but you do not need to invest in intensive training in those areas. You can get this level of education through the internet and by following data visualization thought leaders on social media. If you will be producing reports for clients yourself, then it would be worth investing more time and money into skill development in that area by taking a few online courses or in-person workshops.

At the end of this book, we share a tool that may be helpful for you to use to help guide your personal and professional development as a community consultant. We hope that it gives you some guidance and direction regarding where to focus your time and resources.

5.3 Possible Skills and Knowledge

5.3.1 Leadership and Management

Leadership and management skills involve being able to: help facilitate community activities; mentor community members and organizations; supervise staff; manage human resources; and exhibit financial management competence and business acumen. You will need **leadership humility** if you plan to provide leadership and mentoring with communities, will be working with nonprofits who might want assistance with developing the management or business aspects of their organization, or have your own consulting business with employees or subcontractors.

5.3.1.1 Community Leadership and Mentoring
Community leadership is "the ability to enhance the capacity of individuals and groups to lead effectively, through a collaborative process of engaging, energizing, and mobilizing those individuals and groups regarding an issue of shared importance" (Dalton & Wolfe, 2012, p. 11). It requires the ability to establish trusting relationships with community leaders and members, work with emerging local leaders and their concerns (including the different stakeholders and their priorities in addressing them), work across stakeholder

groups to address issues productively, and support and consult with emerging local leaders to plan and implement action.

As a community consultant, you will rarely, if ever, directly lead communities or community efforts, but you may be called on to help community leaders and members to identify and develop their own leadership potential. This requires that you share what you know about community leadership and work collaboratively with community leaders and members to determine how that can best be applied within their context. For example, Ann often works with new community coalitions and helps them to create the infrastructure (workgroups, action plans, and processes) needed to develop the internal capacity to do the work of community change. She does not serve in a leadership role with the coalitions but works to build their leadership capacity.

There are other ways you can build the leadership capacity of community organizations. For example, helping community organizations understand how systems work and how to work within systems broadens their perspective about the causality of social problems. You might share procedural information, like how to organize a meeting and bring people to the table, or model facilitation and other basic leadership skills. Understanding local codes and code enforcement practices, knowing which municipal department is responsible for what, and how to participate in public hearings are just a few examples of knowledge you might share. You can also share data and facilitate its distribution and interpretation, and help communities understand what data they should use – unbiased and produced through systematic and methodologically sound practices – and what data they should not use – collected using weak methods or intended to mislead the public.

As we have discussed, community consulting is best done in a way that is not top-down but rather performed as a coaching role. **Mentoring** is "the ability to assist community members to identify personal strengths and social and structural resources that they can develop further and use to enhance empowerment, community engagement, and leadership" (Dalton & Wolfe, 2012, p. 11). Mentoring includes being able to advise, model behaviors, and support community leaders to help them to identify and use their own best collaborative leadership style. It may also involve teaching and facilitating effective methods to energize others to engage, encourage critical feedback, and to reflect on their work; as well as helping them to adapt their own style of collaborative leadership. Mentoring potential community leaders is like leadership development since you are helping them to develop their own leadership potential, but is often done on more of a one-on-one, less formal, interpersonal level. As an evaluator with a five-year grant-funded project, Susan worked closely with a program manager. Over time she developed a relationship with her that included serving in a mentoring role. It included providing information about professional development opportunities, helping her to brainstorm ideas to deepen community engagement, and serving as a sounding board for problem solving.

There are several steps you can take to develop leadership and mentoring skills. You might consider taking a leadership and/or project management course or a certification program. You can also take on a leadership role in your work setting if you are not self-employed, or in your community by serving on a local committee or nonprofit board. Observe leaders who have a positive impact and see what they do that makes them effective. To learn mentoring skills, reflect upon what made your mentors effective when they mentored you. Read books and articles about effective mentoring. When you engage in mentoring, ask for feedback from your mentees to identify what you did well. This will help you identify what developmental opportunities you should seek.

5.3.1.2 Budgeting, Financial Planning, and Organizational Management

There are several skills required for budgeting, **financial planning**, and **organizational management** (The Council on Linkages Between Academia and Public Health Practice, 2021; American Evaluation Association, 2018). You will need these skills if you have your own consulting business, or if you are in a management or leadership position within an organization. Having some financial and management knowledge is helpful even in non-management positions. Financial planning and management are among the skills necessary to develop and manage projects and people and are helpful for grant writing and management and organizational management as well.

Financial planning involves being able to assess your organization's current financial status compared to its financial goals. Only then can you create an ongoing process that will support your current business needs while building toward your future goals. For example, if you are a community consultant for a new nonprofit organization, it is helpful to be able to look at its current financial status and sources of income and project forward to determine if, and when, it will need to solicit additional funding to maintain operations and to grow new initiatives. We have on more than one occasion seen nonprofit organizations that are forced to lay off staff because their grants ended, and they did not plan for nor take steps toward sustaining a program or staff position. You don't want that to happen to you! If you have a consulting business of your own, you need to get in the habit of looking ahead to the next six to 12 months to determine when you will need to solicit new projects to maintain a steady income for your business.

Being able to leverage organizational relationships, structures, and functions for **program management** is necessary to navigate your own organization, and those that are part of the system in which you are working. One program Susan worked with was responding to a **request for proposals** for a program that had many components. It was the five-year renewal for the existing program, and the funder added requirements without adding enough funding to support them. One of the requirements was to provide fatherhood services. The program was able to leverage its relationship with another organization that provided fatherhood services through a memorandum of understanding and thus save the money and effort to implement them within its own program.

Another management skill is the ability to develop and implement programs, policies, and procedures. This includes being able to write formal policies and prepare procedure manuals for new and existing programs and services. Making sure program plans, policies, and procedures are clear and documented is important for maintaining program fidelity and ensuring that program staff are clear about their roles and expectations. These skills include being able to document process and develop process flow charts. Policies and procedures should be written in enough detail so that if the whole team won the lottery and walked out, a new team would be able to walk in and implement and manage a program or organization. Program policies and procedures guidance should include procedures for documenting processes, maintaining documentation, monitoring progress, and managing the project. They should also incorporate the timelines for activities.

Most social science programs don't provide accounting, business, or other financial training, but community consultants often find they need these skills. As a consultant, you may need to develop and manage your company's budget; you might write grants that require budget development; or you may assist with program development, which includes budgeting, identifying required resources, and knowing how to budget for them. You might need to conduct cost-effectiveness, cost-benefit, or cost-utility analyses for decision-making. Your role may even extend to preparing and approving funding proposals. Understanding concepts such as cash flow, assets and revenue sources, how to understand financial statements and Form 990s, how to cost out a proposal, and budget development are also important skills if you plan to have your own consulting practice.

Whether you are independently employed, own a company, move up the ranks in someone else's business, or work for a nonprofit, you should understand the financial aspects of running a business or a program. Perhaps you are knowledgeable and are comfortable doing your own taxes. If this is true, you can save money by purchasing accounting software and preparing your own taxes. However, if you are not, you should hire someone to manage your finances. Get referrals from colleagues and be sure to check references. Be sure to interview potential accounting professionals before you retain their services. Some questions you might ask include: How many small businesses do you work with? Have you ever worked with a business like mine? What kind of small business support do you offer? Hopefully you will find an accountant that you trust and you can understand what she or he is saying. It is very important that you feel comfortable in speaking with them and that you understand their advice. This will result in more productive financial discussions. Lastly, when you submit your tax return it is never a good idea to blindly sign the return without understanding your deductions and write-offs.

New consultants who are interested in working with community-based organizations often find the conversations and negotiations for developing contractual agreements to be difficult or uncomfortable. It is not easy to tell a struggling community-based organization that "This is all I can do for you for this amount of money." However, if you either work for or have your own consulting firm, your job or your company will not survive if the amount of time and effort necessary to complete the work (scope of work) far exceeds the budget. That said, have we ever taken on jobs that were insufficiently budgeted for the scope of work required? Of course we have. If we did, we usually had a business reason, or let it eat into personal time rather than our work hours. For example, Ann has donated time to support work benefiting children in foster care because it is an issue she cares about. Susan once provided technical oversight for a statistical community profile for an organization serving a cause she wished to support for a fee that was well below her usual rate. In return for the discounted fee, she negotiated co-authorship on the report that would be publicly released so that she could share it as a work product sample.

Being able to develop, negotiate, and manage contracts is another management skill that is important for community consultants who work directly with contracted clients, or who work with subcontractors. Some consultants retain an attorney with experience working with small businesses to review contracts, but others develop this skill and manage their own contracting and subcontracting.

Having good interpersonal skills as a manager is also an important management competency. Being able to manage personnel effectively includes being able to provide your staff with role clarity, motivate them, and facilitate their development. It also means being able to manage difficult staff members that you either mistakenly hired or inherited in a way that is not disruptive to your operation or other staff members. Good interpersonal skills for a manager also require being able to communicate effectively with other stakeholders. If you are in a middle management position, this will require effective communication with your supervisor and other superiors as well.

Many of these skills can be obtained by taking classes, attending seminars or workshops, or asking someone with the skills you would like to develop to provide you with one-on-one coaching. Check your local community college or university continuing education program for relevant courses on small business accounting, business management, project management, or human resources. If you know someone who is preparing a grant, ask if you can assist to learn how to plan a program and develop the budget. Look for seminars on program planning or grant writing. If you have a local nonprofit capacity building organization, see what they offer.

5.3.2 Community Program Development and Management

Many of the skills described in the previous section are also relevant to this section, especially skills relevant to business, management, and financial areas. Whereas the business and management skills described in the previous section are important for maintaining consulting practices and community-based organizations, this set of skills has to do with developing and implementing new programs.

5.3.2.1 Program Development, Implementation, and Management

Program development, **program implementation**, and program management in terms of skills related to community consulting are "the ability to partner with community stakeholders to plan, develop, implement and sustain programs in community settings" (Dalton & Wolfe, 2012, p. 11). The process of program development begins with assessing community issues, needs, assets, dreams, and resources. The public health competencies add that this includes the ability to implement continuous quality improvement measures and public health informatics practices and procedures.

Facilitating program development, implementation, and management with community partners requires a range of skills. We often begin the process by developing a theory of change, often depicted through a theory of change map, formulating program goals, and identifying measurable process and outcome indicators. This requires the ability to design a program that will attain the goals and fit the cultural and community context. Having management competencies such as staff recruitment and training, budget development, and project management skills is important. Finally, understanding and being able to plan for and ensure sustainability of programs is equally critical, although rarely addressed by many community programs or coalitions.

It is helpful to know some key models and techniques that are useful to share with community-based organizations that have limited resources. In past capacity building work, Susan provided program development workshops that blended the **Getting to OutcomesTM model** developed by Chinman, Imm, and Wandersman (2004) with John Gargani and Stewart Donaldson's **theory driven program design** (2015). Getting to Outcomes provides a concrete, step-by-step process to ensure all aspects of program design are attended to, while theory driven program design incorporates the substantive elements. The workshop also included program evaluation where she incorporated the **Tearless Logic Model** (Lien et al., 2011), a logic model development process that is comfortable for non-evaluators. Nonprofits that cannot afford to hire consultants to assist with program development expressed that this training provided a useful compilation of information.

Obtaining skills related to program design, implementation, and management requires that you read practice-focused program development and implementation literature, attend professional development training, and gain real-world experience. If you have some experience and want to strengthen your skills in this area, you might serve as a reviewer for large federal grant applications. While serving on grant committees to review the evaluation component, Susan has deepened her knowledge of program design by reading the entire proposals and then listening to the program reviewer discussions. If you don't have the time, expertise, or opportunity to do this, read the program design requirements and scoring criteria in a variety of requests for proposals. They will give some structure and information on what you need to include when you help design a program.

5.3.2.2 Prevention and Health Promotion

Having skills in **prevention and health promotion** is "the ability to articulate and implement a prevention perspective, and to implement prevention and health promotion community programs" (Dalton & Wolfe, 2012, p. 11). Being skilled means that you can articulate a prevention-oriented intervention perspective, understand the different types of prevention (**primary prevention**, **secondary prevention**, **tertiary prevention**), and have some knowledge of the prevention literature relevant to your areas of interest. This also requires being able to identify prevention resources and challenges. One of the greatest challenges in working with prevention programs is demonstrating effectiveness. Prevention, via policy or programs, takes time and it may take years to demonstrate outcomes. Furthermore, prevention often requires going beyond interventions at the individually focused program level and making systemic and structural changes through policy or changing cultural norms. These are not quick fixes, which is often where funder interests lie, so the challenge is building a prevention approach into the design and demonstrating progress toward outcomes.

Having prevention and health promotion skills also means that you can work with community partners to develop multi-level prevention programs that link programmatic initiatives to policy and community change. The Australian Psychological Society describes this as being able to coordinate systems to manage projects. An example of such a program is the Health Resources and Services Administration's (HRSA) Healthy Start Initiative which strives to reduce infant mortality disparities. Grantees are required to implement case management and health education programs at the individual level and Community Action Networks (coalitions or collaboratives) to implement the Collective Impact model to promote systems-level change. To affect population-level change, you need to be able to look to the root causes of a problem and develop strategies that will address multiple levels that contribute to or exacerbate the problem.

One of the best ways to develop the relevant skills and knowledge is, first, through reading academic literature, and then studying successful and unsuccessful prevention efforts. As an example of a successful prevention effort, over the years, great strides have been made to reduce smoking by multilevel intervention. Changing laws have made smoking inconvenient and more expensive – who wants to go outside in 100-degree heat or 20-degree freezing temperatures because smoking is no longer allowed indoors or pay more taxes on their purchases? Cultural norms have reduced the popularity of smoking. It is no longer glamorous, and we can no longer puff away to show that we've come a long way, baby (for you younger folks, this is a reference to an old Virginia Slims cigarette ad). Health messaging has gotten through so that people do not want to suffer the health hazards, or worse, expose their children and other loved ones to the toxic danger. Smoking cessation programs have helped individuals to kick the habit.

On the other hand, Project DARE, which was designed to prevent drug use among children and adolescents, proved to be ineffective over the long term (Clayton, Cattarello, & Johnstone, 1996). Learning about its rise to popularity, reading the evaluation results, and then watching how long it took for those shiny DARE vans to disappear from communities is also a valuable lesson. Several years after the evaluation results were released, and even today, communities continued to invest their resources in this program. Knowledge and awareness of successful and unsuccessful interventions will help you support your clients in developing effective community change.

5.3.3 Community and Organizational Capacity Building

To enhance your ability to help build community and organizational capacity, you need to develop specific skills related to capacity building. This section reviews some of these skills

5.3.3.1 Small and Large Group Processes: Facilitation Skills
Skills with small and large **group processes** include using effective communication skills, facilitating meetings, group decisions, and consensus building, providing conflict analysis and assisting with conflict resolution, and using group process for community involvement.

These skills can be useful for a variety of situations. For example, if you conduct focus groups, the small group process skills are essential. To facilitate a small group in a way that keeps the group focused on the task at hand, while ensuring all members participate, is essential to get the information needed from all members. Small group process skills are also useful when participating in or leading meetings or to develop logic models or strategic plans. Community consultants may find themselves on advisory boards, boards of directors, executive committees, or in other positions that require the ability to conduct an effective and efficient meeting. Large group process skills are required for managing events such as community listening sessions or forums. If the topic at hand is emotionally charged, having skills in defusing tensions and making people feel heard are essential for preventing chaos or a mass exodus of participants.

Knowledge of group processes can be obtained by taking facilitation training and reading literature in fields such as social psychology, organizational behavior, social work, and community psychology, among other fields. Participate in group activities and watch the facilitators. Observe and note differences between skilled facilitators and those who are less skilled. Collaborate with a skilled facilitator and ask them to provide guidance and honest feedback.

5.3.3.2 Resource Development

Resource development skills refer to "the ability to identify and integrate the use of human and material resources, including community assets and social capital" (Dalton & Wolfe, 2012, p. 11). It requires the ability to assess community assets and needs, translate the knowledge of them into specific funding aims, develop relationships and partnerships with funders, effectively write grants and raise funds, build capacity to ensure organizations can comply with funding requirements, and develop and present an evaluation plan to ensure the efficiency and effectiveness of resource use. Most organizations will need your assistance to develop financial and human resources.

You may be asked if you can write grants, and this may or may not be something you choose to do as part of your practice or develop within your skill set. If you don't want to write grants, you should develop relationships with grant writers, so you can provide that resource to organizations that need grants written. The ability to write winning proposals can be a useful skill to gain entry to collaboration or work opportunities, and to offer substantive assistance to communities and community-based organizations. Grants sometimes require collaboration between two or more entities and offering an opportunity to receive funding can be a great enticement for another organization to work with yours. Money is often the greatest barrier for communities and community-based organizations to accomplishing their goals.

Being a competent grant writer requires that you have writing skills that include the ability to write for a variety of audiences. Writing a proposal to a local corporation or foundation requires a very different style than writing a proposal to a federal agency. In either case, to write a winning proposal you need to be able to write a clear need statement that summarizes data from a variety of sources to tell the "story" of the focal issue. It also requires the ability to describe a program design (including the theory of change behind it); write a clear implementation or work plan for the program; prepare a budget and justification; and design and articulate a solid evaluation plan.

There are many resources available to learn about writing grants. Many federal agencies, including the Office of Minority Health, post recordings of webinars and other instructive materials online. Classes are available at local universities or through other sources. Working on a grant proposal with an experienced grant writer can also be a valuable experience. If you have sufficient expertise in a specific area (including evaluation), sign up to be a grant reviewer. Federal agencies sometimes have opportunities posted on their websites. Local foundations may also ask for assistance with reviews. Participating in review processes is the best way to find out what scores high, and what loses points.

Developing human resources presents another opportunity for community consultants. Many nonprofit and other organizations need assistance to build the knowledge and skills of their staff. Community consultants can help to develop human resources by providing training, participating in planning conferences, helping organizations to identify staff development opportunities, and mentoring or providing one-on-one training to individuals. Human resource development skills can be developed by attending formal training, co-teaching with more experienced trainers, reading about instructional design, taking advantage of opportunities provided through professional organizations to present or participate in conference programming, evaluating training events, and attending different types of training and observing.

5.3.3.3 Consultation and Organizational Development

Consultation and organizational development skills are "the ability to facilitate growth of an organization's capacity to attain its goals" (Dalton & Wolfe, 2012, p. 12). Having these skills means being able to assess organizational capacity, issues, needs, and assets; creating and sustaining effective partnerships; facilitating organizational learning, problem-solving, and decision-making; and facilitating collaborative strategic planning with organizations. This also includes advocating for learning opportunities within an organization; promoting mentoring and other personal and career development opportunities for the workforce; and ensuring the management of organizational change (The Council on Linkages Between Academia and Public Health Practice, 2021).

The consulting world is inundated with consultants who have developed organizational assessments and canned responses to "fix" the problems identified when organizations complete them. Some are good, many are not so good. Some are very costly, while others are inexpensive "quick fixes." It is a good idea to have a variety of tools and methods in your community consulting toolbox. Having a "one-size-fits-all" approach to organizational capacity building fails to recognize the variation in community-based organizations and their needs.

As a community consultant, rather than adopting the typical "expert models" of organizational development, seek out tools that are participatory and empowering. For example, in their 2013 *Global Journal of Community Psychology Practice* article on community psychology competencies in Italy, Francescato and Bruni described a process called Participatory Multidimensional Organizational Analysis (PMOA) that is taught in European psychology programs to promote organizational empowerment. It includes engaging all levels of the hierarchy in assessing objective aspects of an organization (for example, market share, increase or decrease in customers, staff characteristics) and subjective perceptions such as unconscious representations of work settings, attitudes toward power, and satisfaction. After the in-depth analysis process is completed, the participants develop plans to affect desired changes that are possible using the organization's existing resources.

We recommend that you learn as many tools and methods as possible and fill your toolbox so that you can address the uniqueness of community-based organizations and find the best way to build their capacity. This also requires that you can really listen and attend to the organizational culture, the community culture, and the underlying issues, and gain the trust of leadership through honest dialogue rather than the prescribed talking points that a singular methodology will employ. Susan took graduate courses in organizational psychology, took business classes in an MBA program, and worked in an organization that provided consulting services to facilitate technological change. She has also deepened her understanding of change leadership by becoming a certified **Change Intelligence** facilitator (Trautlein, 2013). These skills are useful for working with organizations or communities who are working to create changes. Susan can help them to understand the needed skills and processes, so their change initiative doesn't fail. For those who are interested in learning more about organizational development, other organizations providing useful resources include the Organizational Development Network and the International Society for Organization Development and Change. Both organizations offer professional development tools and opportunities.

5.3.4 Community and Social Change

Community and **social change** skills include collaboration, coalition, and community development and organizing; public policy analysis, development, and advocacy; and community education, information dissemination, and building public awareness. Each of these represents different approaches that a community consultant might take in bringing about community and social change.

5.3.4.1 Collaboration, Coalition, and Community Development and Organizing

Collaboration and **coalition development** refers to "the ability to help groups with common interests and goals to do together what they cannot do individually" (Dalton & Wolfe, 2012, p. 12). **Community development** is "the ability to help a community develop a vision and take actions toward becoming a healthy community"; and community organizing is "the ability to work collaboratively with community members to gain the power to improve conditions affecting their community" (Dalton & Wolfe, 2012, p. 12). Collaboration and coalition development, community development, and community organizing basically require similar skill sets to those listed below.

1. ***The ability to develop and maintain productive partnerships with clients, residents, organizations, communities, and other stakeholders.*** The public health field describes this as partnering with stakeholders to develop a shared vision; and resolving problems that may affect the delivery of public health services. Community collaboration, maintaining partnerships, and negotiating community asset and resource use are included among these skills (The Council on Linkages Between Academia and Public Health Practice, 2021). The Australian Psychological Society describes the skills as enhancing engagement and collaboration within diverse communities, and the American Evaluation Association describes the "interpersonal domain" which focuses on the human relations and social interaction skills.

2. ***The ability to communicate the value of experiential knowledge of community members affected by an issue and facilitate the process of knowledge use.*** We have too often seen "experts" come into communities with all their knowledge and skills to fix them, only to be left wondering why the problems continue. This is because they too often ignore the community members' knowledge and expertise about their own community and what the real, underlying issues are. They too often assume that what works in their community, or in one article they read, should work everywhere.

3. ***The ability to facilitate inclusive coalition membership and discussion that represents the views of all segments of the community.*** If you look at the coalitions in your community, who are the members? Too often it

is the professionals who work in the community during the day and then drive as far away as they can to their homes in other communities. We have observed coalitions that have been active for years, yet they have failed to affect any real change. Our experience is often that they meet, come up with an individually focused change effort, implement it – maybe even annually – and then celebrate their accomplishment. The only input from the community might be that they express their satisfaction with the event on a survey, or maybe they are provided with an opportunity to respond to a needs assessment survey that included predetermined topics and categories for responses for easier coding and analysis.

Facilitating inclusive coalition membership and discussion representing all segments of the community requires convening gatherings in evenings or on weekends when community members are available, perhaps providing childcare, food, and creating an environment that conveys the message that their engagement is important and valued. It requires that the community determine its own priorities, select the leadership, and define its boundaries. As the consultant, you should remind your community client of the importance of inclusion and be careful to serve only as the organizer and remain in a supporting role.

4. *The ability to facilitate community member efforts to identify issues, resources, and goals, and to generate solutions, as well as to facilitate collaborative strategic planning for initiatives.* This requires good facilitation skills and getting community members comfortable with speaking out and sharing their ideas. It might include sharing data and other information and then helping community members to make sense of it and determine its implications for their community. You might also facilitate their efforts by identifying funding sources and writing grants, organizing meetings, and writing and distributing agendas and minutes. Ideally, the community members will determine what goes on the agenda. They will determine what they want the funding to support. They will determine the real issues that need to be addressed.

5. *The ability to facilitate community efforts to promote systems change, racial equity, and social justice.* Problems that are rooted in racial or other inequities will not go away until racism, sexism, or other "isms" that contribute to their growth and perpetuation are identified, confronted, and addressed. This means community consultants need to develop a level of comfort with being uncomfortable. It requires having the conviction and integrity to speak up when you hear racist comments or microaggressions and recognize that when you are silent you are complicit. Recognizing "code" words is also helpful. For example, when it was no longer acceptable to describe groups by race, many professionals found other terms to disguise their racist conversations. One of our personal favorites is

"apartment people." Think about how you might respond if you heard this term used by professionals in a meeting. Would you be able to openly question the use of the term and its definition?

These skills may be developed by attending specialized training sessions and workshops, and by working with experienced change agents. There are professional associations for individuals engaged in community development such as the National Community Development Association, the Community Development Society, and the International Association for Community Development. There are also very good resources to learn about building coalitions, including books by experts such as Tom Wolff (2010) and Fran Butterfoss (2013). The Community Tool Box is a great web resource with a wealth of tools and information on this topic.

Community organizing skills require the ability to enter communities and work directly with community members. Individual-level skills include listening, building relationships, challenging individuals, and clarifying your self-interest (Speer & Christens, 2015). To effectively practice these skills, you need to have cultural humility, and be an effective communicator and group facilitator. As a community organizer, your role is not to go in and assume a leadership position, but to facilitate the development of leaders within the community. You need to be comfortable with the idea that you may be the expert in some of the technical aspects of community change and empowerment, but that the individuals residing in a community are the real experts on their community. They understand the community's needs, priorities, and how to get things done in their community. You are not charged with setting the priorities, but with helping community members to develop their own priorities and strategies. The goal for empowerment is exactly that – respecting the community members' ability to take control and self-determine the change they wish to see in their community.

To gain coalition building and community organizing skills, it is helpful to attend workshops and training, and read books and articles to familiarize yourself with the theories and models (along with their strengths and limitations). Preparation to work in this area might also include taking courses in conflict management, developing a deeper understanding of community dynamics such as racism and politics, and familiarizing yourself with the variety of stakeholders and their perspectives. Attend coalition meetings and observe the dynamics. See what accomplishments they have made. Identify what works and does not work within specific communities and problem areas. Participate in a local coalition for an issue that is of interest to you as an active member (not as a consultant). For example, if you are interested in early childhood education or maternal infant health, find a local coalition addressing the topic and attend some meetings, and participate as a member.

When you are getting started, it is important also to work alongside individuals who have the requisite community organizing skills. You can gain the underlying knowledge and technical skills through training and education, but because each situation is different, the only way to become adept at community organizing and empowering communities is to engage with them directly. Becoming comfortable and skilled at navigating situations as community groups go through the storming and norming phase, managing conflict, and understanding personal and political agendas require consultants to have exposure to and experience with these situations. Being mentored by someone with more experience and observing someone who is skilled and experienced and how they handle the challenges is helpful.

5.3.4.2 Public Policy Analysis, Development, and Advocacy

Public policy analysis, **policy development**, and **community advocacy** include "the ability to build and sustain effective communication and working relationships with policy makers, elected officials, and community leaders" (Dalton & Wolfe, 2012, p. 12). These skills also include the ability to write policy briefs, present testimony, draft policies and consult with policy makers (elected officials at all levels of government), and to translate research findings into information that can be used to guide policy.

Across fields, these skills manifest in numerous ways. The public affairs and administration field requires the ability to participate in and contribute to the policy process and offer substantive contributions to the design, implementation, and evaluation of public policy. Public health requires policy development skills such as influencing policy, using data and information to develop policy, understanding and describing the implications of policy, and developing and implementing public health policies and programs (The Council on Linkages Between Academia and Public Health Practice, 2021).

If you would like to pursue community consulting work that includes public policy analysis and development, we recommend that you first gain experience working inside government. Susan's experience as an analyst with the U.S. Department of Health and Human Services Office of the Inspector General required that she become familiar with federal and state laws, regulations, and policies relevant to each area in which she worked. The experience was a valuable lesson in how government operates, how policies are made, and how policy can be changed. She found that while most often real change requires that the laws be amended, there are many instances where more effective implementation or enforcement of the laws will result in the changes that are being sought.

Government enacts policies by passing legislation that becomes law. Laws are then semi-operationalized by regulations (for example, see the U.S. Code of Federal Regulations). The responsible agencies or departments then further operationalize them by creating internal policies and guidelines for their implementation. Understanding how to find and read laws, regulations, and policies is the first step required if you plan to engage in policy work. It is not enough to read briefings or articles by other organizations describing them. Always go directly to the source. Also examine whether and how they have been implemented.

Another critical skill set is being able to either design and implement research to assess policies, or at least to identify credible research to address them. We cannot stress the "credible" descriptor enough. If you look at a policy area closely, you will find there is a LOT of evidence being presented on both sides of many issues. Being able to sift through research and determine what is valid or invalid is the important skill set. Look at the research design, the survey respondents or research participants, the location, the findings, and interpretations to determine whether they meet the criteria for credible research. Also, look at who funded or conducted the research. Were they a neutral organization, or do they have an agenda? Get to know which organizations are considered to be liberal or conservative, which are favored by particular political parties. No matter what your own political or other position, it is critical that you remain neutral in terms of which data you use in your work – regardless of whether you agree with the results.

It is important that you are aware of your own political and ideological biases when you are a community consultant. It is too easy to get caught up in advocating for changes that are consistent with your personal beliefs. But what if you find research evidence that does not support the changes supporting your beliefs, or that suggests that the changes may be detrimental to a group of individuals? If you are going to engage in such work as a community consultant, you need to be very sure that whatever policies you are advocating for, or developing, are supported by evidence that they address the problem for the greater good. You also must be willing to decline if you find evidence that such policies will not.

Another important skill for supporting advocacy and policy change is the ability to translate credible evidence into a form that can be easily understood by anyone. This skill includes displaying research findings in a manner that is easily digested and describing how the findings are related to the issue at hand. Data visualization tools and infographics can be very useful and there are numerous free or low-cost programs or applications available. The American Evaluation Association offers resources to learn more about how to effectively visualize and present findings. Another great resource are the free blogs and videos, or paid workshops and training offered by data visualization and presentation professionals such as Ann K. Emery, Sheila Robinson, Stephanie Evergreen, and Echo Rivera to name a few.

Finally, it helps to cultivate relationships with government representatives at the federal, state, and local levels. Learn how to identify the key stakeholders and their staff and how to present information effectively to them and to advocate for positions. Being able to put together an attractive and comprehensive but concise information packet on a topic is critical. Legislators and their staff members have very limited time. Presenting them with concise and eye-catching information is critical. They are not going to read your 50-page research report so you must figure out how to present the critical findings in one or two pages or in an infographic with findings that will jump off the page to grab their attention. It also helps if they get to know you and you are a familiar face and name. Do not be afraid to invite them to important events or call them if you disagree with a position they take. Emailing is good, but there is evidence that phone calls and visits are more effective. Also, subscribe to their email newsletters, which will help you to keep up with their positions on various issues.

5.3.4.3 Community Education, Information Dissemination, and Building Public Awareness

Communication skills such as being able to provide information to community members in ways that they can then use to advocate on their own behalf and engaging diverse groups in dialogue about the information are helpful if you are working with community initiatives. It also helps to develop effective communication skills for consultation, public speaking, writing, and media (including social media).

For effective **information dissemination**, you need to understand the various sources your audience trust and use for information. While consultants often value scientific and research-based information, there are many individuals who do not. Communities that have been exploited by researchers, or that have participated in research only to have their communities described in a negative light, may be distrustful of researchers and their findings. It may be necessary to present credible information in a manner that downplays its validity as "research based" and emphasizes how it will benefit the community. This is not to say you must be deceptive, just that you are careful in your messaging regarding what you wish to highlight.

Understanding how social media works is becoming a more useful information dissemination skill, in addition to the earlier described data visualization and infographic use skills. Keep up with which audience is most engaged with which social media platform. Study effective messaging via these media, and what messaging will appeal to which audience. Susan once conducted a study to identify predictors of risky teen behaviors. She shared the results with a group of teens who had participated in the study and shared her ideas of which findings they might want to include in a newsletter for other teens to share findings. The teens selected several different findings that they wanted to highlight from what Susan selected because they found them more interesting. This is just one example of how understanding the audience, and listening to them, can result in more effective dissemination. Sometimes what we think is interesting isn't necessarily what the community will want to share.

5.3.5 Participatory Community Research

Participatory community research skills include applying basic research skills to help the community identify their needs and being able to build community members' capacity to engage in this research with you. We suggest that you assist the community in conducting needs assessments, resource assessments, and researching program and policy opportunities in a way that fully engages with the community members as co-researchers. Research skills include being able to help communities and community groups to assess and interpret their findings and to build community capacity to use findings from community research to meet their goals.

5.3.5.1 Conducting Community Research – Including Needs and Resource Assessments

Conducting community research is a core skill for many social science and public health professions. For example, the Australian Psychological Society includes conducting community-focused psychosocial research among the skill set for community psychologists, as well as assessing the psychosocial needs of individuals, groups, organizations, and residential communities. Public health skills include analytical and assessment skills such as methods of data collection, data use and application, data collection ethics and data integrity. For community consultants working in health-related fields, such as maternal child health, learning about **epidemiology** and epidemiological methods is helpful. No matter what your discipline or training, as a community consultant it is vital that you learn to use participatory research methods. Community members and community-based organizations should be your full partners in the process.

Understanding basic research methods used for more traditional studies (including survey design, randomization of participants, study design principles) in addition to having training in and understanding statistics is important. Community research needs to be conducted with as much rigor and adherence to solid research design and analytic methods as possible. The difference is that when conducting community research as a community consultant there is a lot less control and you will seldom have opportunities to utilize sophisticated designs.

Community researchers need to be prepared and adept at handling "messy" research. As one example, when you are evaluating a community-based program that works with children or families, attrition may be a challenge. When families move, they may not notify the research team of their new address. If they are from an impoverished population, their phone numbers may be in service intermittently or change frequently. Successfully keeping track of them requires extra effort, resources, and time. Incentives will likely be required to compensate for time spent completing evaluation-related activities.

Understanding how to conduct needs and resources assessments is a useful skill for community consultants. Counties, cities, foundations, and specific funding streams often contract for consultants to conduct needs and resource assessments, community profiles, or related studies. There are numerous books and other resources available to guide such work. One of our favorite resources is Jomella Watson-Thompson and colleagues' chapter "Participatory approaches for conducting community needs and resources assessments" (2015). The authors provide a step-by-step description of eight tasks and skills for conducting such assessments that serves as a useful framework for planning and implementation. They begin with identifying the purpose and end with using the results. The chapter also includes training, education, and recommended experience to facilitate skill development.

Recommendations for developing competencies to conduct needs and resources assessments include training, technical assistance, and applied experiential learning. Training can include both academic preparation and informal resources such as those offered by government or certification courses. Technical assistance with the process may be provided by other, experienced consultants or academic partners. If you are interested in engaging in this work but lack experience, we recommend that you partner with an experienced consultant the first time around.

5.3.5.2 Program and Systems Evaluation

At the time this book was written, the American Evaluation Association (AEA) had adopted a set of evaluator competencies and the Canadian Evaluation Society (CES) identified competencies and implemented a credentialing system for evaluators. The AEA and CES competencies both include a technical domain that includes methodological and data analytical knowledge and skills pertinent to an evaluation context. Both sets of competencies also include knowing **program evaluation** foundations such as guidelines and practice standards, as well as being familiar with evaluation fundamentals. Evaluation-specific skills are cited, such as determining program evaluability, specifying program theory, and understanding the evaluation knowledge base, such as theories, models, types, methods, and tools.

The AEA methodology domain indicates that being a competent evaluator means having a wider range of skills than research methods and statistics courses. It requires an understanding of how these skills translate to use for evaluation. Whereas research is used to generate knowledge and support or refute hypotheses, the Evaluation Toolbox defines evaluation as "a structured process of assessing the success of a project in meeting its goals and to reflect on the lessons learned" (Evaluation Toolbox, 2016).

AEA's competencies also include a context domain that focuses on understanding the unique circumstances and settings of evaluations and their stakeholders. Evaluators must be able to describe the program; determine its evaluability; identify and understand its context; respect and respond to the uniqueness of the context; identify and engage stakeholders for planning and conducting an evaluation; attend to evaluation use; and consider the broader context in which the evaluation is performed.

For many community consultants, program evaluation is the core of their practice. If you are an independent community consultant, evaluation will likely be your major source of income, unless you have developed and demonstrated expertise in other specific areas. Many communities, especially those where there is no formal evaluation training program, are filled with individuals providing evaluation services who sorely lack the appropriate training or experience. Being well-trained and experienced as an evaluator (meeting standards set forth by the AEA and the CES) can be of value to you and the communities and organizations in which you work.

When Susan was awarded a contract with one grant-funded program that had been working with a prior evaluator, she was surprised to find reports that included the wrong program name, use of inappropriate graphs, numbers in text that did not match figures, and other fundamental errors. We have heard similar stories from other evaluators who received reports that had been prepared by other "evaluation experts" who had been paid handsome sums of money for worthless and useless reports. There is a need in many communities for competent evaluators who have the requisite skills and competencies to provide useful and accurate information to facilitate decision-making.

Assuming a **utilization focused evaluation** approach is also essential for community consultants (Patton, 2008). Far too many community-based organizations have hired evaluators who collected a lot of data and presented them with a big report, but there was absolutely nothing useful in the report for decision-making or program improvement. They merely ended up with a lot of numbers to give to their funders. Evaluation as a community consultant requires that you design and implement evaluations that meet all the organization's needs, not just provide them with numbers for reports. This competency requires that you learn to ask the right questions in the beginning of the evaluation and to design evaluations that answer them. Susan was working with a project whose state funder required that they participate in the state evaluation of their coalition. The university-based evaluation team conducted a social network analysis and sent them a fancy drawing of their network density. This information had absolutely no utility for the project, which was struggling with how to engage community members and move their coalition from one that met and talked to a group that acts to effect community changes.

In addition to being skilled at doing evaluation, you may also want to develop skills with building evaluation capacity in nonprofit and other organizations. The skills are like the capacity building skills described earlier, but in this case, they are specifically focused on evaluation capacity. Both of us have done this with large national organizations and with smaller organizations such as public libraries, community coalitions, and local nonprofits.

There are many ways to gain expertise as an evaluator. First and foremost, enroll in graduate courses and attend training workshops, conferences and other opportunities that will provide a solid foundation and continuing education. There are certificates and master's programs available through universities and other resources such as Michigan State University, Claremont University, and The Evaluator's Institute. If your graduate program did not provide you with sufficient evaluation training, or you want to develop more credentials in the field, these are excellent resources that are accessible through the internet. Additional training opportunities are offered through the AEA, including webinars, the AEA Summer Institute, and the AEA annual conference. If you plan to focus on evaluating educational programs, the American Educational Research Association offers professional development opportunities. It also helps to read books, such as Michael Quinn Patton's *Utilization Focused Evaluation* (2008) and E. Jane Davidson's *Actionable Evaluation Basics* (2013).

In addition to education, you need experience to gain expertise as an evaluator. Begin by working with an experienced evaluator. Make sure they have specific training and experience with evaluation. Work across a variety of types of evaluation and become familiar with different approaches, methods, and how the concepts you learned play out in actual settings. Ask to be involved in the design, proposal preparation, implementation, analysis, and reporting. Learn different reporting styles and how to prepare reports for different audiences.

Memberships in professional associations provide a means to access mentors and to learn about education and training opportunities. We are both members of the AEA. Many other countries also have national evaluation professional associations, such as the CES, the African Evaluation Association, the European Evaluation Society, and the International Development Evaluation Association to name a few. There are also local affiliates, such as the Atlanta-area Evaluation Association, the Chicagoland Evaluation Association, the Texas Evaluation Network, and the Washington Evaluators. These are all excellent resources for networking with evaluation professionals, identifying mentors, and finding professional development and training opportunities.

5.3.5.3 Communicating and Using Research and Evaluation Results

Several skills are required for communicating and using research and evaluation results. One is being able to think critically and synthesize information, as well as being able to use information to solve problems and make decisions, including ethically contributing to decision-making by using evidence that recognizes stakeholders' competing values. Public health skills add in being able to retrieve, describe, and apply scientific evidence regarding public health concerns; discuss the limitations of the research; and discuss, critique, and explain the scientific foundations of the field and the lessons learned historically. Social work competencies describe being able to distinguish, appraise, and integrate multiple sources of knowledge, including research; and analyze models for prevention and intervention. Advanced social work practice requires the ability to differentially select and implement strategies for assessment and intervention using evidence-based and best practice methods.

European community psychologists encourage pluralistic interpretations of social problems that integrate objective and subjective knowledge and broaden the viewpoints from which a situation can be considered. This is an important skill set for community consultants to consider when applying research and evaluation results. To draw on a singular perspective will likely not take all sides of an issue into account and can breed more conflict than collaboration if the consultant appears to be promoting one side of an issue rather than the full range. In an article in the *Global Journal of Community Psychology Practice*, Francescato and Zani (2013) described a technique called community profiling and network building that is a structured, participatory action research to gather information about an issue or problem through the eyes of different groups and determine the changes they each desire. While it can take two to six months to complete the process, in the end the combination of objective and subjective information, and the networking required to complete the process, has been demonstrated across studies to be an effective foundation for creating social change.

Applying results from community-based research, needs assessments and evaluation can provide an opportunity to give voice to community members or groups that might otherwise never be heard. When speaking with community members, avoid the urge to only present the community's "problems" or to describe its members as the problem. Susan evaluated a community-based conference where a teen attendee commented that she had attended a session on teen pregnancy and that it was very uncomfortable for her to sit in the audience and see herself presented as a problem. It is important to gather perspectives that help to present new and affirmative scripts and roles – in other words, rather than showing only a map of where a community has been and is, work with community members to identify routes they can take to move their community forward.

5.4 Key Points

- The focus of your community consulting practice will determine the types of skills you will need to develop.
- Use the tool provided at the end of this book to help you decide which skills you need to focus your professional development activities on, and to what extent. The tool includes personal qualities, knowledge and values, and technical skills. Focusing your professional development on the skills you need will help you to expend your time and resources most effectively
- To fully develop a set of skills takes time, effort, and experience. If you are not prepared and lack skills in an area, you can ultimately end up hurting your reputation, so be patient and put in the time and effort and then wait until you are ready before engaging in work that requires that you apply those skills.

6 Setting Up Your Practice and Managing the Practical Matters

Business success does not lie in growing something quickly and massively, but rather in building something that's both remarkable and resilient over the long term.

—Paul Jarvis (2019)

In Chapter 6 we talk about what you need to do if you plan to set up your own community consulting business. This includes how to prepare a business plan, decide on your business structure, market your business, choose clients, find work, and get paid. We also share tips on how to manage the practical matters of owning a consulting practice. Some of the information shared in this chapter will be useful for those who work for consulting firms, to help understand the bigger picture of the business.

So, you're contemplating dipping your toes into opening your own consulting business, or maybe you have already decided to dive in. Before you get started, you will have to prepare. You would never dive into water without knowing how deep it was, right? In this chapter, we will discuss the details of starting a community consulting business and provide readers with the knowledge they need to determine their business structure and set up their business. For detailed information about how to set up your business structure and the detailed steps you will need to take to establish it, we recommend you consult with your local Small Business Administration office or other business expert, such as a business attorney or accountant. Even if you are not setting up your own business, there is information throughout this chapter that is applicable to other situations, such as writing proposals (for example, budgets, staffing), marketing programs, and expanding your professional knowledge. This chapter will be helpful to you as well.

After your consulting business is up and running, you must set up structures and processes to manage your business to ensure continued success. Managing the business includes understanding contracts, establishing accounting practices, paying all appropriate taxes, acquiring the necessary insurance coverage, establishing time management strategies, and marketing the business. It is at this stage that many consultants get stuck. Unless you went to business school, you may not feel you have the necessary skills to start and/or manage a business. But don't panic, there is help available.

6.1 Setting Up Shop

Should I hire a lawyer? This may be the very first question to ask yourself. We want to say at the outset that neither of us consulted a lawyer when we started our consulting business. Ann worked with her Certified Public Accountant (CPA) who helped her file her papers of incorporation. Her CPA filed the necessary paperwork with her local city and state; Ann reviewed and approved. Susan used an online company that completed all her paperwork. That said, hiring an attorney that specializes in small business is advised if you have a partner, even if (maybe especially if) that partner is a friend or family member. We have seen a lot of partnerships devolve, resulting in stress and sometimes financial consequences. There are other times when you might seek legal advice. Ann hired a copyright attorney to trademark her podcast, *Community Possibilities*, and to copyright some of the resources she offers on her website.

There are many ways to structure your business. The structure you choose will depend on several factors. First, do you want to work with others and, if so, how do you want to define your relationships with colleagues? Second, what is your tolerance for financial risk? No matter what structure you choose, it is a good idea to consult with a **Certified Public Accountant (CPA)** to determine what business structure best suits your personal financial situation. You may also want to consult an attorney, especially if you decide to partner with another consultant. It also may be helpful to contact your local Small Business Development Center for more help in this area. Finally, there are books and internet resources available if you want to further research many of the things we discuss in this chapter. We mention several resources in this chapter and share more information and links to them in Appendix 2. Our goal is to get you started thinking about these important elements that will have a direct impact on your success.

Finally, you will need to choose a company name and reserve a website domain name. Be sure and research the name you choose. You don't want to select a name already used by someone else. Building your website is a must for businesses. Although you can do this on your own, you may at least want to get some advice so that your website ranks high in Google searches by using **search engine optimization (SEO)**.

6.2 Prepare a Business Plan

Before you make any decisions or set up a business structure, you should prepare a **business plan**. Guidance provided by the Small Business Administration provides a listing of all the sections that should be included in your plan. The sections they recommend are: an executive summary; company description; market analysis; organization and management; service or product line; marketing and sales; funding request; financial projections; and an appendix with key documents.

While it may seem tedious, writing a business plan will help you make some important decisions as you set up your business. Your business plan will serve as a guidebook for you to follow, and a point of reference for check-ups as you develop your business. A good business plan does not have to be long or overly detailed. It just needs to summarize your mission, vision, brand identity, your services, your ideal customer or customers, and your strategy for reaching them. You can develop it in Microsoft Word, but Ann developed hers in PowerPoint. We recommend that you review the plan at least annually to determine whether you are on track or if there is a need to revise and update it. No doubt, as your business matures there will be changes in your situation and you will need to change the plan accordingly.

6.3 Going Solo or Tandem

One of the first thing you need to decide is whether you want to be in practice alone or with a partner or partners. Neither of us wanted to be financially tied to someone else. But we do know other consultants who have partners and are happy with their choice. Cheryl Holmes-Hansen, who does have a partner, has some specific advice if you choose to have a partner. Cheryl and her partner started off by having many conversations about their relationship and what they wanted their partnership to be like. They used a resource on the *Fundera* website while they were early in the planning stages for their partnership, and found it incredibly helpful as they discussed if, and then how, to move forward. The next part of this chapter reviews various types of business structures.

6.4 Deciding on Your Business Structure

There are multiple types of business structures and no single one is the right one – there is only the right one for you. In this section of the chapter, we will provide descriptions of the various types of business structures so that you can decide which structure best fits your situation.

6.4.1 Sole Proprietorship

We contend that many people attracted to consulting are the independent type. If this describes you, then you likely enjoy working alone. You may want to avoid the complications of other types of business structures or the risks inherent in partnerships. If this describes you, you may choose to set up your business as a **sole proprietorship**. A sole proprietorship is the simplest and most common business structure. As the name implies, a sole proprietorship is an unincorporated business owned and run by a single individual. There is no legal distinction between the business and the owner (you). Although you are entitled to all the profits generated by the business, you also assume all the business's debts, losses, and liabilities. You do not have to take any formal action to form a sole proprietorship, but you may need to obtain licenses or permits depending on the type of business and state and local requirements.

If you decide to use a name for your business that is different than your own, you may have to file a fictitious name, also known as an assumed name, trade name, or DBA name, short for "doing business as." You need to choose an original name, so be sure to conduct a thorough search and make sure the business name you choose has not already been used by someone else. In most states you can find an online search tool on the website of the secretary of state or other state agency that is responsible for business entity filings. You should also search the U.S. Patent and Trademark Office (USPTO) online database for similar trademarked names to yours.

You need to be aware that because you and your business are the same, you will not file separate taxes for your business. The revenue generated by your business is reported on your personal tax return. As a sole proprietor in the United States, you are responsible for your own **self-employment taxes** (Social Security and Medicare). Keep in mind that you will be paying this amount times two – because you are covering *both* the employee and employer's share. You can find more information about the tax implications for sole proprietorships on the Internal Revenue Service (IRS) website.

There are advantages and disadvantages to a sole proprietorship (Viola & McMahon, 2010). Advantages of this type of structure include being your own boss and having complete control over business decisions, the ease and low cost of starting your business, easy tax preparation, and being able to close your business when you want or need to. Disadvantages include the unlimited personal liability, potential difficulties with raising money, lack of business continuity if the owner dies or is unable to work, and the burden of having to do everything yourself.

If you have a full-time job and are only taking contracts on the side, this structure may work well for you. When Susan and Ann were in graduate school, they both consulted as sole proprietors; that structure worked out for them at that time. Consulting was a means to supplement income from their graduate assistantships. When Susan decided to take a full-time job, the transition was simple since she had only one contract at the time, and it was with her new employer. She found an evaluator who could step into the role and the organization easily agreed to the change. Once she was divested of the contract, the organization could hire her without conflict of interest.

6.4.2 Partnerships

A partnership is a business structure in which two or more people jointly own a single business. Each partner contributes to all aspects of the business, including money, property, labor, and/or skill. In return, each partner shares in the profits and losses of the business.

Because partnerships entail more than one person in the decision-making process, it is important to communicate clearly and agree on specific issues regarding running your business before you begin. Make sure you get along and that your skills are complementary. But be aware that many partnerships often end, and not always in an agreeable way. So, although partnership agreements are not legally required, they are a good idea. The partnership agreement should clearly detail how future business decisions will be made, how the partners will divide profits, resolve disputes, and how to dissolve the partnership. Be sure to schedule periodic check-ins to discuss how the partnership is going and, if anyone is dissatisfied, make any changes needed. We discuss this more in depth in the next chapter.

There are three general types of formal partnership arrangements:

1. In **general partnerships**, all profits, losses, and management duties are normally divided equally among partners. If you opt for a different arrangement, be sure to document the percentages assigned to each partner in the partnership agreement.
2. **Limited partnerships** are more complex and allow partners to have limited liability and limited input into management decisions. These limits are dependent on each partner's investment percentage. This type of partnership is sometimes used for short-term projects.
3. **Joint ventures** are general partnerships but are usually only in place for a limited time period or for a single project. Joint venture partners may decide later to continue their ongoing partnership, but they must file the proper paperwork if they choose to continue.

You will need to register your partnership and file an "annual information return" that reports the partnership's income, deductions, gains, and losses from the business's operations. However, the business does not pay income tax. The business profits and losses "pass through" to its partners and their respective share of the partnership's income or loss on their personal tax returns. As with the sole proprietorship, this structure has its advantages and disadvantages as well (Viola & McMahon, 2010). Disadvantages include the potential for contrasting opinions, increased cost to the client for team consultation, that partners may be held liable for actions by other partners, and that there may be disagreements about sharing profits. Severing the partnership can be difficult if there is some type of conflict that was not covered by the partnership agreement. However, there are advantages to a partnership. First, they are easy and inexpensive to form. Clients benefit from a greater knowledge base, larger network, and broader experience of the partners. Together, you may have more capital due to pooled resources and greater borrowing capacity should the need arise. If the partnership dissolves, it is easy to change your legal structure.

6.4.3 Corporations

In many cases, setting your business up as a **corporation** is recommended by business experts. It is a legal entity with a specific purpose, established by one or more individuals, and is separate from its owners. It carries with it all the legal rights and responsibilities of an individual person. Advantages of a corporate structure include certain tax advantages, credibility for seeking financing, management flexibility, potential ease of ownership transfers, and the corporation can have a perpetual life that outlasts you. Disadvantages may include rates of taxation, legal and administrative costs, the complexity of forming the corporation, and potential additional paperwork for government entities.

You can find more specific information through the Small Business Development Agency's website or in Gail Barrington's book, *Consulting Start Up and Management*, but the following subsections briefly discuss the types of corporate structures.

6.4.3.1 C Corporation

A **C corporation** (C Corp) is a legal entity owned by its shareholders. Profits of the corporation are taxed and then taxed again when shareholders are paid dividends. C Corps are more complex and are therefore a structure used by larger companies. You will likely not select this structure for your consulting business.

6.4.3.2 Limited Liability Company

A **limited liability company (LLC)** is a "pass-through" structure used by many small businesses. Owners get most of the personal asset protection of a corporation and are taxed similarly to sole proprietorships or partnerships, depending on who owns the business. Advantages of this specific type of corporation include the ease of setting it up, not having to sell and keep track of stock, limited liability, and flexibility in the number of owners (Viola & McMahon, 2010). Disadvantages include that not everyone is eligible to create an LLC, you may have to pay self-employment tax, and you may have to pay a yearly "franchise tax." Susan's company was set up as an LLC and it works well for her. In the state of Texas, LLCs do not pay a franchise tax until their gross income is over $1.5 million per year. Susan dreams that someday she will have to pay the franchise tax!

6.4.3.3 S Corporation

An **S corporation** (S Corp) is a corporation created through an IRS election. The corporation must first be registered in the state where it is headquartered. An S Corp files a tax return but, like an LLC, the business's profits or losses pass through to shareholders' income tax returns. There can be up to 35 shareholders in the S Corp. Ann has used this type of structure since establishing her company in 2004. Benefits and disadvantages are like those associated with LLCs.

Note: There is a difference between your business entity and the business's tax status. An LLC can elect to be taxed like an S Corp, resulting in potential tax savings, while still being an LLC (business entity). This is the set-up Ann uses for her business.

6.4.4 For-Profit versus Non-Profit

The difference between for-profit and non-profit companies is their purpose. For-profit companies are typically designed to create income for their owners and employees, while nonprofit companies typically, but not always, have a humanitarian purpose or are mission-driven. Nonprofits primarily rely on grants and donations and for-profit companies generate revenue through sales. If you decide to pursue nonprofit status, you must file paperwork with the IRS and your state for tax-exempt status (Viola & McMahon, 2010). You will be required to have a **board of directors** and **by-laws**. You will also have to file a Form 990 with the IRS each year and report details such as salaries, revenue sources, and expenses. While a nonprofit is a more complex business form, it can be advantageous if you plan to hire staff and grow. You can still have private clients, such as government and community-based organizations, and are also eligible for government and foundation grants that are unavailable to for-profit entities.

6.5 Are You Eligible for Special Status?

Perhaps not at the beginning of your business, but once you have your basic infrastructure, you might consider applying for special status for your business if you are eligible. If you are in the United States, this might include being certified as:

- A **Historically Underutilized Business (HUB)**.
- An **8(a) firm**, a small business that is owned and operated by socially and economically disadvantaged citizens. This program is administered by the Small Business Administration (SBA), the U.S. agency charged with supporting the growth and development of small businesses.
- A **Women-Owned Small Business** and/or Women-owned Small Business Enterprise. Several organizations provide these certifications; check your state for these entities.

As an example, in the state of Texas to qualify as a HUB, the applicant owner must show at least 51 percent ownership and daily control of the business and must be "economically disadvantaged" as a(n) Asian Pacific American, Black American, Hispanic American, Native American, American woman, and/or Service-Disabled Veteran with a service-related disability of 20 percent or greater (Texas Comptroller of Public Accounts, n.d.).

6.6 Getting Paid

Before you think about how much to charge for your services, if you have not already developed a business plan, do it now. Remember, the business plan includes a market analysis to find out what your local market will support. You likely will not be able to find out exactly what other consultants are making but you can ask your peers to share their rate with you if they are comfortable with sharing that information. If they do not feel comfortable sharing, ask them if they can provide a range. You can also check in with a few local headhunters or search a website such as Glass Door. Keep in mind that hourly fees will differ based on your education, experience, the clients you are serving, and where you are located.

Before you settle on your hourly rate, there are a few things you need to do. The *first* thing you should do is get comfortable talking about money and setting fees. It is important to be fair to your client, but you also need to be fair to yourself. Be confident in your skills and ask for what you deserve. But, as a community consultant, there is some negotiation that occurs during talks about fees. It is OK to ask potential clients about their budget and then scope the work based on what the client can afford. This can be especially challenging when you are working with smaller nonprofits that have limited resources, but it is the reality of being in business to serve communities.

We recommend that you always ask the client for a budget during the initial meeting or call. If you find out what they can afford at the very beginning, it will help you to focus the scope of your conversation. You might also want to ask if they have the funds on hand, or if they will need to raise the funds to do the project. One of the toughest transitions for community-minded professionals is when they need to put on their business hats. If you are going to survive, it must be done.

Too often formal requests for proposals do not provide information about how much is available for the project, and worse, they don't always include contact information if you do have questions. If they do include contact information, don't be shy about using that contact information to ask how much has been budgeted for the project. If they will not reveal the amount, then include all costs of doing the work as it needs to be done to provide a quality product and scope the project as best you can. If the potential client found you on your website or reached out to you directly, they are more likely to share the budget.

Over time, if you track your time for various tasks performed within each project, you will have a cadre of information that can help you estimate how long it will take to do various tasks (for example, design a logic model, develop a strategic plan, develop and offer training, or write an evaluation plan).

Now you are ready to calculate your rate.

6.6.1 Getting Down to the Number

Gail Barrington's (2012) book describes a straightforward way of setting fees. We recommend Gail's book for more details on rate setting, but we provide a few tips in this section of the chapter. You will find advice from other consultants as well on the web. MBO Partners provides one helpful website that helps calculate an hourly rate. Another method used by some consultants is to choose an hourly rate of pay, then triple it to cover overhead and profit. But how do you choose your starting salary? One way is to start with the salary at your last place of employment and use that to calculate your daily and hourly rate.

Sounds simple enough, right? But before you come up with a number and think you are done, think again. After several years in business, Ann went to her business-savvy husband with this dilemma. Although she had a good number of contracts, she felt like her company was not making a profit. And indeed, that was true, because she wasn't including a profit margin or, worse, covering any overhead costs!

Likewise, Gail Barrington (2012) asserts that you need to think about these and two other important issues that will impact your business. Namely:

1. What is the actual cost of running your business? Otherwise known as overhead, this includes accounting fees, printing services, office equipment, insurance, legal services, professional development costs, office rental expenses, utilities, office supplies, and so on. You get the picture.
2. How many days and hours can you reasonably work? Unless you plan to work 365 days per year, you will need to subtract weekends, vacation days, holidays, and sick days. If you have administrative duties, and you will as a business owner or partner, you will need to subtract days for managing and marketing your business. If you take advantage of professional development opportunities, which you should, you will need to consider that time as well.

So, what is a more accurate way to get to your billable rate? Start with the number of workdays available (260 excluding weekends) and subtract your vacation, sick days, and holidays and the time for professional development, administrative time, and marketing. You now have your total number of possible billable days. Make sure to be realistic!

Next, calculate your total costs as desired salary plus overhead. This is where we, once again, recommend Gail Barrington's book, because she gives a very complete list of all possible overhead expenses. When you calculate your estimated taxes, keep in mind that it will include self-employment taxes. Also, if your taxes will be reported on your personal return and you have a spouse, estimate your tax rate for your combined incomes. Susan forgot to consider that one year and it led to a very unhappy April 15. Now divide your total by the number of possible billable days. Add in your desired profit and you now have your daily rate. Divide this number by the number of hours in a workday (eight) and you have your hourly rate.

6.6.2 Value-Based Pricing

An alternative to the pricing methods described above is **value-based pricing**. Value-based pricing is a strategy of setting the price of a consultancy primarily based on a client's perceived value of a product or service (Beattie, 2020). Value-based pricing is different than **cost-plus pricing**, which we have described. If you can make the argument that you or your company offers unique value, that your services are better than your competitors, and will deliver at a high level that meets their needs you might consider using value-based pricing. Steps to do this are: (1) conduct market research; (2) conduct competitor research; (3) analyze the market; (4) calculate the value; and (5) test your prices (Qualtrics, n.d.). If you decide to adopt this pricing method, you will still need to calculate your cost of doing business.

6.7 Growth Brings ... Complications

If your business grows and you add staff, deciding on your hourly rate becomes *a lot* more complicated. The upside is that if you have staff that are junior to you and who make less than your hourly rate, you have an opportunity to be a lot more competitive when bidding for projects. You may want to offer a blended rate. It is also common practice to add an amount to each person's rate to partially cover company profit and overhead. So, you may have several rates for staff or consultants based on their experience. In this case your salary is an average of your rate, plus the rate of any staff junior to you (like your graduate or undergraduate assistants). Your office manager or other administrative staff (if you have them) should be calculated into your other overhead costs. You still need to be mindful of the actual number of billable days you are available to work and add your profit margin.

6.8 Retainers

Ann was once asked if she would consider accepting a retainer. A retainer is a fee paid to you by the client who then has ongoing access to you for a specified number of hours per week or month. You are paid the fee whether they use your services or not. The nonprofit was small and did not feel it had the budget for an internal evaluator, nor did it have the budget for an external evalua-tor. It did have some internal expertise and felt like it could do some basic evaluation with a little technical assistance. This agreement did not happen, but you may want to incorporate retainers into your portfolio of service offer-ings. If an organization is interested in this type of agreement and wants you to consult with it on a specific number of projects during a specific timeframe, you can calculate the amount of time you will dedicate to work on its projects. Alternatively, you can come to an agreement on the number of days per week you will work for that organization, then multiply your daily rate by the num-ber of hours you plan to work.

6.9 Calculating Project Budgets

Many of our clients have a specific budget in mind for the consultation they need. However, they don't always say so. You need to get comfortable with asking potential clients about their budget. When they share their budget, you can provide a realistic idea of the cost of the work they were hoping for. If their budget is smaller than their desired deliverables, you can scope a project given what they can afford. Sometimes, we provide a "good, better, and best" estimate so they have a better idea what they can get for various price points.

Neither of us work under contracts that are "**time and materials con-tracts**" (contracts that pay you by the hour plus any project-related expenses). If you budget correctly, **fixed-fee contracts** (a contract in which the fee does not change no matter how many hours you dedicate to the project) can work for you. However, if you fail to control **scope creep** or have a very difficult-to-please client, you can very quickly fall into a financial hole. Scope creep is when the client asks for things outside the signed contract. When this happens, it is in everyone's best interest to discuss the situation right away. If there is flexibility in the contract you can negotiate and provide the needed service. If not, you should estimate the cost of the additional work and seek approval. We do not recommend that you provide the work without a discussion. In any case, you should provide a change order, a document the specifies the task or deliverable to be added, the amount of effort needed, the date it will be com-pleted, and the cost.

Do keep detailed and accurate records. Over the years, we have been able to accurately (well, fairly accurately anyway) estimate the time it takes to do specific tasks. The inevitable scope creep comes in and neither of us is very good at saying no. But if you have kept careful records of how long specific tasks take, you can use your findings to renegotiate your contracts in subse-quent years.

6.10 Billing

There are different ways you can bill for your projects. You can bill an hourly rate and invoice monthly or at some other interval for the number of hours worked. The advantage of this method is that you can be sure you are paid for every hour you work. The disadvantage is that you must then share your hourly rate with the clients and prepare monthly invoices. Susan used this approach for her first few years in business and transitioned away from this because it is time-consuming, and she found that she just really does not enjoy preparing all those invoices every month and tracking every hour. Also, it is easier for her to budget if she knows exactly how much she will get from each contract. Keep in mind that if you invoice only for the hours you work, you may end up leaving money on the table if the project takes less time than anticipated.

Another way is to bill by deliverable. The client is invoiced each time you deliver a product. In this case, you will break down the project by deliverables. Some examples of deliverables might be a finished report, facilitating a meeting, or presenting an evaluation framework. Another way is to cost out the entire project and timeline and request payment at certain times. If you are retained as a consultant on an ongoing basis, you might request monthly or quarterly payments. Another way would be to request half of the money up front and half when the final products are delivered. Whichever method you choose, the best way to calculate project rates is to clearly define what the project deliverables are. Most often clients will not ask to see your rate information unless you are responding to a formal request for proposals (RFP). A detailed spreadsheet can help you manage projects and determine the accuracy of your cost projections by comparing estimated versus actual project costs.

In the past few years, Ann makes it a habit to include in every **scope of work (SOW)** or contract the caveat that any work requested outside the SOW will be charged at a specific hourly rate. We recommend this so that if the client asks for additional work, you can refer back to the agreement and develop a change order or new contract.

6.11 Staffing or Subcontracting

Staff size for your business can range from one (just you) to as many as your business will accommodate. Susan decided from the beginning that she never wanted to hire or manage staff. To expand the size of her business, when necessary, she partners with other consultants. Ann, on the other hand, decided to hire staff or consultants as her business grew. Each of us were successful in accomplishing what we had planned, and each way works in a way that serves our business. When you are thinking about size, you must also think about the various levels of responsibility of each position and how many people are needed at each staffing level (Lyons & Harrington, 2006). You can also consider a hybrid design with some paid staff and some consultants who fill in on projects as needed.

6.11.1 Setting Up Subcontractors for Success

Set your subcontractors up for success by developing a formal agreement with them that details all their responsibilities, the expected hours they will contribute to the project, their fee, and invoice schedule. Make clear if they will be billing by the hour or if their contract is fixed price. Provide them with guidelines or standard operating procedures (SOP) for work that must be done in a specific way. SOPs are helpful for tasks such as updating dashboards, sending quarterly reports, or formats and procedures for producing reports. Make sure that you provide subcontractors with the details necessary for them to create products in a way that is consistent with your brand. The more clarity and detail you provide your subcontractors, the more likely it is that they will be successful and provide you with the support you need.

6.12 Locating and Setting Up Your Business

6.12.1 Home Office versus Renting an Office

Since 2020 and the COVID-19 pandemic, many people who had not worked remotely before were forced to do so. Before deciding if you will permanently set up your office in your home or outside of it, you need to really do some serious self-examination. You need to ask yourself if you have the self-discipline to ignore the pile of laundry and dirty dishes and sit down to work. If you have a dog, will it be barking during conference calls? Will your neighbors drop by presuming you are available? Can you handle working alone at home? If you can handle distractions and discipline yourself to work diligently at home, then a home office may be right for you.

A home office has the advantage of avoiding the cost of rent (which is overhead passed on to your clients) and you may qualify for a home office tax deduction. But be warned, to take a home office tax deduction, you must make sure that everything in your home office relates solely to your business. In other words, you don't want it to double as your children's study area or your craft closet. A home office can also be more comfortable than a rented space, you avoid a commute each day, and you don't have to take time to dress up to "go to work." Best of all, nobody steals your lunch out of the refrigerator, and you can guarantee that the microwave and bathrooms are clean!

Renting an office has advantages and disadvantages as well. A dedicated office outside your home residence obviously provides a quiet, private space for you to work and meet clients. It provides a professional presence in the community and is essential if you find you cannot "leave work" when your office is at home. However, depending on where you live, it may be a significant monthly expense. You will also need to pay for utilities, internet, phone, and insurance to cover the office and office equipment. You will likely be asked to sign a multi-year lease and, depending on your tolerance for risk, that may not be something you are comfortable with.

Alternatively, you may be able to sublease space from another business, thereby avoiding some if not all the costs for internet and possibly utilities. An increasingly popular strategy is co-working spaces where you have a dedicated office and share other spaces and amenities, such as a conference room, break room, receptionist, and office equipment, with others. A "virtual office" is a similar model in which you rent an office and drop in when you need to.

6.12.1.1 Office Equipment and Supplies

Whether you're equipping your first office or just re-stocking your current one, the checklist in Table 6.1 will help you determine and track which furniture, equipment, technologies, and supplies you may need to help your business run more smoothly. Some are "must haves" and others are optional. For example, if you need to make copies you can always visit a local office supply store. As technology evolves, we are finding that our office equipment and supplies needs change.

Get to know your local office supply stores to see if there are benefits to opening a business account, find out if they deliver, and how you can lower your costs. You might also check your local membership-only warehouses to see if it is worth getting a membership if they offer good prices on items you will buy in bulk. Check online sources as well but be aware of any shipping fees. Sometimes it is less expensive to pay a little more and shop locally.

6.12.1.2 Services and Software

You will also need to shop carefully for various services that will support your business. It is helpful to have a domain name for your website that can be used for your email address too. Your website provider can set you up with email addresses specific to your company. Google email is free and convenient but is not as professional as an email that includes your company name.

You may wish to purchase software packages to support your business. You will need software for word processing, spreadsheets, and presentations, such as MS Office. You may also need analytic software for statistical or qualitative analyses. If you do your own accounting, you will need some type of bookkeeping software. You may also want software that supports data visualization or other specialized services. To make such selections, reach out to other consultants to find out what they are using and research online to compare costs and features with your capacity and needs.

Table 6.1 List of office equipment and supplies: absolute and possible needs

Category	Needs	
	Absolute needs	Possible needs
Office furniture and equipment	• Desk • File cabinets • Overhead and work lighting • Fire extinguisher • Ergonomically comfortable chair • Bookcases • Worktable(s) • Paper shredder • Wastebasket • Recycling bin	• Fireproof safe • Postage meter or scale • Office decorations • Labeling machine • First-aid kit • Wall whiteboard and markers • Alarm system • Client seating
Computer hardware and accessories	• Desktop or laptops computer with docking stations and monitors • Surge protectors • Online computer back-up service • Scanner • Keyboard and mouse • Printer • Battery back-up unit	• PowerPoint projector • Tablets
Communication	• Internet connection • Smartphones • Zoom, WebEx or other conferencing service	• Telephone land line • Toll-free line • Fax machine • Cordless headset • Desk telephones (speakerphones) • Digital recorders
General office supplies	• Business cards • Printer cartridges • Pens and pencils • Cleaning supplies • File folders • Envelopes • Postage stamps • USB drives • Printer paper • Notepads • Flip charts	• Stationery

You will likely also need some type of web meeting services. There are free services such as Skype and Google Hangout. There is also FreeConferenceCall .com, which is a free online conference call service. These work reasonably well and are improving all the time. For additional features you might consider one of the paid services such as Webex, Zoom, or GoToMeeting. If you will be doing a lot of remote work with individuals or groups in other cities or need to host group meetings, we recommend one of the paid services. They allow for easy desktop sharing, recording of your meetings, polls and audience engagement, and other useful features.

6.13 Managing Your Money

We highly recommend that you establish separate bank accounts and credit cards for your business. Establish a relationship with a local bank and shop around for one that offers additional benefits for business customers. For example, Susan's bank offers business customers free notary services which she has used on several occasions. They also offer free checking and savings accounts, and a special window for transactions (with a shorter line) when in-person banking is required.

When you shop for a credit card, look for one that offers special benefits. Susan's card offers airline miles for her most frequently used airline and a free checked bag which saves her a considerable amount of money. Having separate accounts for your business and personal life is very helpful for keeping your personal and business expenses separate. Many a businessperson has gotten into trouble by mixing their personal money with that of the business. Don't do it.

Unless you have basic accounting skills and are knowledgeable about tax laws and deductions, you may need to contract for accounting services. An accounting firm can help you with payroll (if you hire staff), tax preparation, and other financial matters. Viola and McMahon (2010) recommend that you meet with a few before selecting one to ensure that you are working with someone you trust. Be sure to get referrals from other small business owners.

Since her business was small and simple, Susan chose not to use the services of an accountant. She uses Quicken for invoicing, preparing 1099s, and accounting, and an online tax service to prepare her taxes. That said, we would be remiss if we did not mention that she has had two accounting courses (one at the master's level) and has assisted with professional tax preparation in the past. Ann uses Quicken, too, but hired a CPA to manage her payroll and quarterly and yearly tax filings. Her office manager handles invoicing, accounts receivable, and accounts payable.

You might also wish to retain the services of an attorney that specializes in small businesses, particularly those that are consulting business. Viola and McMahon (2010) present a number of reasons an attorney might be helpful. These include setting up your business structure, handling collections problems with clients, disputes with creditors or employees, helping with copyrighting your products, and reviewing leases and contracts. If you do not use the services of an attorney to review contracts, review them very carefully and *read every word*. Do not be shy about asking potential clients for changes to the terms. Susan read one contract carefully and found that if she met all the costly and unnecessary requirements, such as paying for drug and background checks, she would end up making almost no money. The contractor was willing to remove nearly all of them when she brought it to their attention. This was a standard contract they used with many provisions unrelated to the work she would be doing.

Business cards are also important. Do not skimp on cost by printing your own. Investing a few extra dollars to get cards that are very professional looking and include your **branding** (logo, tag line, colors) is worth it. Order plenty because you want to hand out many of them as you network. There are inexpensive online resources that offer professional-looking cards.

6.13.1 Invoicing and Accounting (Taxes)

There are some things related to your business that you can, or may want to, handle on your own. You may or may not want to hire an accountant, depending on your experience, education, and comfort level. As we mentioned earlier, when Ann first started her company, she hired a CPA who helped her file the incorporation papers. For a short time, until her business grew, she handled all the invoicing and payroll herself. Her CPA filed quarterly and yearly payroll taxes. Susan, on the other hand, has an accounting background. She manages all the finances related to her business, including invoicing, and quarterly and yearly tax filings.

Invoicing is often simple when you first start your business. You might have a few clients and if you choose to bill quarterly, invoicing is a snap. Once you get multiple clients, or if clients need to be billed according to several schedules, things get complicated. It's easy to get behind and, the next thing you know, you are waiting for payments on multiple projects. Our advice? Make sure you invoice your clients as specified in the SOW and do not allow them to be late on payments. To do so hurts your business and sends the message that paying you is not important.

6.14 Insurance

There are many consultants who do not carry insurance. But not carrying insurance is like walking out in the rain without an umbrella. It is a bad idea and bad business practice. Although you may believe it is unnecessary, carrying insurance, just like paying for a computer and software subscriptions, is a cost of doing business.

What types of insurance will you need? Obviously, you need to carry **automobile insurance**. Even if you don't own any company vehicles, if employees drive their own cars on company business, consider getting non-owned auto liability to protect your company in case your employee has inadequate coverage or no coverage at all. If you rent an office outside your home, you will need **property insurance** to cover the cost of loss or damage due to theft or fire or other reasons. General or **business liability insurance** protects you from claims such as bodily injury, property damage, personal injury, and other situations that can arise from your business operations. **Professional liability insurance** protects you from negligence and other claims that may be initiated by clients. **Errors and omission insurance** protects you from claims that you failed to render professional services or did so improperly. Your general liability policy does not provide this protection. **Worker's compensation insurance** provides wage replacement and medical benefits to employees injured while working on the job. In exchange for these benefits, the employee gives up his rights to sue his employer for the incident, unless the injury is caused by an intentional act. Worker's compensation insurance protects you and the company. State laws vary, but all states require you to have worker's compensation if you have a certain number of **W2 employees**. Penalties for non-compliance can be steep so check with your state's Department of Labor. A **business owner policy** (BOP) package may be appropriate and bundles all required coverages a business owner might need. These types of policies will include business interruption insurance, property insurance, vehicle coverage, liability insurance, and crime insurance. You can adjust the BOP coverage depending on the needs of your company and you may be able to save money by doing so.

It may feel like a daunting task to think about all these various types of insurance. First, don't panic. Start by talking to your personal insurance agent. Even if they can't help you directly, they may be able to point you in the right direction. You should also check with any professional associations to which you belong. Several provide some insurance for their members. You can also reach out to your professional network to see where your colleagues get their insurance. This a common topic for one of the listservs we belong to. We don't want to provide specific company names here but there are a few companies that specialize in small business insurance.

As your company grows and you bid on larger contracts, you will likely find that carrying insurance is required by some potential clients. If you read the fine print in a contract and find the potential client requires a higher coverage limit than you carry, don't hesitate to ask if the amount can be negotiated. We have yet to have anyone say no to our request for an adjustment to the contract.

6.15 Finding Work

From the very start, and ongoing, you will be looking for work. Ideally, you will have a good balance of smaller projects and larger projects (Lyons & Harrington, 2006), and short-term and long-term projects. The remainder of this section will provide some ideas for how you might find various types of projects.

6.15.1 The Power of a Good Referral

In our experience, most of our contracts have come from referrals from past or current clients that were happy with our work. Other consultants attest to the same experience. In her book, Gail Barrington (2012) shared that 29.6 percent of 125 projects were attained through referrals from former clients, colleagues, former workshop participants, or other people with whom she worked. If you have specific skills and content expertise, produce useful reports and products, and deliver them on time, you stand a good chance of developing a good reputation. It is a sad fact that there are many consultants who do not produce good work. So, when someone rises to the top and is excellent at what they do, the word quickly spreads. This is especially true, we believe, among small- to mid-size nonprofit organizations with close professional networks and limited budgets. They are very likely to reach out to their peers for recommendations when they need a consultant to develop a strategic plan, train their staff, help design a community intervention, or conduct an evaluation.

6.15.2 Certifications and Vendor Lists

Once you become an "official" business, you may be eligible for a variety of certifications. These include Small Business, Small Disadvantaged Business, Woman-Owned Business, Minority-Owned Business, Historically Underutilized Business, and a Veteran's or Disabled Veteran's Business. These designations have advantages that include being able to use them on marketing materials and website listings, eligibility for certain grants, or for technical assistance or other business support (Viola & McMahon, 2010). You will likely need to apply for such certifications at the federal, state, and local levels. To learn more about your eligibility and how to become certified you will need to do some research for each of these designations.

Another step that can be helpful to generate business is to get your business placed on vendor lists. Many school districts, some foundations, local government entities, and even some larger companies pre-approve a set of vendors that they can call upon when they need someone for a specific project. Some entities will issue RFPs and only approved vendors are eligible to compete for the projects.

6.15.3 Become Involved in the Community

Another great way to generate leads is to be involved in the community in which you live. Besides giving back to your local neighbors, you will develop your skills and your reputation at the same time. Working in the community is no easy task, and what better way to hone your skills than working in your own backyard? Pro bono work with nonprofits in your local area is also an important way to contribute to social change in your neighborhood or state. For example, Ann served on a high school's school governance council and offered her expertise in substance abuse prevention, data visualization, and evaluation planning. She currently serves on a nonprofit board.

If you do not want to do pro bono work, consider doing projects for select organizations at a deep discount. This can be especially advantageous if you negotiate being able to share the report you prepare as a work product or being able to list the organization as a client on your website. Susan did a project for a small branch of a national organization for a substantially reduced price. She primarily did it because it was an organization and a cause she was happy to support. Three years later it paid off when she won a substantially larger competitive bid for the national organization, partly because she had direct experience with the local affiliate.

6.15.4 Networking: Attend Professional Meetings

Investing in your own continuing professional education is important. It helps you stay current with new and changing techniques and exposes you to the latest research in your key content areas. So be sure to include conferences and other professional development expenses in your projected budget. Reading peer-reviewed journals and publications are two ways to do this, but attending professional meetings and conferences provides the opportunity to reconnect with existing colleagues and meet new ones. Find out which professional associations (national, state, and local) represent your disciplinary background (for example, sociology, psychology, evaluation) and which ones are related to your specific content area. For example, if a large part of your work is in maternal and child health, you might also want to investigate the opportunities offered by CityMatCH. In fact, the two of us first connected at an American Evaluation Association (AEA) conference several years ago and have since collaborated on several presentations and worked together to chair the AEA's Community Psychology Topical Interest Group (TIG) and the Nonprofits and Foundations TIG. In fact, Ann and Susan first met many of the colleagues they work with through AEA.

When you attend conferences, make it a practice to bring your business cards and gather cards from your new contacts. Make a note on the back of them with a brief reminder as to how you met the person. Be sure and follow up with them shortly after you return home. If they are local, schedule a time to have coffee or lunch. If they are not, consider setting up a Zoom call.

Once you make a new connection, what should you look for in a potential colleague? We recommend that you seek other consultants who have skills you do not have. For example, if you have strong quantitative skills, you may want a few contacts that have strong qualitative skills. If you are strong at planning but less strong at report writing, team up with someone who is skilled at synthesizing and communicating information. If there is a skill you want to learn, see if there are opportunities to partner with someone who has the skills and experience, and what you might be able to offer them in return.

6.15.5 Respond to Request for Proposals

RFPs, **requests for applications** (RFA), and **requests for quotes** (RFQ) are the most commonly used methods to solicit proposals from community consultants. When we refer to RFPs, we are referring to all of these potential solicitation types. Consultants use the information provided in the RFP and their own expertise to suggest a solution and associated costs. The organization can then choose among the proposals to select the consultant they feel best meets their needs or narrow the field down to a few finalists. In our experience, RFPs are typically funded at a higher level than work that comes to you from a referral. If you want to grow your practice, responding to proposals is something you should consider. What makes RFPs particularly frustrating is the lack of ability to work with the client to discuss the problem that led to the proposal, as they see it, and work with them on collaborative solutions. It is this creative process that we find rewarding. If you prefer a participatory process like we do, blind RFPs are particularly frustrating.

However, there are two ways you can use RFPs to support your clients. First, look out for RFPs for programs and services your potential clients might be interested in and share the announcement with them. This creates good will and keeps you in their mind. If there is a good opportunity to partner with them, let them know how you can help. Second, watch for RFPs that are a good fit for your business and apply only if it fits within your portfolio of products. We share more information about how to find and respond to RFPs in Chapter 9 of this book.

6.16 Define Your Scope of Work

For each project, you need to define a contract that includes a SOW. The SOW defines specific project deliverables, a timeframe for each deliverable, project costs, and an invoice schedule. Base the deliverables and timelines included in the SOW on the client's plans as communicated to you in your initial conversations. You will likely have to go back and forth with the client a few times before you can both agree on the SOW and sign it.

But as you will find out if you haven't already, clients' plans often change for a host of reasons or as you specified in a formal proposal. For example, stakeholders may pull out, community priorities change, or things take longer to implement. Don't be surprised at all if you need to redefine your timelines or deliverables. As a professional, just make sure that *you* are not the reason timelines or deliverables need to be revised. When specific deliverables change in any significant way or if timelines need to move, we highly recommend that you write a change order, an addendum to the SOW that specifies the changes that need to be made. You (the consultant) and the individual that represents the organization should sign the change order.

Ideally your SOW will detail, very specifically, all the deliverables you agree to provide to the client. Deliverables should reflect the purpose of the project and lead to actionable steps that the community-based organization or coalition will implement to achieve their goals. So, it is important to be very clear about what information or products the client expects the project will yield. It is good practice to draft a list of deliverables and share with the potential client for their input, allowing you to discuss anything that is not clear. Sometimes it is helpful to share notes or a brief concept paper after the initial meeting to ensure that you correctly understood the potential client's needs and goals. This is a good opportunity to check that the due dates you assigned reflect the needs of the client. Don't forget to ask about any funder deadlines that need to be considered. You and the person responsible for oversight and paying you should sign the SOW.

6.17 Managing Your Time and Projects

One of the most difficult things for any consultant to learn, maybe more so for the community consultant, is time management. Time is something you will need to learn to manage if your business is to survive and thrive. Community projects get complicated quickly so don't be surprised if you are asked to attend local community events or other activities that were not specified in the SOW.

First, you need to distinguish between paid (billable) and unpaid activities (nonbillable). Billable time is time that is directly related to your work. This includes communication tasks (such as emails, phone calls, reports, and meetings) and project work (training, focus group data collection, quantitative analysis, and so on). Nonbillable time should be kept to a minimum. As a business owner, you may have more nonbillable time than your staff or contractors because you are responsible for administrative tasks that cannot be directly billed to the client. However, the company's profit margin is dependent on how much you control nonbillable time. So, think about a goal for nonbillable versus billable time for each staff and periodically review estimated versus actual. There is even less wiggle room for subcontractors on fixed-priced contracts.

You will need to develop a way to track your time for everyone who is working on a project. The simplest way to track project time is to use an Excel spreadsheet. You can organize it by client and/or project and track estimated versus actual time (see Chapter 9 in Gail Barrington's book). Ann used this method for a while until her business grew and she added staff.

Then you might use software to help manage time tracking. Once Community Evaluation Solutions (CES) started to grow, Ann switched from Excel to a program called Toggl, a relatively low-cost option that tracks billable time by project. That worked for a time, but CES wanted a way to track estimated versus actual by staff member and project. Ann then switched to an online service called Function Fox. The method you choose should be driven by your company's needs. There are many other software programs that help with simple time tracking such as Clockify or Harvest. If you need help with project management than you might consider Function Fox, Asana, Monday.com or others. With a little research, you will find a solution that works for you.

6.18 Marketing

6.18.1 Social Media

These days, most businesses and organizations have some type of **social media** presence to reach potential and current clients. Most of us of a certain age have heard of Facebook, Instagram, LinkedIn, and Twitter. There always seems to be some new social media platform and it can be difficult to keep up. Keep in mind that the demographics of people who use each of these platforms are very different and often change. You will want to think about the people you are trying to reach – their interests, demographics, and where they get their information. What social media platforms do the organizations you want to connect with use?

There are two common mistakes made by businesses regarding social media. To begin, some businesses assume that social media is unnecessary or superfluous. The benefits of social media for businesses include being actively engaged both with others in their field, and with their clients. Whereas traditional marketing tools such as billboards and television ads only allow businesses to publish advertising material, social media allows businesses to receive direct feedback from their audience. This is an invaluable source of information for both for-profit and nonprofit businesses. Another benefit for a community consulting firm is to provide support and awareness for social issues of interest to clients.

The second mistake is that some businesses attempt to be present on every social media channel available. A good social media consultant helps their client choose which platforms to engage. Facebook and Twitter are no longer the only widely used social media platforms: Snapchat, Instagram, Periscope, and Group Me are a few of the other platforms that have taken a prominent role in the world of social media. By the time this book reaches print, there will likely be several more platforms or possibly something we could not yet imagine.

You may be able to organize your own marketing strategy using social media, or depending on your budget, hire a social media consultant (perhaps one of your media-savvy children) to help you. A social media consultant can use their expertise and experience to find material that is of interest to your company's ideal audience and then schedule daily posts, monitor your page and encourage community engagement, and, hopefully, generate business.

At Community Evaluation Solutions, we determined that our audience typically uses Facebook, LinkedIn, and Twitter, so our social media strategy has focused on those three platforms. It is certainly possible that we may expand to include other platforms in the future. However, it would not be beneficial to spend resources trying to break into new platforms without first building the base of our strategy on the platforms with which our audience already engages. We would also want to do some marketing analysis to determine if our clients are using new or different platforms. For now, we share our experience in the field of evaluation and post engaging material that is relevant to our clients. Topics we post about include evaluation, evaluation comics, substance abuse prevention, public health, community coalitions, and systems change – areas in which we work and have some interest. We use Hootsuite to schedule posts across multiple platforms to be more efficient. Although, when we see something we want to share with our clients and followers, we post immediately. We also retweet "favorite" items from our clients and other organizations so that we remain an actively engaged social media partner.

6.18.2 Blogging

Ann will admit that she was a reluctant blogger. It was while attending EVAL2013, the AEA's annual conference in Washington, DC that our evaluation colleague, Chris Lysy, issued a challenge for evaluators to start blogging. Ann has always enjoyed writing, so she decided to respond to that challenge. You can check out her **blog** on her website. There is a link to it in Appendix 2. Many people are now blogging. Blogging provides another way to communicate your values, interests, and expertise with others to reach your ideal customer. If you have a specific expertise, say training community coalitions, then blogging is one way you can share that expertise with others. You may be able to turn followers into clients!

A word of warning, though, is that if you start blogging, try to be consistent about it so that you can develop a following. Susan is getting better at this, but admittedly, still needs to be more consistent. You can find her blog on her website. Also, be careful about what you write so that it is well-written and would not offend someone. Remember, you are a businessperson and need to appeal to a broad base and give an impression of professionalism.

6.18.3 Website

We contend that you really will not be acknowledged as a legitimate business these days without a website. Arguably, you can have a presence using social media alone. But a bona fide website allows you to present your company in a professional way and will prove to be useful if you have a need for e-commerce (selling materials, products, or training). A website can make a one-person shop have more of a presence and increase your profitability. You can spend thousands of dollars on a custom-designed site but there is no need to spend that much. For a minimal investment (anywhere from $10 to $25 per month) and a few hours of your time, you can use online web design services to create an attractive website. Just like social media, technology is constantly changing, but there are a host of low-cost website building companies. You might want to research *PC Magazine* or other online resources. Keep in mind that if you later decide to change hosting companies, your site may not transfer, and you may have to start over. Of course, if you are technically challenged, you should have no problem finding a website designer in your local area.

Whether you design your website yourself or hire someone, make sure the website is user-friendly, and the important things are easy to find. Nothing is more frustrating than having to dig through a website searching for something that should be obvious. Things to think about presenting on your website include:

- *Branding* – make sure your logo and colors are prominent and reflect your company.
- *Pictures* – people are more likely to stop and view your website (and blogs, tweets, and so on for that matter) if you use pictures.
- *Services and expertise* – what do you offer and how is that different from others?
- *Personnel* – show off your education, experience, and interests along with those of your staff.
- *Case studies* – help your potential clients understand what you offer by describing some of the work you have done. Use examples to demonstrate your services.
- *Testimonials* – ask a few of your clients to provide a short testimonial about what you or your company helped them achieve.
- *Social media* – be sure to include the icons that link to your social media sites; some websites present a live Twitter feed on the landing page.

- **Contact us** – make sure your clients and followers know how to reach you. List your business address, phone number, and your email address.

6.18.4 Direct Mailers

Although neither of us has tried this approach, direct mailers (brochures, letters, newsletters) are another way to reach potential clients. You will likely be approached by marketing companies that promise you a specific list of potential clients, for a fee of course. We think that if you want to use this approach, you are much better off doing your own study of potential clients and reaching out to them in this way. Keep in mind that if you choose an electronic newsletter company rather than a paper newsletter, such as Mail Chimp or Constant Contact, you will need the client or potential client's permission to send them your newsletter. You run the risk of being barred from these services if a high number of contacts reject your solicitation.

6.19 A Word of Caution: Choose Your Clients Wisely

It is hard to believe, but often true, that community members and organizations don't always think the evaluation plan or community change strategy you so painstakingly helped them develop is a priority. More often, they are hard at work at providing their service and not so keen on collecting data, following through with implementing their strategic plan, or ensuring a participative planning process. This is true of organizations that have been around for quite some time as well as younger organizations. It is also true of simple and complex organizations and immature and mature organizations.

We have found in our practice that some organizations seem very engaged until the contract is signed. Even when we emphasize that it is important for the community or organizational leader to remain involved throughout the change process, they do not always engage. Based on our experience, we try our best to avoid working with these types of organizations. Typically, we have found when the leader is not involved throughout the process the project will suffer. For example, if the product you have been hired to develop, like an evaluation plan or strategic plan, is not supported from the top, it will not be supported by staff either. When staff fail to buy in for a myriad of reasons, they are less likely to be engaged and more likely to withhold important information. When the leader disengages, consultation methods and the results are often questioned or rejected outright. This is equally true of other types of community change initiatives. You will want to ensure that a potential client is ready for change and committed to the work you will be facilitating at all levels.

We also caution that you take time to determine the stability and readiness of the organization. In our practice, we have encountered organizations that really needed to work on their structure and internal processes and culture before they would be ready to engage in evaluation, strategic plans, or strategy development. For example, if the organization has an interim director, make sure the board of directors is aware and supportive of what you will be doing and considers it important enough that they would encourage new leadership to engage with you. Some organizations need to build stronger infrastructure before they can move forward with service expansions or enhancements or implementing an effective evaluation or strategic plan. If the organization simply has too many priority issues that it must address (for example, serious funding problems, large and frequent leadership turnover, unstable board, or internal discord), then it is acceptable to point out that perhaps they first expend resources on working through those issues, so they can reap all the benefits of what you are offering.

6.20 Additional Practical Matters

In this chapter we have touched on some, but admittedly not all, of the practical matters involved in starting your community consulting practice. The types of things you decide to handle versus those you contract out will depend largely on your comfort level with these tasks. Some tasks are relatively easy, or at least low-tech, like choosing a company name. Other tasks are more technical, like setting up QuickBooks, and you may want to work with a professional to help you. Table 6.2 depicts some of these tasks and who might be responsible for each task. As the owner, you will always have primary responsibility but there might be times when you need some assistance. In the table we note where you might want to get advice from an attorney, an accountant, or other professional like a marketing expert or website designer, For example, you might write a contract for a client, but ask that your attorney review it. You might develop some ideas about how you would like your website to look and function but hire a website designer to build it for you. Keep in mind that some of these tasks can be done simultaneously.

6.21 Key Points

- There are many things to consider and tasks to complete to start a community consulting practice. They include determining the business structure and setting it up; purchasing insurance and equipment and supplies; and bringing in business. You can do this yourself but may want to seek help from an attorney or CPA.

Table 6.2 *Dealing with the practical matters*

Task	Owner	Attorney	Accountant	Other
Write a business plan	✓			
Pick a company name	✓			
Pick a corporate structure	✓		✓	
Apply for local and state licenses/permits	✓			✓
Develop a marketing strategy (define your ideal client and how you will reach them)	✓			
Choose a website domain name	✓			✓
Apply for special status (women-owned business, small business enterprise, disadvantaged minority-owned business, etc.)	✓			✓
Build and update your website	✓			
Apply for a Unique Entity Identifier (UEI) and Employer Identification Number (EIN)	✓			
Create contracts for clients and subcontractors	✓	✓		
Pay invoices	✓		✓	
Pay quarterly and yearly state and federal taxes	✓		✓	
Interview and hire employees and subcontractors	✓			
Document corporate meetings	✓			
Develop standard operating procedures	✓			

- Think carefully about whether you want to share ownership of your business. The advice we share about being a good collaborator certainly applies to having a business partner. Choose your partner or partners carefully. Talk about how you will handle disagreements and how you will handle it if you or your partner decide not to continue the partnership. Develop a partnership agreement. Make sure you build in time for periodic check-ins.
- It is important to plan carefully and lay the groundwork from the beginning, and make sure you are ready to open your doors with necessary structures and supports in place.
- Develop a SOW for each contract and for each subcontractor that will be supporting the work. Include all the deliverables, the due dates, amount of the contract, payment schedule and terms, and any other details (data ownership, data security, and so on).
- Invoice regularly and make sure you receive payment as outlined in the client's SOW.

- Track your billable and nonbillable time. This helps you understand if you are budgeting appropriately. As a business owner, you can't reasonably expect to be 100 percent billable. You need to budget time to manage projects and the business.
- Get all appropriate insurance. If you cannot afford insurance, then you are not ready to be in business.
- Appearances matter regardless of how good you may be at what you do. Taking time to present a professional appearance with a website, logo, and consistent branding colors can make a difference.

7 Collaboration with Colleagues

> Entrepreneurs have a natural inclination to go it alone. While this do-it-yourself spirit can help move you forward, adding an element of collaboration to the mix can make you unstoppable.
>
> —Leah Busque (2012)

In Chapter 7 we share strategies to facilitate successful collaboration with colleagues. We make a case for collaboration, share ideas on how to find colleagues for collaboration and what to look for, and provide tips for how to be a good collaborator.

Whether you consult inside companies or have your own consulting practice, it is highly likely that you will, at some time, be required to, or will need to, collaborate with other people. At times you may need to hire staff or contract with other consultants. In either case, you need to know how to be a good collaborator. This chapter will provide you with information you need to consider when choosing and collaborating with colleagues.

7.1 Why Collaborate?

There are many reasons why you might wish to collaborate with other colleagues, or members of other organizations. You are likely familiar with the ancient proverb, "many hands make light work" (Heywood, 2008). Some projects or initiatives are just too large for one or two people to do well. Collaborating with colleagues lessens the workload for everyone.

Another benefit of collaboration is that you can build an **interdisciplinary** team. Collaborating with colleagues trained in different methods, theories, and approaches expands the expertise available on any project. We regularly collaborate with colleagues who were trained in public health, education, social work, evaluation, anthropology, medicine, history, and other disciplines. In doing so, we not only expand the range of work that is available to us, but we broaden our own perspectives and knowledge as we learn from our colleagues.

Collaboration with colleagues has the potential to result in much better products and client experiences than you can produce on your own. When you collaborate, you have more input and ideas and more eyes on the products. The team brings energy and creativity and there is a synergy created when everyone is brainstorming or reviewing and putting their thoughts into a deliverable. Working with a team has another benefit as well. In working with communities, sometimes one person on the team may not connect as well with the community or a specific community member as a different team member might. When we collaborated on work in rural communities in Texas, Ann had a lot of experience and is more comfortable in rural settings than Susan, and that was helpful. Community members knew Susan had come from one of the large Texas cities. We were able to build trust more quickly as a team when Ann talked about the work she had done in rural Georgia.

Finally, collaborating with colleagues makes the work more fun! There is a certain excitement that comes about when a team is planning and implementing a project that someone working solo just cannot generate. When things go well, you have someone to celebrate with, and someone to commiserate with when things don't go as planned.

7.2 How Do I Get Started?

7.2.1 Finding and Choosing Colleagues

So, you're working on your own and you finally land that big contract. You realize it's a little more than you can handle. Or perhaps you identify an RFP but it requires expertise that you do not have. Where do you find potential highly qualified colleagues with whom you can collaborate? Barrington (2012) and Weiss (2016) suggest that you plan ahead for your human resource needs. You should establish a cadre of people to whom you can turn should the need arise long before you need them. This section of the chapter suggests ways to find potential collaborators.

7.2.1.1 Start Locally
Look within your own community and state for like-minded colleagues at professional association meetings, trainings, and conferences, and among colleges and universities. Become involved in local affiliates of national professional organizations for which you are a member. Your community likely has special groups focused on specific industry sectors. For example, the American Evaluation Association (AEA) has 31 affiliates across the country. If you don't have a local affiliate of your professional organization, you might try organizing your own group of consultants who are doing similar work. It's as simple as emailing all the contacts you have, making a reservation, and meeting for coffee, lunch, or happy hour.

Most communities have Chambers of Commerce or other groups where local business professionals can connect. Many communities have associations for women in business or other specific groups. Be sure and check with your local Small Business Administration (SBA) office. The SBA sponsors workshops and trainings on marketing, financing your business, becoming an 8A (a small business run by someone who is economically or socially disadvantaged), and other important topics that can help grow your business and connect you with others.

7.2.1.2 Think Nationally

We have already discussed the benefits of joining professional associations. Joining professional associations is a good way to expand your networking nationally beyond your local community or city. National conferences are a great place to network. By getting involved in committees or interest groups, you will have the opportunity to meet others who you might not have met otherwise. Become active by volunteering in the association in some way. Volunteer to write an interest group newsletter or chair a committee. Get to know your new contacts and find out what their interests, experience, and expertise are. Schedule virtual meetings to get to know them better. Keep in mind that to really benefit from and develop professional collaboration opportunities you need to do more than just be a passive member.

Susan and Ann met at an AEA conference several years ago when they were paired on a panel presentation together. They started talking and soon learned that they were both community psychologists with many interests in common. Susan invited Ann to come to the Community Psychology (CP) Topical Interest Group (TIG) meeting and the rest is history. Since then, we have co-chaired the CP TIG and the Nonprofits and Foundations TIG, written articles, written proposals (and this book), worked on evaluation and training projects, and presented nationally and internationally together.

7.2.1.3 International

Do you have a desire to work internationally? There are professional consultants that work with communities all over the world. Our international experience is limited, but we have asked our colleagues about how someone can enter the international arena. They shared that perhaps the best way to get started is to find employment in an organization dedicated to international work and get to know the consultants they work with. If you are a member of a professional association that has an international committee or interest group, get involved. Attend the business meetings and the presentations they sponsor to identify and connect with potential mentors. Find websites and listservs where you can virtually meet other professionals and learn about international consulting opportunities. Take advantage of workshops and other professional development opportunities where you will meet other consultants who work internationally. Attend conference presentations to see who is doing the type of work that interests you and then stick around to chat with the presenters. Learning a second, or perhaps a third, language would certainly make you more attractive in the international arena and differentiate you from others. You might also consider volunteering or even an internship opportunity for an international nongovernmental organization to gain international experience.

7.2.1.4 Get Social

Consider joining listservs to communicate with other professionals in your field or areas of expertise and get your name out there. When possible, answer the questions posed by others and pose some of your own. Develop an area or areas of expertise. Be a thought leader, someone who is viewed as an influential leader in their field, by sharing your expertise. This, in turn, will help you develop your personal brand, that is the thing that makes you unique.

These days, a website is a starting point to develop brand recognition but it is not the only necessity for a business. It is also important to develop a social media presence. Start by identifying the platforms that your potential collaborators use. Where do the people you most want to meet and collaborate with spend their time? I know, you're too busy, right? Ann thought so too. Susan is still hesitant but making progress. Consider blogging or hosting a podcast. Ann's podcast, *Community Possibilities*, is gaining steam and has a growing list of subscribers. These days, communicating through a website and social media presence is a requirement. Regardless of the social media platforms you choose, be intentional about them. You don't want to waste your time posting to a medium your ideal clients or collaborators don't use. Keep in mind that the algorithms used by social media platforms change frequently and new platforms are being developed all the time. See Chapter 10 for more on developing a social media presence.

You should also consider some not-so-obvious ways to find collaborators. For example, Barrington (2012) suggests you look on bidders' lists for potential collaborators and research others who have done work or published in your key areas. A bidders' list is the list of the consultants and firms that apply for a grant or proposal. Pay attention to participants on bidders' calls and reach out to potential collaborators. Set up a networking call to get to know them; identify their areas of strength and interests. You may find opportunities to maximize each other's strengths on the next proposal.

7.2.2 Some Things to Think About When Selecting Collaborators

In a small business, your reputation is everything. So, before you enter a collaborative relationship with anyone, interview them just as you would any other employee. Barrington (2012) suggests that you do more than simply have lunch with them. She suggests that you observe them as they present and ask for writing samples.

If you were hiring an employee, you would ask for their résumé, wouldn't you? So, don't be shy about asking a potential collaborator for their résumé or curriculum vitae. Naturally, you want to make sure they have the commensurate education and experience needed for the work. You would need someone reliable, so look for gaps in their employment history. You may want to see that there is some progression in their responsibilities as their career progressed. You should consider how long they have been a consultant. Many people start consulting after a career in an industry and company. That is fine, but you need some assurance that they are committed to the work and have the necessary temperament for the inevitable ups and downs of being a consultant. We are not saying you need to check references as you would a new hire, but you do need to speak with others with whom they have worked.

Something that can't be observed but that you need to understand is whether you share the same work ethic and work process. These are critical to your mutual success. You might consider collaborating on a smaller project before collaborating on a larger, more complicated project. We started collaborating on leadership and projects through our professional association. Overtime, we collaborated on smaller, then larger projects, and now work together often.

From our experience, we have learned that there are people who we just do not work well with. Either they are competitive and not collaborative, they prove to be unreliable, or they don't contribute to the project. In any case, we already know from those interactions that we would not consider partnering with them on a consulting project. For example, Susan once worked with someone who waited until the last minute to submit her parts of the work, if she was on time at all. That caused stress and anxiety for Susan, and made the team look bad in the eyes of the client.

We highly recommend that you look for someone with complementary skills. For example, if you have amazing quantitative skills, you may want to look for collaborators with a deep background in qualitative data design, collection, and analysis. If you aren't super organized, you want to look for people who are. It is important that you and your collaborator or collaborators respect each other. If you think you bring more to the relationship than the person(s) with whom you are collaborating, then it probably does not bode well for the longevity of the relationship. Have this conversation before entering into an agreement with anyone. And be very honest about your own shortcomings and strengths. In other words, if you are not super organized, the potential collaborator needs to know that before entering into a collaboration. It might be a deal-breaker for them.

That brings us back to the soft skills that we talked about in Chapter 3 of this book. Being a consultant requires a level of friendliness and ease. If you need this collaborator to have client interaction, you will want to partner with individuals who have good social skills. When you're considering collaborating with someone, ask yourself, "Is this someone I would feel comfortable putting in front of my client?" If the answer is no, then you should consider if there is a role for them behind the scenes.

Then there is the question of style. If your style is more of a low-key marketing approach and your partner is more of a hard-sell type, that could either be a strength or just plain awkward. Ann once worked with someone who had a more assertive marketing style and even though she was the lead on the project, the person collaborating on the project kept bringing up the next contract. There were significant problems with the organization's board and Ann was not sure if this was a project that they *should* pursue. Even though they discussed this ahead of time, Ann's colleague continued to bring up future work. It was a little awkward.

7.2.3 Collaboration Requires Some Ground Rules

If you choose to subcontract with someone as a consultant, request a statement of work just as you would provide to your client. In it, the subcontractors should outline the scope of work, specific deliverables, and due dates. Make sure the agreement specifies the length of the contact, terms of payment, and invoice dates. Gray (2010) outlines other specific items you may want to include such as cancellation provisions, instructions about how to handle documentation, non-compete clauses, and clarity about tax responsibilities. We have worked together for years now, but still would not think about entering a subcontract with one another without a written agreement.

You have your subcontractor(s) identified, now what? Barrington (2012) suggests, and as we mentioned earlier, we agree, that at first you should start your new collaboration with a straightforward piece of work. See how your subcontractor(s) perform and test your communication before you enter into a more complex or costly endeavor.

In addition, we want to offer you five ground rules for collaboration. These ground rules are based on our experience – they are not gleaned from an extensive literature search.

1. *Communication*: Sometimes communication is not just about speaking the same language. Have you ever met someone who you just didn't click with? Like no matter what you say and how hard you try, you just can't seem to understand each other? You want to avoid that.
2. *Honesty and trust*: We don't know about you, but we would rather work for and with people with whom we can be completely honest and trust

than someone who tells us what we want to hear. Honesty also means doing what you say you will do. The last thing you would ever want is to enter into an agreement with someone, make a commitment to a client, and then not fulfill your commitments. Sometimes, even when you do your due diligence, things don't work out. Ann once landed a contract with a national organization. The Friday before a Monday morning kickoff meeting in another state, the person with whom she chose to subcontract called her to say she herself had landed a large contract and could not attend the kickoff meeting. After discussing the situation, they reached an agreement that the other consultant would attend the kickoff meeting but that would be the extent of their involvement. To the best of your ability, make sure that when *you* make a commitment, you carry it through and do what you have promised. Your reputation with your colleagues is just as important as your relationship with your clients.

3. *Define roles*: Contracts consist of many types of deliverables and tasks. You really don't need to be an expert at everything you do, but you do need to be very clear with the others with whom you are collaborating regarding the role you each will take. Are you the lead contact with the client, or is that someone else? Who will make sure the deliverables are met, who will analyze the data, or write the final report?

4. *Check your ego*: Consultants can be a stubborn, independent lot. Try to remember, you don't *always* have to be right. One of the biggest benefits to collaborating with others is that you get to learn from people that have areas of expertise different than your own. Likewise, you also do not *always* have to be in charge of things. No matter what level of experience and expertise you have, it is OK to sometimes step down and let someone else lead.

5. *And finally, never, ever disagree in front of the client*: No matter what you do, if you disagree, try your best not to argue in front of your client. Take a break if you need to and discuss in private. If you must, kick your partner under the table.

7.3 Being a Good Collaborator

What is a good collaborator? If you do a search on the internet, you will find dozens of articles on what makes a good collaborator. Some of these qualities we have already explored in our discussion of what to look for in a collaborator. Now we want to turn inward and think about what types of qualities will make *you* a good collaborator.

Susan will admit that on one of her first collaborative projects she was not the best collaborator. OK. Full transparency. She was not a good collaborator at all. She had just left a position in a highly competitive environment and was not at all good at things like trusting her collaborator and being comfortable not being the top expert. Susan held the contract and was project lead. In this role, she did not always communicate with her collaborator or let her know everything that was going on, she did not rely on her to advise and seek her input regularly. Finally, her collaborator called her out on it (very professionally and appropriately) and they were able to communicate about it. By being a poor collaborator, Susan probably lost any chance of working with this very talented consultant again.

The first step in becoming a good collaborator is to do an honest self-assessment of your strengths and weaknesses. Only by doing so will you identify how you can become a good collaborator. Of course, everyone has strengths and weaknesses. What are yours? For example, if you are a great "big picture" person, but not as strong on details, understand that and share that with your potential partners. Ideally, you will want to partner with someone who is detail-oriented. Perhaps you have strong qualitative skills (for example, are a great interviewer), but are less familiar with the specifics of quantitative methods. Again, sharing that honestly with your potential collaborative partners is important and will go a long way in ensuring a smooth relationship.

Doing a thorough self-assessment to identify where you are strong and where you are less strong is not a one-time activity. A periodic self-assessment should become part of your ongoing professional development. Be patient with yourself; developing your own collaboration competence takes time and experience. Also, be honest with yourself. Be accepting that although you are likely good at a lot of things, there will also be areas in which you don't shine. But mostly, when you own what you aren't so good at, or own whatever "issues" you have that may get in the way of being a good collaborator, you open space for growth. If Susan had continued as she was, there is a good chance we would not be writing this book together (and Susan is saying this, not Ann).

One of the surest ways to gain understanding is to get feedback from those who know you best. Ask your family and friends about your strengths and shortcomings. In addition, be sure to ask other professionals with whom you have worked in the past to describe your strengths and developmental opportunities. If you find the feedback you get reveals a pattern, then you need to seriously consider that there may be truth in what you hear and make a plan to develop your competence where it is necessary and accentuate your strengths.

When you are collaborating with others, make sure that you make time for the team to work together. When the team has a meeting, honor that as you would any other obligation. Never take your colleagues for granted. It is important that your collaborators know that they can count on you to be available as needed and to show up. At the end of a project, take time to debrief with the team to discuss what went well and what you could do better.

When you decide to collaborate with others, it is important that you share resources and information. If you are going to develop products together, make sure you have agreed ahead of time about ownership and use of them. We have done a lot of training together, so we share materials and slides. We have found that in our consulting industry, we are competitors with one another and our colleagues in many ways, but by maintaining a supportive and collaborative community we all lift each other. The same can be true if you work within a company or at a nonprofit organization. When you work with individuals from other organizations, you may often compete with them for funding from the same foundations, but if you focus on the mission of the collaborative project and partner in a way that capitalizes on each organization's strengths, you all get further ahead than you might on your own.

What can you do to improve those areas where you are not strong? Consider finding a mentor, coach, or trusted peer with whom you can get ongoing support. Take advantage of regular continuing education and training opportunities. Some of our favorite training includes the annual AEA conference and the AEA Summer Institute. AEA's annual conference offers pre- and post-conference workshops designed to build the skills of evaluators. The Summer Institute, held yearly in Atlanta, offers practical and skills-based training that includes topics such as handling conflict, evaluation design, conducting focus groups, data visualization, and many more topics. Other national training opportunities include the national meeting of the American Public Health Association and other professional conferences that may be related to your content area. Take advantage of training offered in your local communities sponsored by associations related to your field, or other fields. For example, even if you are not a social worker, some of the programs offering social work continuing education units may be relevant to your needs. If you live in a larger city, you may have an organization that provides training to nonprofit associations, often at a reasonable cost. Check out your local university's continuing education program.

Finally, to collaborate effectively, you need to be OK with relinquishing control on components of a project that your colleagues are in charge of or are better suited to manage. After all, you can't truly collaborate if you don't trust your colleagues or acknowledge the areas in which they have more expertise/better fit. Even if you have similar skills and experience, you don't always have the lead. But when you are the leader, avoid micromanaging your collaborators. Micromanaging your colleagues also indicates a lack of trust in their expertise and ability to do that work. When you are overly controlling, you aren't really getting the benefit of collaboration by failing to let your colleagues take things off your plate.

7.4 Maintaining a Collaborating Partnership

Cheryl Holm-Hansen recommends conducting periodic reviews of partnerships. She was kind enough to share the questions used during the Midwest

Center for School Mental Health's quarterly partnership review that we mentioned earlier. While they debrief specific projects or activities along the way, they also meet quarterly just to take a step back from the work and check in with each other.

7.4.1 Midwest Center for School Mental Health Quarterly Partnership Check-in

- Overall, how are things going? What is going well? What isn't?
- How much time are we each putting into the center? Is time being spent equitably? If not, do we need to take steps to make it more equitable or consider allocating payments unevenly?
- Is the amount of work manageable? How much more work do we have the capacity to take on if we maintain equitable time contributions? Could we take on more work if we shift the time contributions?
- Are our respective roles appropriate? Do we need to make any shifts in the way we are splitting up the work?
- Are we comfortable with the ways that we are making decisions? Do we both feel that have a voice in shaping what we are doing and how we are doing it?
- How effective is our communication? Do we need to change the frequency or format of communication? Do we each have the information that we need to complete work effectively and efficiently?
- How do we feel about the specific projects that we have taken on? Do they seem like a good fit for our capacity and expertise? If not, how do we realign our portfolio?
- What is our long-term vision for where we want the center to go? What should we be doing now to lay the groundwork for that long-term vision?
- Are there any other issues or concerns that we want to share?
- Do we want to do anything differently as we look ahead to the next quarter?

7.5 Dealing with Challenging Colleagues or Collaborators

No matter how much introspection you do, or how well you plan your teams, you may from time to time encounter a challenging colleague, supervisor, or client. Who is a challenging colleague? Someone once said that what you hate in others is what you hate in yourself. Someone you perceive as a challenging colleague may be perceived by someone else as the perfect partner. We have found that to be true. You need to start by understanding what pushes your buttons. For Ann, it's when someone does not do what they say they will do. For Susan, two of her pet peeves are indecisiveness and disorganized people who don't stay on top of things.

Develop a strategy for working with challenging colleagues. This may include processes and procedures that help you structure your work. Schedule weekly or monthly meetings or phone calls to discuss the progress of the project, and more calls if necessary. Share your work on reports frequently and provide your partner with constructive feedback. Communicate regularly, constructively, and openly. Do not let resentment build and do not gossip to others about this colleague.

What do you do if you find it difficult to work with someone with whom you have entered a contract? Obviously, you do not want to dissolve a collaborative relationship in the middle of an engagement. Finish the work as best you can. When the project is over, have an honest discussion and end the work on as good a note as possible. Before you have the discussion, do some soul-searching to see what role you played in the less than satisfactory collaboration. When you have the discussion, own up to your responsibility for why the relationship was less than smooth. Brainstorm together what went well and what didn't go so well. Be careful not to let this evolve into a blame fest, but think about how different actions might have produced better results. Even if the professional relationship ends, you both will have learned things that can help you to improve your skills and relationships in the future.

7.6 Contracting versus Hiring

You've landed that big contract, or maybe several little contracts at once. The deliverables are piling up and you need help. Having followed our advice, you have a pool of highly qualified consultants to whom you can turn for support. Or maybe your business has grown so much you need a long-term human resource solution. How you structure this solution will depend on several important factors.

First, you need to understand the difference between an employee and a contractor. To determine the difference, you need to first understand your relationship with the other person. If the person you are considering hiring will direct what they do and how they do it, but you maintain control over the result of the work, that person is an independent contractor. An independent contractor is self-employed and responsible for paying their own taxes.

The person you are considering hiring is an employee, and not an independent contractor, if they perform services that can be controlled by you, the employer. That is, if you have authority over what they do and how they will do it, then this person is an employee. That includes telling them where they will do the work, and during what hours and days. In this case, an employer–employee relationship exists, and earnings are subject to FICA (Social Security tax and Medicare) and income tax withholding, which you, the employer, are responsible for.

According to the Internal Revenue Service (IRS), under "common-law rules," anyone who performs services for you is your employee *if you can control what will be done and how it will be done.* This is true even if you give the employee freedom of action. The deciding factor is whether *you* have the right to control the details of how services they provide are performed. There are three types of control that you should examine (IRS, 2022). First is behavioral control. Do you control when and how this person will do their job? Second is financial control. Do you control how this person is paid, whether expenses are reimbursed, and provide the tools (computers, software, and so on) for them to do the job? Third is the relationship of the parties. Is there a written contract or oral agreement describing the relationship? Will the relationship continue past this one engagement? Is the work that is being performed a key piece of the regular business of the company?

You need to consider all these questions when determining whether a worker is an employee or independent contractor. The answers to some questions may indicate that the person you are considering hiring is an employee, while other answers indicate this person should be classified as an independent contractor. There is no specific number of factors that determines their status, and no one factor stands alone in making this determination. It is important to consider the entire relationship and to consider the degree of the right to direct and control the work. You should document how you made your determination. If after considering all these factors, you are still not sure of their status, you can file *Form SS-8, Determination of Worker Status for Purposes of Federal Employment Taxes and Income Tax Withholding* with the IRS. The form may be filed by either the business or the worker. The IRS will review the facts and circumstances and officially determine the worker's status. You should know that it may take at least six months to get a determination. Fair warning, if you classify an employee as an independent contractor but have no reasonable basis for doing so, you could later be held liable for employment taxes.

7.7 When You Have No Choice But to Collaborate with Someone

If you are an employee in an organization or have been contracted individually and added to a team, you may not have a choice about collaborators. You might be assigned to a project with a co-worker that you would never choose to work with. What can you do then? Begin the work with a meeting with the co-worker(s) and your supervisor to clarify project roles and expectations. Be very detailed, including plans for communication (frequency, who is included), task expectations for each collaborator, timelines, descriptions of anticipated deliverables. Take notes about what is decided, share them back with the team and make sure everyone agrees. That way you will have something to go back to if there are any disagreements.

If one or more of the other collaborators show themselves to be less collaborative (competitive or worse), then bring it into the open as early as possible. Do not do this in a way that sounds accusatory toward any individual but present it indirectly as a challenge requiring a solution. Some examples of behaviors that may undermine your performance might include being given incomplete information, being left out of communication loops, or even outright sabotage. It is important that you do not immediately assume certain comments or behaviors were intentional. Sometimes people just forget to include someone or forget to give some information. Say, for example, you were "accidentally" left off an important email communication. Rather than confront the person directly with "You left me off the distribution list for that important email," you might phrase it as "I think moving forward we should figure out what can be done so that I am not left off future important emails." Phrases such as this bring forward the issue in a way that is neither accusatory nor finger-pointing. You never know if the omission was accidental. If it wasn't, it alerts the individual who omitted you that you will bring the behavior to the forefront and do something about it. If you need to complain, do it with someone outside of the situation who has nothing to do with the work and who does not know the parties involved. And then, don't name names. If the situation continues or intensifies, take it up with someone who has the authority to do something about it.

Enter collaborations with the assumption that all members of the team will work together and be collaborative. Most of all, even though you did not select your collaborators, work to find common ground with them and BE a good collaborator. Start the collaboration by first establishing expectations, roles, and group norms for behavior. Make them explicit and keep them at the forefront. Do not think of it as a competition and maintain the mindset that nobody shines unless the whole team and each member shines. Do what is expected of you and meet all your deadlines. Most of all, communicate regularly and often. Try to reframe difficult collaborations as good developmental opportunities.

7.8 Key Points

- As a community consultant, regardless of whether you are an independent consultant or working for an organization, you will likely collaborate with colleagues at some time. Start the process with self-reflection regarding what qualities are important to you in a collaborator, and what qualities you bring with you to a collaborative relationship.
- Select partners carefully so as to ensure the smoothest collaborations possible.

- Be attentive to your own performance as a partner, and work to meet the needs and expectations of those with whom you are collaborating.
- Throughout the collaborative process, and afterwards, review how the work went. Be honest about your own strengths and weaknesses and identify ways you can improve.
- Sometimes working relationships just don't work out, but communication along the way and at the end of the work can go a long way in at least ending the professional relationship as well as possible.

8 Collaboration with Clients and the Community

Alone we can do so little; together we can do so much.

—Helen Keller (Lash, 1980)

There is immense power when a group of people with similar interests gets together to work toward the same goals.

—Odowu Koyenikan (2016)

Chapter 8 provides tips and resources to help consultants to enjoy better collaboration with their individual clients, and to foster collaboration among community members and community-based organizations. It includes descriptions of some challenges the consultant might encounter and how the consultant might overcome them, such as conflict between community members.

8.1 Relating to Clients from a Community Perspective

Long before Steven Covey encouraged people to "Seek first to understand," the ancient prayer attributed to St. Francis implores God to "Grant that I may not so much seek to be ... understood, but to understand." St. Francis is not asking to simply understand someone; he is saying that understanding someone else is much more important than having ourselves be understood. Putting aside our own self-interests and perspectives is hard to do, especially when relationships are difficult. Let's start this chapter by beginning at the start of relationship building.

The first step in any new relationship is to get to know each other. To become friends, you need to really connect and understand who the other person is. What are their likes and dislikes, their history, their goals, and their values? Think about a first date. If you try too hard to sell yourself, talk too much about yourself and your interests, chances are there won't be a second date! Assuming you make it past the first few dates and go on to have a long-term relationship, the way to maintain it is to work to understand where your partner is coming from. When you're amid a disagreement, that can be hard to do. Working in the community is no different. Your need to take time to get to know the community members, their likes, dislikes, fears, hopes, and vision for their community. You need to build the relationships.

8.2 What Might You Face as a Consultant in the Community?

It is quite possible that when you first enter a community as a consultant, you may be welcomed into the community with no issues at all. The community may accept you as a welcome partner. Maybe they won't see you as an outsider, you won't experience any obstacles, and you and they will get right to work.

Although we have certainly experienced some communities as more welcoming than others, at some point, you are likely to experience some level of resistance. In many cases organizations and communities don't engage a consultant unless they are required to do so by a funder or board member, so expect some level of friction. The resistance may not be immediate, but eventually as you make suggestions and community members begin to understand the implications of real change, don't be surprised if there is some pushback.

Resistance may come in many forms and from different people. You might experience acceptance from some community members, and resistance from others. If this happens, you should first work to clarify whether this is coming from true feelings, or whether the differences have nothing to do with you or what you are doing but are grounded in another dynamic altogether. This is where it is helpful to know the history of the issue under consideration within the community, and the history of community members' interactions. You may find that one group was resistant to inviting you in, or even that they had advocated for another consultant that they preferred. It could be that some community members are resentful of dollars being used to fund your work rather than programs and services.

Both of us have encountered passive and even overt resistance when we worked in communities. For example, Ann has done a lot of work in substance abuse prevention, and it is quite common for community members to focus on the perceived weaknesses of substance abusers rather than on some of the community norms or policies that support youth substance use. Ann once had a client that was enthusiastic when she was first engaged but as soon as it was time to take the community needs assessment from information to implementation, the client resisted. Several important community stakeholders were much more comfortable talking about treatment than the environmental prevention strategies which the grant required. It is much easier to talk about *why* people use (they make poor choices, are lazy and unemployed, and so on) than to think of substance misuse and addiction as a risk for everyone then designing an appropriate community-wide public health prevention strategy.

Susan has experienced resistance to change based on an interest in maintaining the status quo. One coalition she works with was required to adopt the Collective Impact model and to include community members. Many of the professional members of the coalition make their money by having the community members as their "clients." Despite the grant requirement, the professionals created numerous barriers to engaging community members. "Their neighborhood is too far to drive to." "We can't meet during evenings and weekends." These and other assumptions manifested in real barriers that kept community members, the ones experiencing the problem, from being a part of the conversation. While the coalition coordinator expressed agreement with Susan's recommendations, she has yet to implement any of them. Ironically, when the coordinator brought in another consultant to facilitate a strategic planning session, the other consultant made the same recommendations as Susan! This next section will provide you with some tips for overcoming such resistance.

Before we explore how to help your community client deal with conflict, we want to spend just a moment on how *you* handle conflict. How do you react when people disagree, whether in your presence or with you personally? In some cases, you may experience straight up hostility to your ideas or maybe your very presence. Fortunately, we have not yet encountered this, but we will not be surprised if we do in the future. In an AEA365 blog, Elizabeth Grimm (2021) offers three tips. First is to trust your gut. Get in touch with your body sensations and let them help to guide you. Second is to schedule time for reflection. Schedule time to read, reflect, and apply what you have learned. And, third, she suggests that you "honor your no." It is OK to sometimes be unavailable, to not accept a project, or to set boundaries as needed. This kind of self-care is essential to maintaining effectiveness in the community.

8.3 Overcoming Resistance

The first step in collaboration is to learn about the community. Who lives there? What is their political background? What are their religious traditions? Who are the important players at the table and, just as importantly, who is *not* at the table that should be? For example, Ann works with a lot of community prevention programs that are working to prevent youth substance abuse, but in many cases, the youth of the community are not involved in the coalition. In this case, your role is to point that out and encourage the community to engage these groups.

Don't be surprised if you get invited to community events or a Sunday church supper. How will you react if you are? You need to examine your level of comfort and be comfortable in these scenarios. If you are politically conservative, will you be comfortable in a community that is politically liberal? If you live in a rural area, will you be comfortable working in an inner-city neighborhood?

8.3.1 Learn the Community's Stories and Traditions

Every community has a history. And that history, revealed through its stories, is the essence of the community. It may be stories of teens who died in a car crash after leaving a party. It may be a story about a teen who committed suicide after being bullied about their sexuality. Communities have positive community stories too. Stories of a community member who feeds their neighbors, churches helping to rebuild a neighborhood after a storm, or a community member starting a nonprofit or program that gives back to the community. All these stories contribute to the culture of the community. They also provide a lot of useful information to understanding the community culture, history, and viewpoints.

Collaborating with communities also requires that you share some of yourself as well. It does not require that you tell community members all your deepest secrets but sharing some information about yourself does help you build good will. For example, Susan might share that she is a dog lover or mention that she has grandchildren. Ann loves to cook, bake, and hike. Usually, the sharing is intentional to identify a common bond between ourselves and the community members. It is personable enough to make us seem like real people, but not so personal as to somehow influence personal opinions of us or cross over into the realm of inappropriate sharing.

8.3.2 Learn the Current and Past Issues That Affect the Community

Communities have a past, present, and future. As a community consultant, you need to be attuned to them. Community issues are often about growth and how to handle that change or it may be about a contraction of growth and loss of jobs. In Ann's own community, a new town formed only ten years ago, there is conflict about how to handle growth. One group wants to maintain the rural nature of the town and believes the local politicians have sold out to developers; the other side is pro-growth.

Conflict about growth is just one of many community issues common in other areas of the country. For example, in Georgia, over that last several years, many rural hospitals have closed. In some communities, an influx of refugees is a very real issue as families move in and children who do not speak English, many who have experienced significant trauma, enter schools. Their parents need to get the family settled and find work within a short time. Community members already present may react with concern over the stress put on the school system, housing, and available jobs. They may also be suspicious or fearful of refugees.

Just as our national history is relevant to our current policies and events, the same is true for local communities, such as counties and cities. When you work toward a necessary policy change, if you don't know the history of the focal policy, you may not fully understand sources of resistance to the change. You also may not be using an effective strategy that addresses the history in a way that can overcome such resistance.

8.3.3 You Don't Have to Be the Star or the "Expert" – in Fact, You Aren't

We think the value that underlies our vision of community consulting is *service*. When you consult in the community from this point of view, then you come from a humble position. You aren't the star of the show; you are in the chorus or maybe a backup singer. You might even be one of the roadies. Your role is not to show how much you know about research or randomized control designs, multivariate analysis, or group facilitation. Your role is to provide support, ideas, coaching, encouragement, resources, and suggestions to help the community meet their goals.

It's helpful to remember this tip: It's not what *you* want, it's what *they* want. There have been many situations in which we truly believed the coalition or collaborative with whom we were working was making the wrong decision or decisions. Perhaps they chose an intervention approach that is not supported by science; or they chose not to evaluate something the way we feel they should; or they failed to implement their action plan. You might be concerned that their goals are too ambitious. Perhaps they've planned more interventions than their capacity can support. Our strategy would be to provide our best advice. But, ultimately, it is the organization or community group that must make the decision on what they want to do and how they want to implement their chosen activities. Time will tell how things will develop. Ann always tells her clients, "It's all learning." As community consultants and evaluators, we believe that information resulting from the evaluation of community interventions need to be used to improve the community initiative. This is true even when the community outcomes are not what was hoped for or intended.

What the community decides to do, and how they choose to assess their outcomes, is ultimately up to them. You need to remember that although you may be the expert in designing community interventions or research, the client is the expert in their community. Respect their community knowledge by viewing and treating them as an equal partner in the work. We recommend that you assemble an internal committee that includes the director, representatives of the community groups within whom you are working, frontline staff, any key stakeholders such as board members, and you, the community consultant. Paul Mattessich's (2003) book, *The Manager's Guide to Program Evaluation*, is a practical, easy to read guide for program managers and Ann often recommends it to the community leaders with whom she works when she is consulting for evaluation. It offers practical information that is useful for not only evaluations but community interventions. The author defines a process of planning and design, implementation, monitoring, and gathering and using information. Each chapter clearly defines the roles and responsibilities for consultants and program managers and staff throughout each phase of the work.

Of course, there is one exception to leaving everything to the community. If your coalition or community-based organization has received funding and is accountable for specific activities and outcomes that are defined by the funder, and you were hired by the funder as the evaluator or to provide technical assistance, you will need to speak up and remind them of the obligation. If the community feels strongly that they are the wrong outcomes or activities to meet their community's needs, you may be able to use your "expert" position and provide support if they decide to push back with their funder. If your community coalition or the organization decides they are unwilling to meet the funder's requirements, you may be able to help them secure new funding or make a plan to move forward without that funding source.

8.3.4 What Did You Say?

By far, one of the most difficult things to do when working in communities is to understand the "language" of the community. We are not talk about language in the traditional sense. Rather we mean something much subtler; we mean the words they choose and the way they use these words. At the same time, we need to be careful about the words *we* choose and how what we say is perceived.

To facilitate communication with community members, we need to learn to do a few simple things. First, we need to learn to understand and speak the language of the community. Second, we need to be able to explain our strategies and ideas using common terms. For example, if we are designing an evaluation of a community intervention, we need to explain what we mean by "outputs" and "outcomes."

Sometimes difficulty in communication happens around expectations about the work you have been asked to do. Some of your clients may not exactly know how to use your talents and skills. They may not understand your role and how you can help them reach their goals. You need to be clear during initial meetings with the person that hired you, and with community stakeholders, about what you can offer the clients.

Sometimes the community consultant must help set priorities between what the community's funders want and what the community wants. Often the community organization has multiple funders all with various requirements and reports. You may need to help the community prioritize what they need to do and simplify the related tasks in a way that reduces burden. Ann advises organizations to stay true to their mission and vision and not to become side-tracked by responding to every RFP that comes along. Yes, funding is important, but becoming scattered to the extent you lose sight of why the organization was formed is not wise.

8.4 Why Can't We Be Friends?

Conflict is inevitable, so it should be no surprise that conflict within communities often arises among people that are passionate about concerns within their community. Conflict arises throughout the life cycle of any group or organization. In the beginning stage, a community organization may experience conflict about their purpose. They may disagree on who the leader or leaders should be or what the coalition should work on first. They may disagree about group structure, such as who should be on the steering committee. Once up and running, a community organization often experiences conflict over what interventions to choose. Community leaders may come and go, causing strain and frustration. Some people may become frustrated if they feel they are among the few who are doing the work. Once established, it is not unusual for conflict to occur over sustainability plans. For example, we have seen community organizations argue about whether the community organization should apply for 501(C)(3) status.

So, what is the community consultant to do when the community cannot get along? First, it is important to normalize conflict. Disagreement is a normal part of group dynamics. While those of us who work with groups are familiar with the stages of group process (forming, storming, norming, performing; Tuckman, 1965), community members may not be. You need to recognize the stages of group process, point that out to the group where it is appropriate and encourage community members to find common ground. While community members have their own biases, priorities, and agendas, as members of a community coalition, partnership, or collaborative, they need to maintain focus on the things they have in common. Moreover, people often come to coalitions and collaboratives looking through the lens of their special interest groups.

For the group to function effectively, each person needs to put aside the agenda of their organization and, instead, focus on what is best for their community. In the case of community coalitions and collaboratives, having a shared vision and mission helps generate support and awareness, to identify and attract partners, and reduces conflict and confusion about the group's purpose (Butterfoss, 2013). For example, a community drug free prevention coalition may attract treatment center representatives. Although it cannot be argued that treatment centers are necessary, the primary interest of this type of community group is prevention, not filling hospital beds. A clear mission and vision will help define the group's purpose and clarify expectations and appropriate actions of members. Some of the coalitions Susan works with also have members with self-interests, such as medical insurance providers and for-profit dental services. It is important to foster their inclusion but not to the extent that they are able to exploit their membership.

Fran Butterfoss' 2013 book, *Ignite*, offers advice on how community coalitions can avoid conflict, and much of this can apply to any type of community group that is collaborating. First, having a clear vision and mission helps gather partners and raise awareness for the cause and helps reduce conflict because it makes clear the purpose of the organization. Defined roles and responsibilities of the steering committee, established by-laws, job descriptions for staff and volunteers, and memorandums of understanding (MOU) for partner organizations and members all help to reduce conflict (Butterfoss, 2013). Knowledge and awareness of group dynamics is important. It is essential that the community organization commit to and foster a culture of collaboration that unites community members to the shared vision, practices shared decision-making, addresses diversity, and resolves conflict in productive ways (Foster-Fishman, Berkowitz, Jacobson, & Allen, 2001). These elements are linked to member satisfaction (Butterfoss & Kegler, 2009). We both routinely include measures of coalition member satisfaction in our work with coalitions and collaboratives.

Sometimes people, for whatever reason, just don't get along. Sometimes, conflict within a group occurs because of interpersonal conflict, some of which may pre-date the current collaboration. No matter the source of the group conflict, at the heart of each is a breakdown in communication. You can help set some basic ground rules for the group to help reduce intergroup conflict. For example, a "No parking lot conversations" rule helps limit gossip and jockeying for power outside the group. Members should be encouraged to air all ideas, issues, and disagreements within group meetings. Interpersonal conflict, therefore, group conflict, can be reduced through good basic active and reflective listening techniques. For example, the use of I-statements ("I feel …", "When you …") can facilitate listening. Processing the conflict within the scope of the mission and vision in a way that depersonalizes the issues can sometimes help to get the group back on track, focused on mission rather than personalities. If you have done all you can to help the group normalize conflict and deal with it when it does occur, encourage your client to get conflict resolution training, perhaps by bringing in a consultant with communication expertise. When conflict becomes untenable and when outside mediation does not work, it may be time to disband the coalition (Butterfoss, 2013).

8.5 Collaborative Solutions

Assuming the community group or coalition you are working with manages their conflict effectively, there are things you can do to help them work collaboratively. If you are interested in building community collaboratives or facilitating better collaboration to fulfill a mission or build an initiative, we highly recommend Tom Wolff's (2010) book, *The Power of Collaborative Solutions*, which presents a model for true collaboration. We will briefly describe Wolff's six principles in this section of this book.

8.5.1 Fostering True Collaboration

The first principle is to encourage "true collaboration." Himmelman (2001) defines a continuum of collaboration, differentiating it from **networking**, **coordination**, and **cooperation**. The first level, networking, refers to the exchange of information for mutual benefit. Typically, when there are networking events or opportunities, people gather for the purpose of meeting one another. In this scenario, there aren't usually formal activities focused on any type of action. The next level is coordination. Coordination includes information exchange and activities with mutual benefit. For example, two organizations serving a similar population might establish a shared referral system or develop a process that ensure services are not offered at the same time. Coordination involves little disruption within each organization and no actual sharing of resources. The third level is cooperation. Cooperation includes networking, coordination, and sharing resources for a common purpose. Community-based organizations might cooperate by planning and implementing an event together, such as a community substance abuse prevention summit, or by presenting a program or training together, such as trauma-informed training for teachers.

Collaboration incorporates all the above levels and involves activities and processes that enhance the capacity of another organization. In this scenario, organizations that collaborate experience mutual benefits, but at the same time, pursue a common purpose while sharing risks, resources, responsibilities, and rewards. As an example, in 2020 to 2022, as the pandemic spread across the globe, organizations within many communities (for example, schools, non-profits, public health, churches, chambers of commerce, and others) came together to meet the needs of their neighbors.

8.5.2 Engaging the Full Diversity of the Community

Collaborative solutions require that the members of the groups that are most affected by the problem are included in the work. Earlier in this chapter Ann noted her surprise that communities who were combating youth substance abuse were not including youth in the solution. Susan has struggled with coalitions whose stated mission is to reduce infant mortality disparities, but they never engage the women who are experiencing the problem in identifying solutions. Your role as a community consultant is to advocate for the inclusion of all community members in the discussion, design, implementation, and evaluation of the community change effort.

8.5.3 Practicing Democracy and Promoting Empowerment

We view the role of community consultant as one that goes beyond any one task but rather includes attitudes and activities that encourage civic engagement, especially among groups that are typically disenfranchised and have the least amount of power. For example, if youth are "at the table" then the adults must learn to listen and allow them to fully participate. Likewise, when professionals come to the table with community members, *the professionals* must be trained and prepared so that they do not treat community members like "clients," but acknowledge them as equals and allow them to determine the actions that will be taken on their behalf or within their neighborhood. As a community consultant, you should set this expectation and model the behavior you hope to see.

8.5.4 Applying an Ecological, Strength-Based Approach

According to Lewin (1936), behavior is a function of a person in interaction with their environment. Too often, when groups or community members get together to collaborate and address a social or public health problem, they focus very quickly on individual-level behavior and attitude changes. If obesity is the problem, they plan events to teach people to eat better and exercise. For breastfeeding, they might have a campaign to encourage women to breastfeed. These simple, individual-focused interventions are doomed to fail unless the environment in which these behaviors is also addressed. For example, at the same time we are teaching people to eat healthy foods and exercise more often, we need to make sure that they have easy access to healthy food and safe places to exercise. The same is true for breastfeeding. How many women return to work after maternity leave and find out there is no sanitary, private, comfortable place to pump their breasts and that taking time out to do so will hurt their career status? How many women have been shamed for breastfeeding in public spaces? An ecological, strength-based approach focuses on identifying strengths and assets and building an environment that will support changes.

8.5.5 Addressing Issues Based on a Common Vision

How many meetings have you been to where the focus is on the problem? Sure, identifying the scope and nature of the problem is important, but until there is a vision for an alternative, typically nothing moves forward. Creating a common vision can be an important exercise to get all the collaborative members on the same page, it is motivating because it helps people to see the possibilities, and it provides an end goal to guide actions and objectives for the group. As noted earlier, a shared vision also helps to reduce conflict.

When you are working to create a common vision, rather than using "problem focused" approaches toward planning, consider using strategies such as appreciative inquiry and focusing on dreams to build the vision. Think about how you go about planning a trip. You don't typically start by exploring your route to find everything wrong and plan a whole trip around overcoming travel obstacles or find everything bad about the location you want to visit. You plan based on what you want to see and do, what will be enjoyable, and how you can get the most from your travels given your resources. The same mindset should apply when you are facilitating community change. Plan for it based on how the community can use the assets it has to move toward its dreams and vision.

8.5.6 Engaging Spirituality

Spirituality transcends religion. Many of the best community consultants we know come from a wide range of beliefs. They include Catholics, Baha'is, Jews, Quakers, Baptists, Methodists, Hindus, Muslims, Buddhists, agnostics, and atheists. They all base their community change work in principles such as appreciation, interdependence, acceptance, and compassion. The members of the collaborative need to explicitly recognize the power that exists in unity and how much stronger they are when they capitalize on their interdependence rather than engage in competition. As a community consultant, you need to base your community engagement in universal spiritual principles or virtues such as truthfulness, authenticity, commitment, respect, graciousness, integrity, patience, and kindness and embrace the values we described in Chapter 4 of this book.

Tom Wolff points out factors that prevent the current helping system from really making a difference. They include the focus on deficits in communities, the lack of grounding in social justice goals, interactions restricted by racism and lack of cultural humility, and a system whereby professionals from outside communities dominate the generation and implementation of solutions and resources. The current funding system, with its deficit focus, is also set up so that helping organizations are in competition with one another for funds and other resources. It is not designed to reward collaboration, nor is it designed to build strong communities. In fact, we would go so far as to argue that the current system is set up to survive only as long as people and communities continue to have problems. If we solve the problems, there will no longer be a need for what is frequently described as the "nonprofit industrial complex" and the people who work within this system will eventually lose their power and their jobs. What started centuries ago as help based on spiritual purpose has become just another business.

Tom Wolff offers suggestions to overcome the limitations of current "helping" systems. We will briefly share them here but recommend reading his book to gain an in-depth understanding of how to incorporate spiritualism into your community consulting work.

1. Work to shift from a deficit to an asset focus. Approach communities with appreciation for strengths and assets.
2. Work toward social justice based on principles of interconnection and interdependence. Incorporate ecological models and systems perspectives into your work.
3. Overcome limitations of racism and lack of cultural humility by embracing acceptance and the value of all people.
4. Base your work in the principle of compassion to overcome the "professionalization" of community work. Open yourself fully to the community members' whole life situation rather than focusing on a single problem. Wish them well by working shoulder to shoulder with them and respecting that you are there to learn from them rather than being the "expert."
5. Develop collaboration rather than competition across helping systems. Bring providers together with the spirit of meeting the needs of everyone in the community, recognizing interdependencies.
6. Focus more on social justice and social change rather than efficiency and business management styles.

8.6 Communicating about Programmatic Changes

Community coalitions and other community-based organizations often change plans or shift course as needs arise. As a community consultant, you may not always be aware of these changes, especially if you don't live in the community. There are a few things that we use in our practice to stay up to date with our clients. Ann conducts monthly calls with all her clients. During these calls they discuss any changes that have happened in the community or the organization since the previous month. They review new needs or impending deliverables and timelines and, if needed, negotiate changes. Ann typically keeps notes on the calls so that if there is any confusion about decisions that were made, she can refer to them as needed.

As we all know, these days, email is the most common form of instant communication. Emails provide you easy and quick access to other people (assuming they answer emails right away). Email is a great way to document information and changes, but it does have drawbacks. First, it is sometimes hard to read someone's emotions in an email. Have you ever written an email and thought you were being clear, but the recipient didn't understand what you were trying to say? Or worse, they misinterpreted your intent or feelings? So, what should you do to ensure that email communication is clear? In our offices, we try to abide by the guideline that if an issue is not cleared up in two emails, it's time to pick up the phone and call the person with whom you are communicating. Of course, nothing can beat old-fashioned face-to-face meetings to build your relationship with the client and with community members. If face-to-face is not possible because of distance, time, or a worldwide pandemic, then it helps to use conference calling technology, such as Zoom, Microsoft Teams, or Webex.

8.7 Communities and Organizations Are Always in Flux

Communities and organizations are ever changing. People move in and out of communities. Staff and leadership move in and out of organizations. Over time, demographics shift. The community members who lived there before may accept these changes or tensions may arise among community members. If you are lucky enough to work in a community over a period of time, you may experience this yourself. Your role as someone who works with community organizations is to help the community understand and react to these changes positively if that is practical or, if necessary, act. Your role when communities are changing will depend on what the community members want. Many outsiders to a community often view gentrification as something good. New housing is developed, or old homes are renovated. New businesses move in, and gentrified communities often become the new "hot" neighborhood. Community members often experience gentrification as the beginning of the end of their community. New housing and renovation may drive up home values to the extent that the existing residents cannot afford their property taxes. The residents may want to take action to stop these changes so they can maintain their community. Rather than promoting a positive attitude toward such changes, your role may be to help the community to organize to fight against the change.

8.8 Sometimes You Just Have to Walk Away

There are times when you are collaborating with a community that you may find the collaboration is not working in a way that is best serving the community. This can occur for a variety of reasons. Maybe you just never quite connected with the community members in a way that would support a good working relationship. Maybe you don't have the skills or insights this particular community needs. The community or organizations may not be ready to do the work or embrace the changes needed. Sometimes the organizations or communities may not want to hear what you have to say. When the relationship is characterized by consistent and unresolvable conflict, or your presence is more disruptive than constructive, then you will likely need to just walk away.

8.9 Key Points

- The first step in any new relationship is to get to know each other. This applies to working in new communities and with new community organizations too. In order to become friends with a new community, you must get to know them and they you. You need to understand their history, their values, and their vision for their future.
- Conflict is inevitable, especially among community members that are passionate about the concerns of their community. Help your client understand that conflict is normal and happens throughout the life cycle of any group or organization. If the group can't get past their conflict, consider bringing in an expert. If the issues still cannot be resolved, the community coalition may need to disband.
- Collaboration can be thought of as a continuum, from networking to coordination, connection, and then, finally, true collaboration. True collaboration involves activities and processes that enhance the capacity of another organization. It results in mutual benefits, and the organizations involved share a common purpose, risks, resources, responsibilities, and rewards.
- Communities are always changing. The residents must adapt to the change, or fight against it, depending on their needs to maintain community.

9 Money Matters

I don't want to make money; I want to make a difference.
—Lady Gaga (Blasberg, 2011)

In Chapter 9 we talk about how to find requests for proposals/quotes/applications for your organization, or for community organizations you are working with, how to write a good proposal, and things you can do when money is tight.

If you are a full-time consultant in your own company, you will need to generate revenue. If you work in a consulting team, you may be asked to help write proposals. Even if you have chosen your career based on your values or because of a personal mission, you probably want to make a comfortable living. It is important that you develop a level of ease with earning what you are worth. After all, if you don't understand your own value, it will be difficult for others to understand it. Sometimes consultants from less privileged backgrounds and consultants of color fail to recognize the added value they bring to the table. They have experiences, cultural understanding, and other assets that bring added worth.

In Chapter 6 of this book, one of the methods we mentioned to generate business is to respond to RFPs, applications, or quotes, which we collectively refer to as RFPs. The content in this chapter helps you understand how to consider and respond to RFPs from government agencies, foundations, and other sources as a means of bringing in revenue. The information we provide is applicable whether you are seeking funding for yourself, your organization, or seeking funding on behalf of a community organization. The information we share is admittedly less applicable for responding to academic research RFPs, although a few tips we provide may be helpful. Academic research proposals require more specific guidelines than we present here. If this is the type of consultation you want to do, we advise that you seek guidance specific to National Institute of Health (NIH), National Science Foundation (NSF), and other research grants.

Let's be honest. Responding to RFPs is time-consuming. It takes about as much time to respond to an RFP as it does to write a comprehensive report. Furthermore, if you are an independent consultant, you aren't paid for the time it takes to write proposals, though this time can be included in your overhead costs. There are myriad factors that affect whether you will win the proposal. This chapter will provide some guidelines that will help you determine if it is worth investing the time to respond to RFPs and less formal proposals, such as when a potential client asks you to provide a bid. We also present tips for developing a budget, defining the scope of work, and preparing a work plan. We end the chapter by sharing tips on how to bring in extra money during lean times.

9.1 How Do I Find RFPs?

Finding opportunities and proposal announcements requires time and research. As we described in Chapter 6, these often come in the form of RFPs (request for proposals), RFAs (request for applications), or RFQs (request for quotes). The first step is to define your scope of interest and area(s) of expertise or identify the community need. If there are organizations you would like to work with, do your homework and familiarize yourself with their mission, programs, and capacity. If you are seeking funding on behalf of clients or organizations, define their scope of interest and closely examine their mission and vision to ensure they are not going after funding that will take them too far afield from their purpose. Make sure that they can handle the financial and reporting requirements.

Once you have defined the interests and scope for yourself, your organization, or your clients, start researching potential funding sources. Here are some tips to get you started:

- Google can be your friend here. Look at your interests, identify some key words, and start searching.
- If you or the organization you are representing are a member of an eligible minority group, a veteran, a person with a disability, or women-owned business and have applied for your certifications locally or within your state, your information may become public and larger organizations may reach out to you.
- Use foundation directories to learn about relevant foundations. You can find these online or access them at no cost at a local library or center that supports local nonprofits. Then visit their websites and do your homework. Register for their mailing list. Note their funding cycle and when they issue their requests each year. Put these dates on your calendar.
- Be a good collaborator. Network with other community consultants and let them know your interests and learn about theirs. When we find RFPs that do not interest us, we usually share them with other organizations or consultants that may be a good fit.

- If you, or the organizations you are working with, are interested in federal or other government funding, identify the relevant federal, state, and local agencies, and study their websites to see what they have funded in the past. Read the terms and conditions and grants policy statements. Sign up for notifications so that you receive notices about RFPs. If you have the opportunity, talk with government officials and see if they are able to provide guidance or information that may be helpful. Federal agencies sometimes hold regional conferences. Attend them, interact with federal program staff, and learn about trends and future funding priority areas. Network with others who have received funding from sources of interest and learn what you can about their experiences as well.

There are many ways to find RFPs. It is just a matter of spending some time researching potential sources, networking, regularly scanning relevant websites (for example, grants.gov, websites for state agencies), and getting on state and federal email lists. It is worth the investment of time and effort.

9.2 Should I Respond to This Request?

RFPs come into our email inboxes somewhat regularly and will come into yours as well. You may be tempted to respond to many of them. However, in most cases, after we review the RFP, it goes into the e-trash bin. The reality is that very few of them are fitting opportunities for one reason or another. Being able to distinguish between what is a possibility and what is not worth your time will save you frustration. Here are a few tips we can offer you to determine whether an opportunity is worth investing time and effort.

9.2.1 Are You and Your Organization Eligible?

The first question may seem obvious, but your first step is to determine whether your organization is even eligible to apply for a funding opportunity. Some government, foundation, and even corporate **Funding Opportunity Announcements (FOA)** have restrictions regarding who is eligible. They may be restricted to certain types of organizations, specific geographic locations, or other factors. If you, your organization, or an organization you are representing is ineligible, think about whether you can identify an eligible organization that you could partner with, and approach them with your interest.

9.2.2 Can You Meet the Deadline with a Quality Proposal?

Another fundamental question to ask is whether you or the organization submitting a proposal can meet the application deadline. Outline all the steps that will need to be taken and determine whether it is realistic to apply. If specific letters of support must be included, will you be able to get them in time? Do your partners have hoops they must go through to submit such as approvals by department heads? What are their deadlines to submit internally? Do you have time to put an appropriate team together? Writing the proposal may be your introduction to this organization. You don't want to be remembered as the person who submitted the sloppy proposal.

9.2.3 Consider the Required Scope of Work and Resources Needed

Once you determine if you or the organization you are writing for meets the basic requirements and can develop an excellent proposal, determine if you or the applicant organization have the time and resources to successfully complete the work. For example, most proposals require specific skills and sometimes (although not always) content expertise may also be required. For example, a proposal may require content expertise in child development or clinical psychology and that consultants have that appropriate professional certification. If the project requires specific content expertise or certification you should either identify a potential partner or pass on the opportunity.

If the proposal is for a large project that requires a team and you do not have access to a one, you might also decide not to submit. For example, if the project requires a large telephone survey that includes a random sample of community residents and you do not have the staff and software needed to do the survey well, it may be more than you should take on. The same would be true for an organization pursuing a program. If they do not have the requisite resources available to them, even with funding, then it is best to pass.

Again, if you lack the required resources, but know of another community consultant or organization who has them, consider collaborating with them. This is an effective strategy used by many independent consultants who work individually to obtain larger contracts, or smaller community-based organizations desiring to participate in larger initiatives. We recommend that you constantly work to build your network so that you have a pool of potential collaborators.

9.2.4 Is the Budget Sufficient?

As much as most of us do the work because we care about our communities and our neighbors, we do need to be paid fairly for our work. Do some analysis to determine if the budget will allow you to do the best job possible. Sometimes it is good to start your process by roughly thinking through what you would do (the scope of work) and how much that would cost. If you find that there is not enough of a budget to do the job well, consider passing. Otherwise, you will either not do the project justice, or you may end up losing time and money trying to make it work. You may also miss out on a more lucrative opportunity because you have not invested your time well. Keep in mind, your name will be on the final report and many organizations post their reports on their websites. There won't be a place on the website for you to provide an explanation that there wasn't enough money to do the job you really wanted to do. If they end up unhappy with the work, it will be you they blame.

9.2.5 Do You Have Time to Do the Work?

Before you respond to an RFP, you need to examine your workload. Be sure to look at your calendar starting from the time the project will start through the end of the project timeline. Then ask yourself whether this work fits in with your other projects and work. Be sure to consider the time it will take to do the work, the timing of other projects like conferences and workshops, and time for travel if that applies. If the potential project will overlap with another project for a month or two, and you can do it even if it means working some extra time or getting some help, then go for it. If the overlap is greater or there is no way you could do this project well without shortchanging your other work, then it's better to pass. Again, your reputation is on the line and your reputation is your most valuable asset. Besides, doing work that is less than your best is just not ethical.

9.2.6 Are You the Best Consultant for This Job?

If you are considering a competitive RFP, be honest with yourself about whether it is within your area of expertise. Give careful thought to your experience, education, and interests. These are the things that make you uniquely qualified for the work. It is important to do an honest assessment of your skills, abilities, and experience and compare them with the requirements in the RFP. If you feel like you really need to stretch your description of yourself or your organization, it won't be worth your time. Even if you write the proposal, you likely won't win it anyway. Better to focus on RFPs that are more in line with your experience and interests. If you are still interested in the project, perhaps because it is a new area that you want to break into, consider contacting a colleague who has the required experience and knowledge and ask if they would be willing to partner with you on the proposal.

For example, while Susan has experience working as an internal evaluator for a large school district, this is still not her preferred area, nor is it her area of expertise. In her community, a local university has a large school of education that often is the go-to organization for this work. There are also several evaluation consultants in the area that specialize in education-focused consulting projects. Because of this, she typically does not respond to education-focused RFPs because the likelihood they will choose them over her is high.

Likewise, if you are working with an organization that wishes to respond to a large RFP that is not within their realm of experience, try to discourage them. Susan regularly sits on federal grant review committees, and one of the criteria is often the organizational capacity or the applicants – including their experience. If the organization you are working with cannot write about having experience, then they will not be able to respond adequately, and thus, will not score well. They will also have expended a large amount of staff time and other resources for nothing.

When you think about whether you are the best consultant for the job, take stock of your unique experiences and skills. What makes you special that may make you the exact consultant for this job? Did someone in the organization or who knows the organization well send you a copy of the RFP? Do you know someone in the organization that you have developed a good working relationship with? Do you know of a specific methodology or strategy that is the best fit for the need described in the RFP?

9.2.7 Is the Project Interesting to You?

Let's just be honest here. We all do our best work when we are doing work that is interesting to us. If you take on work that is not interesting to you, you likely won't have time on your calendar when the right project *does* come along. If this project is not interesting but is large and long term, unless you absolutely need it to survive, then think long and hard as to whether it is worthwhile. Once you sign a contract, you will be committed and that will be time you will not be available for things you *want* to do.

9.2.8 Who Is Your Competition?

Like it or not, being in business as a community consultant means you will compete with other people. Working to secure funding on behalf of a nonprofit organization can also be competitive. Knowing your competition and distinguishing yourself by identifying how you are uniquely qualified to do the work will help you win contracts. Here are a few tips for identifying your competition:

- Investigate whether there is an incumbent in the consulting role. Do some research by looking at their website and talking to your contacts. If you can't find any information, it is OK to ask. You want to discover if they are happy with their consultant. Obviously, you can't be that forward, but if they are unhappy, it should be somewhat obvious.
- If there is an incumbent, you need to try and discern if the organization is just going through the motions of the proposal process. Sometimes, they are perfectly happy with their consultant, but their funder or their own by-laws require they elicit a certain number of bids. If this is true, you are likely wasting your time.

- If you suspect that the organization may already have someone in mind, research who they have used in the past for similar work. For example, if they are looking for someone to facilitate a strategic plan, see if their previous plans are posted online, and look to see who did them. If you see that a specific organization has done their last four plans, it is likely they will use them again. Tapping into your peer network for information might be helpful as the organization that issued the RFP will never admit to any preference. You may, however, get a hint of this if you know someone in the organization. In one case, Susan was told "If you respond, please do not spend too much time on the proposal." She did submit but did not spend a lot of time on it. Was it worth it? In this case, it was because she got her credentials in front of this organization and was later hired for other work.

- If you are considering responding to an RFP on behalf of a community-based organization or client, ask your client if they know of other organizations that might be seeking the funding. Similar to the situation where there is an incumbent consultant, you need to understand if the RFP is for a competitive grant renewal. Your client may be viewed negatively by the incumbent organization as well as other organizations in the community if they compete for the funding. They will need to decide if it is worth the potential risk of not being seen as a collaborative community partner.

- Ask whether the community beneficiaries will be supportive of the project. You do not want to find yourself on the wrong end of a project that a community is fighting against if you ever plan to work in that community again.

At this point you may find you just can't be sure who your competition is. We suggest you read between the lines. One clue the proposal may not be a genuine request is if the turnaround time is ridiculously short. Look for requirements for very specific experience, expertise, or tools. If they require at least three years of experience working with their project, they likely have already made the selection. Likewise, if they are asking for experience with a proprietary software that is unique to their organization. Read carefully and think about the requirements. If your intuition tells you that a requirement in the skills and experience section seems very specific, then consider passing on submitting a proposal.

9.2.9 Have You Done Your Homework about the Organization and Project?

No matter how much money is on the table, there are some organizations you may not wish to be associated with. This is especially true if they have a poor reputation in the community because of weak or harmful work. If they are having financial difficulties and may not be able to pay your invoices, you may want to check out the organization's financial information. If it is a nonprofit organization, there will be a Form 990 on file. Finally, you want to investigate the capacity of the organization. Ask if there is a strategic plan and ask to see it. Find out how long the executive director has been in place.

Susan was once approached by someone who was starting a new program and wanted to develop its evidence base. Further conversations with the developer indicated that he was most interested in getting the project to move forward so he could sell it. The project had not been tested and was of questionable validity. It lacked research support and an adequate theory of change. She told the program developer the steps that would be necessary to validate the program and begin developing an evidence base and informed him that she was unwilling to engage unless he was willing to do it right. He came back and said that he found someone who would do what he wanted and would not be using her services. That was OK with Susan. Keep in mind that *your* reputation as a community consultant is important and being associated with a poorly developed program or an unhealthy organization is not in your best interest.

RFPs may or may not clearly describe what the organization is looking for. Although many organizations hold meetings or calls (called bidder's calls) for potential respondents, it can still be difficult to determine what they are looking for. Some proposals, depending on their focus, require a program development plan or a well-developed evaluation plan. Although it has never happened to us, we do know of consultants who provided detailed plans and were not hired but found out later that the organization implemented the plan without payment. The main difficulty from our perspective is that you usually don't have the opportunity to get to know the people with whom you will be working. We think that is important. Some relationships just are not meant to be.

All this confusion may be intentional. Sometimes organizations are required by their own internal policies or that of their funders to gather at least three bids. They may already have someone in mind and are just going through the motions. They may also be trying to assess if they can do the work themselves. Susan once responded to an RFP and was asked to do a presentation. After her presentation, she received a call stating that they would be issuing a new RFP and invited her to respond to it. The new RFP included some aspects of the project that she had included in her proposal! She responded a second time (barely tweaking the original proposal) and then was informed they had selected a different vendor for the project. It was obvious that the potential client liked the community focused and participatory aspects she had incorporated, but they likely selected the vendor before the first RFP was issued.

If you are responding to an RFP that does not include sufficient information to decide, then don't be shy about emailing the contact person listed. You might ask if they have determined a maximum budget amount, confirm their timelines, and ask any questions you have about the project or organization. We have both seen RFPs for large projects only to find out that the amount they budgeted would never be enough to cover the project needs and complete quality deliverables.

9.3 Responding to the RFP

It's time to make the "Go" or "No go" decision. Once you do your due diligence, weigh the pros and cons, and decide to go, it's time to write the proposal. You *will* have competition. If there is a lot of competition, the reviewers will look for reasons to eliminate proposals and narrow the field of applicants. This section of the chapter will give you some tips on how to increase the odds that your proposal will be successful.

You want your proposal to catch someone's eye, so it should look attractive and professional. There are some things that you can develop as "boiler plate" but most sections and the detail of the proposal will be specific to the potential client and request. Assuming you have the right expertise for the job, and you decide to proceed by submitting a proposal, there are a few things you should know.

Check for details like margins, type size, spacing, and fonts. It matters. If you don't follow directions, they likely will think you will not give them the product they expect either. If they ask for two work samples then send two. Resist the urge to send as many as you have in the hope that they will like one of them. Make sure you check spelling and grammar. Proofread the proposal several times. Have someone else give it a cold read to catch the errors that you may have become blind to after reading it 100 times. Provide ONLY what is requested and provide EVERYTHING that is requested.

In summary, here are some tips to writing a competitive proposal.

1. Follow directions. It may seem basic, but it's important to pay close attention to the instructions and provide answers to the questions proposed.
2. Provide a clear description of the project. Include enough detail and justify why you are recommending the approach you suggest.
3. Assemble a winning team. If the project requires that you work with others, identify colleagues or staff that have the requisite experience.
4. Work systematically. Review all the proposal requirements and make sure you meet all the requirements, attach all supporting documents, and submit the proposal as directed and on time.
5. If one is provided, review the proposal draft through the filter of the scoring rubric.

If you can do these four things, then you should be able to write a winning proposal.

9.3.1 Applying for a Federal Grant

If you are working on applying for a federal grant either for your organization or with a community partner, there are additional steps the organization should take at least one month before the proposal is due. First, the organization will need to know and provide its North American Industry Classification System (NAICS) codes. It will next need its Unique Entity Identifier (formerly known as the DUNS number). Information about obtaining this number is presented on federal funding websites. The Unique Entity Identifier is emailed the same day.

The next step is to register in the System for Award Management (SAM. gov). This can take five business days to be processed and then another day before the applicant can log into Grants.gov, the system where the actual proposal will be submitted. SAM registration must be renewed each year. The final step is to register with Grants.gov. Registration in Grants.gov must also be updated annually and passwords must be updated every 90 days. Since completing all these steps can take several days, if your client waits until the last minute, they may not be able to submit a proposal. If they complete these registrations and do not use them, there will be no harm. There should be no expenses associated with these registrations so you and your potential client should avoid organizations that offer to do this for a fee.

9.3.2 If You Are Working on a Collaborative Proposal

Writing proposals collaboratively can be a great experience, or one you never want to relive. It is important to set up a successful collaboration from the start.

9.3.2.1 Determine Who Will Take the Lead

The organization that will take the lead should be the strongest organization with the greatest potential and capability to manage the project. If one organization has a history of successful federal grant management and you are applying for federal funding, then that might be the lead organization. The most important factor is the organization or individual's capacity to assume the leadership role, as well as who will look best on paper as the lead.

It is also possible to share leadership. For example, one organization may take the lead for the financial obligations, while another assumes leadership for project management and a third takes leadership of analysis or reporting. In this case, each organization would assume leadership for the area in which they are strongest. This type of arrangement will still require that someone is overseeing everything to ensure that all requirements are met, and activities and reporting is timely and of sufficient quality.

9.3.2.2 Collaborative Strategies for Preparing the Proposal

To prepare a proposal with a group requires that everyone has very clear guidelines regarding tasks and timelines, as well as expectations for final products. Build in check points for task completion and accountabilities throughout the process. Set up regular meetings, but not so many that time is wasted in meetings that could better be spent working on the proposal. Prepare a written process with timelines and specific responsibilities just as you would for a project. Make sure that the individuals who are assigned to specific components have the capacity to complete them. If an organization volunteers to prepare a need statement, be sure the individual who will be assigned knows how to write a good need statement. Make sure the plan plays to each organization or individual's strengths. Using shared platforms, such as OneDrive or Google, will allow collaborators to monitor progress and review and edit each other's work.

9.3.3 Developing the Scope of Work

Now it's time to develop the scope of work (SOW). In some cases, the proposal may require a very detailed SOW, in and other cases you may develop a less detailed plan until after you or your organization have received notice that funding has been awarded. Developing the SOW requires that you fully read and understand the RFP and are clear on the work it includes. The SOW should detail how you will accomplish everything. While you may want to offer to do something extra, consider the cost implications and keep in mind that whoever issued the RFP may not want it.

9.3.4 Determining Time, People, and Other Resources

When you are determining the amount of time or people hours needed, number of people to staff the project, and other resources (that is, administrative help, transcription costs, printing), do not cut corners. Start by creating a timeline of activities. Then add the staff/consultants that will be assigned to the project. Finally, add how many person-hours each activity requires. Look at the hours expended relative to the timeline and make sure it is possible. Your proposal will not be strong if it appears that one person will be performing 80 hours of work in one week. Be realistic in how you lay out the work relative to people and hours available. Be mindful of the skill sets required for each activity.

If you or your current team members do not have a specific skill set, then you will need to add someone to your team who has the requisite skills. If your business strategy includes regularly responding to RFPs, it helps to have a clear understanding of your core services and skill sets. Also, having a list of pre-screened go-to collaborators and subcontractors is essential so that you can quickly mobilize them and submit the SOW on time. For example, if you pursue projects that require translation services, find a good service, and know how much they charge as well as their typical availability and turnaround time. Contact them to confirm that they are able and willing to be written into the proposal. The same may be true for other services such as transcription, data collection support, or statisticians.

When determining time, people, and resources, think about each activity that comprises the project. Consider all supplies, skills, and each task associated with each activity. Walk through the project as though you are on a tour and want to see every detail. Sometimes mapping the process can be helpful to identify where data collection points might happen or when extra resources may be needed.

9.3.5 Preparing an Implementation Plan

Your implementation plan should be very detailed. Someone should be able to read the plan and know exactly how, when, and by whom each activity will be conducted. A detailed implementation plan shows the potential client or grantor that you are highly organized and can immediately hit the ground running. The funder should also be able to look at your plan throughout the project and know exactly what phase you are in, and which activities are underway at that time.

Sometimes creating the implementation timeline is easier if you start at the project end date and work backwards. At this point, you should have all the project's activities and tasks identified. The implementation plan should detail which activities precede other activities. They can overlap when necessary. For example, someone can be conducting qualitative data collection at the same time the quantitative data are being analyzed. One way you might lay out such a plan would be to use a Gantt chart. Table 9.1 is an example of the chart we used when we wrote this book.

This tool was useful for planning this book and may be helpful as you write proposals and SOWs. You can also lay out the information in a table that depicts who has primary responsibility for each activity. This will provide clarity regarding who would do what and when each would do it. The Gantt chart made it easier to quickly process the information visually. Having these tools in place provides a level of accountability, or in our cases, induced a great deal of guilt whenever we fell behind schedule. Having an implementation plan kept us moving forward and can help you complete your projects on time. Most of all, including this in the SOW shows the funder or client that you have a specific plan.

Table 9.1 *Gantt chart example*

Chapters	Task	Month 1	2	3	4	5	6	7	8	9	10	11	12	13	14	15
1 and 2	Write	■														
1 and 2	Revise/edit		■													
1 and 2	Ex. reviews											■				
3 and 4	Write			■												
3 and 4	Revise/edit				■											
3 and 4	Ex. reviews											■				
5 and 6	Write					■										
5 and 6	Revise/edit						■									
5 and 6	Ex. reviews												■			
7 and 8	Write							■								
7 and 8	Revise/edit								■							
7 and 8	Ex. reviews												■			
9 and 10	Write									■						
9 and 10	Revise/edit										■					
9 and 10	Ex. reviews													■		
11	Write											■				
11	Revise/edit											■				
11	Ex. reviews														■	
Appendices	Write		■	■	■	■	■	■	■	■	■	■				
All	Revise/edit											■	■			
All	Submit															■

9.4 Determining the Budget

If you have completed a clear and detailed implementation plan then you already know what resources you will need, including time, people, and other resources. The budget should flow easily from there.

9.4.1 The Cost of Time, People, and Other Resources

We talk to many new consultants and some of the most frequent questions are about how much they should charge for their services. Figuring out how much you are worth can be tricky. In her book, *Consulting Start-Up and Management*, Gail Barrington (2012) provides a very detailed method for determining fees if you are working independently as a consultant. There are also many articles on the internet and in other books about determining fees. If you are part of an organization, then they have defined billable rates for each staff position depending on education and experience. If you are an independent consultant, then your fees will include your salary, profit, and overhead as well. Overhead includes insurance, rent, utilities, and other business expenses.

As with planning for resources, you don't want to pad the budget unnecessarily, nor do you want to charge too little and end up absorbing the excess costs. Be realistic and make sure you budget adequately. Look closely at the

RFP to ensure that you are including only allowable expenses. If the RFP does not specify a mileage rate, use the current rate set by the Internal Revenue Service. It changes annually so check each year. If overnight travel will be required make sure you check airfare, hotels, and ground transportation. To estimate meal expenses, use the U.S. General Services Administration's (GSA) per diem rates. Include expenses such as airport parking and car rentals and taxi fares. Do not include personal expenses that may be associated with travel such as dry cleaning, boarding your pets, or an extra day you tacked on to sightsee.

The budget should clearly reflect the costs associated with the implementation plan. Reviewers should easily be able to see how the two match up. If you include an in-person meeting that is out of town then you should have travel expenses in the budget. You will likely need to prepare a budget justification and include it with your budget which details how you computed each line item in the budget.

9.4.2 When the RFP Does Not Specify a Maximum Amount or It Is Insufficient

One of the greatest challenges and frustrations we have encountered in responding to an RFP is when the issuer fails to specify a maximum amount of funding available. Sometimes they simply do not know how much the project will cost. Other times they just will not specify the amount or reveal it if asked, for fear applicants will go straight to the top of the budget. If you don't know the budget and you decide to go forward and submit anyway, cost out the project for a reasonable amount and submit. Do not try to cut corners in the hope of being competitive if it risks not getting an adequate amount to cover your time and expenses. For example, if you know you will need at least a minimum amount for travel expenses, then be sure to budget a reasonable amount so that expenses do not exceed reimbursement and cut into your potential profit.

Likewise, if the organization specifies an amount and it is not enough to cover time and other expenses to do the project right, then pass on the project. When we receive an RFP, the first thing we do is look at how much is being offered versus the desired/required deliverables. Then we think about what it will take to complete the project and determine whether the maximum allowable amount will cover the work. If you are really interested in the project anyway, then only shortchange yourself if there will be some other benefit, such as a foot in the door for more work or an impressive reference.

9.5 Final Tips for Writing a Good Proposal

We will briefly reiterate some of the key tips. A good proposal is one that is clear, concise and answers all the questions or requests posed in the RFP. Read each question carefully and be sure to answer what is being asked. Provide everything that is requested and keep in mind that less is more. It is important to be concise yet thorough.

Make it easy for reviewers to see how you have addressed all of the information that is requested. Make sure everything is written in the correct section of the proposal. Reviewers should not have to work too hard to find that you've met the criteria. Be obvious with your answers, make sure your proposal is organized according to instructions, and write clear sentences that do not ramble. To make sure you have addressed all items, read not only the instructions, but read through the scoring criteria carefully as well. It is OK to be obvious. For example, if the criteria are that "the applicant demonstrates they have direct experience working with the focal population" you can write something very direct like "Our organization has extensive experience working with *focal population*." And then go on and give concrete examples of work you did with that specific population.

Link what you plan to do to evidence-based or otherwise established best practices. Be able to explain why what you plan to do is the best way to do it. If you are helping with a program grant, make sure the theory of change underlying the program is explained. Do use visual representations such as process maps or flow charts. Lay information out in tables to organize it, such as your data collection and analysis plans. Being able to see how goals and objectives align with measurement tools and the plan to analyze the data will help you make a compelling case.

Be strategic in preparing your proposal. Plan to submit your proposal early, so that if there is glitch in your plan you will have time to recover. For example, set the date to receive all letters of support if required at least a week or two before the deadline. People mean well when they promise to meet your deadline, but sometimes things come up. Select partners and supporters who will enhance what you are doing and who will also stay ahead of the game to complete their part of the project. Be sure the reviewers can see what they will get for their money. Provide clear descriptions of the deliverables. If possible, tie them to the budget.

9.5.1 If Your Proposal Is Being Considered

If all goes well, you be one of the two or three candidates asked to make a formal presentation (in person or virtually) to the decision makers. This will likely be the executive director and a few staff or perhaps the organization's board. This also involves a good deal of time with no guarantee of the outcome. You must make sure you prepare a very professional presentation and are ready to answer almost any question that might come your way.

9.6 If Your Proposal Is Not Funded

Do not take a non-funded application as a failure. If it is a program grant, sometimes it is possible to review, revise, and resubmit it, or submit it to another funding agency. Use any feedback you may have from the last proposal to correct those items that did not score well. If the organization does not provide feedback, such as comments from reviewers, with the notification, always ask what you could have done that may have strengthened your proposal. If the organization is willing, set up a meeting with the hiring manager or project officer. Do not specifically ask why you did not get it. Questions should be less direct so as not to put anyone on the spot. For example, you might ask if they can offer you advice for how you might prepare a stronger proposal next time. If possible, find out who was awarded the funding and see how their organization may differ from yours. The funder may not want to share specifically who they chose, but they may share something about the characteristics that made that organization a stronger fit for their needs. Occasionally you will hear either through your grapevine or find out by doing a Google search.

Sometimes you can write a great proposal, but there will be an applicant with some type of edge over you, such as more experience or known expertise. For example, Susan recently submitted a strong proposal in response to an RFP and found out that one of her competitors won the project. She could easily see why without needing to investigate. His offices were geographically closer, and he would not have been required to travel. His experience is more closely aligned with the project content, and he has a larger team available to do the work. So, even though Susan would have done a great job on the project and wrote a strong proposal, there was someone who was a better fit for this particular project.

9.6.1 Surviving Lean Times

Inevitably, there will be times in your career that you experience challenges. Oftentimes, even getting your first job is difficult. And even experienced consultants go through lean times when the job does not pay as well as you would like, or contracts come more slowly than they had in the past. The rest of this chapter will present ideas and insights into how to survive these lean times or bring in added income to pay off student loans or save a down payment for a home.

9.6.2 Working "On the Side"

Some consultants have started their businesses while they continue to work as full-time staff at an established organization, and they worked on their first few consulting projects "on the side" during evenings and weekends. This can be challenging if your client is a nine-to-five organization, and your full-time job is also nine-to-five. However, a lot of work can be accomplished through conference calls or during your lunch break. Be very careful to keep your consulting work strictly to off hours and do not sneak in a call or two during your work hours. Maintaining those boundaries is very important as your employer would not be happy about paying you to work for someone else. Make sure you aren't violating any non-compete clauses too. These are common in some consulting firms. Some organizations may restrict you from working on outside projects while employed and/or for a period of time after your employment ends. You might also consider negotiating an agreement with your employer that would allow you more flexibility to manage your full-time job and consulting work. If you do this, it will be important to make sure you do not shortchange your employer in any way.

When Susan was getting started as a consultant, she taught as an adjunct professor at two universities. Teaching provided that little bit of extra money she needed as she built her business. Adjunct teaching also has several benefits. Being associated with a university can help to increase your prominence and prestige in the community. University affiliation provides additional benefits. If you eventually consult full time, having university connections is helpful for getting interns to help with your projects. Besides, it's fun to interact with students. Working at a university gives you an opportunity to meet faculty that might be interested in partnering in the future. Lastly, being affiliated with a university is helpful when you need to access academic literature to prepare a good proposal or conduct literature reviews.

Susan once left her consulting practice for a short time to work for another organization and realized that wasn't working for her. When she left her job to return to consulting, she realized it was going to take some time to rebuild her practice. In the meantime, she took on a less than half-time, temporary six-month job to fill the gap. The six-month job lasted three and a half years and at the time this book was written, she is still working with the organization as a consultant.

9.6.3 Applying Your Skills and Knowledge for Smaller or Unrelated Jobs

When you are getting started, no job is too small if it pays you what you are worth (or close to it!). It is great when you can land a couple of good-sized contracts, but sometimes the small jobs are worthwhile. It does not take many small jobs here and there to add up to a salary you can live on. We have both found that small projects often lead to future work. For example, perhaps a local community-based nonprofit has problems organizing their data for evaluation. If you are good with setting up spreadsheets and data entry systems, you might be able to help them out for a small sum of money. If smaller projects occur over multiple years, they can provide a base business and larger projects can provide periodic infusions of work. Ann tries to manage a portfolio that includes smaller projects that have long funding periods and larger projects that tend to last between one and three years.

Take stock of your skills and knowledge. Then, think about how you might translate some of them into specific small jobs. Are you good with statistics and data analysis? Can you write grants? Do you have a certification that may be in demand? Let local nonprofit organizations and other programs know that you are available to do these small jobs for a reasonable price. Nonprofits may be able to afford to pay for a task that will help them build their evaluation, development, or management capacity even though larger scale efforts may be out of reach for them. You can help them to build a long-term plan that includes a series of smaller jobs rather than one large effort. Perhaps to start you can help them define their theory of change or prepare a logic model with measurable goals and indicators. Later you can review and refine their data collection instruments and so on. As their capacity grows, your opportunities to serve them may grow too.

You might also consider jobs outside of the consulting realm. While less than ideal, they are a means to an end if they will help you to get your business off the ground or support you while you move into a career that suits your values and goals.

9.6.4 You Have Expertise – Share It!

Do you have some expertise that you can package and share? Another way to supplement your business during lean times is to teach workshops. If you have access to a venue, consider offering workshops or seminars. Market yourself as a trainer for organizations. For example, a development office at a reasonably large nonprofit, educational, or medical institution might benefit from a private grant-writing seminar. In addition, many local academic institutions may have continuing education programs.

You can also offer online courses using an online course platform. There are several available and while all charge a subscription fee for their premium services, some do have free plans. There are online learning platforms, sometimes called online course marketplaces, that allow learners to search and pay for courses directly. There are also learning management systems that can be used to create, host, deliver, and sell online courses. The advantage of creating your own course marketplace compared with providing a course through platforms such as Teachable, Udemy, Skillshare, or Coursera is that you keep your revenue and user data.

Research the requirements for continuing education providers in your state across professions. Look at the listing of the types of training required each year for social work, nursing, psychology, and other professions and compare it with your own expertise. If you find a match, apply to become a Continuing Education Credit (CEU) provider in your state. It may cost a small sum but also may be worth it. If you want to develop and teach workshops, being able to provide CEUs can expand your potential audience. If you are tech-savvy and have the right tools, consider developing some online options.

Another way to benefit financially from your expertise is to develop a specific product. This often takes time to develop, test, and validate, but may not if you come up with the right product. A great example is Laura Keene of Keene Insights who developed the Consult Tracker software for independent consultants. The software helps them to track financials, prepare invoices, and keep track of projects and client relations among other things. As an independent consultant, she recognized what she needed, developed it, and now sells it for a very affordable price to other independent consultants.

Likewise, after years of providing consulting for change management to a variety of organizations, Barbara Trautlein of Change Catalysts developed and validated a Change Intelligence, or CQ, framework over many years. Coinciding with the release of her book, she developed a CQ facilitator certification process and has certified facilitators worldwide. In addition to the additional income, she and her clients benefit from the expertise she has continually developed along with this product. The certification process provides other consultants with a useful set of skills and tools to expand their repertoire at the same time. As a certified facilitator, Susan has found the framework useful to supplement workshops she currently teaches.

9.6.5 Take Advantage of Slow Time

Slow time is financially difficult but can also be productive time. Here are some ideas for how you might use your slow time:

- Put your writing skills to work. Use the time to publish articles, write or edit a book, develop a blog, write an article to post on LinkedIn, and otherwise show off your expertise. You can get your name out there and establish yourself as a thought leader while you continue to build your résumé or CV.
- Network, network, network. Connect with other community consultants who may need to subcontract work. Look for RFPs that require a team and reach out to colleagues for collaboration opportunities. Check in with past clients to see how they have benefited from the work you did and if they have any current needs.
- Use this time to take a critical look at your website and other marketing materials. Make sure they have a current look and a clean and attractive

layout. Update your LinkedIn profile and find ways to use it to your advantage. Develop a social media strategy. Write a pile of blogs that are ready for release during times when you are busy. Update your CV or résumé.

- Explore new lines of business or new products to better serve communities. Develop your entrepreneurial spirit! Take courses or training, obtain a certification if there is one that would be of benefit. Take time to read the books and journal articles that have piled up.

- Consider just taking a break. Indulge in some self-care so that you can recharge before business picks up again. Clear your mind, engage in new healthy habits, adjust your daily flow.

- DO NOT panic and go after work that is not within your area of expertise or desperately seek anything. This is not a time to jump on work that does not interest you or that you may not do well.

9.6.6 Surviving Psychologically

Perhaps the greatest challenge during slow times is trying to maintain a positive attitude and not succumb to despair. Every business owner encounters slumps or slow times. Be proactive and prepare for them financially. The psychological impact is lessened if you know you can get by for six months with no business, especially if you at least have some money coming in.

One way to survive psychologically is to find ways to use your slow times productively as we described above. In addition to benefiting your business or organization, you will feel like you are moving forward rather than stagnating or trending downward. Slow times are good times to clean out your office and organize your files. Is there an article or book you have been meaning to write? This is a good time to do it. If you've been saving for a vacation, now might be the time to take it, before business picks back up once again and makes it difficult to schedule.

All businesses and careers go through ups and downs, and yours will probably be no exception. Accept it and do not let yourself become discouraged. Do not allow yourself to start sleeping late, watching daytime TV, or otherwise becoming distracted. Whether you work at home or for another organization, go to work and produce. Look at where you are and where you need to be, then make and implement a plan to get there.

Social support is critically important. While we all want to appear to be very successful to our peers, it is OK sometimes to let them know that you are going through a slow period. They may be swamped and need to subcontract work. Even if they don't, they may offer a great source of support, leads, or ideas. Let your friends and family know and allow them to support you, too.

As hard as it can be, it's very important that you do not become discouraged and lose motivation. That said, if you are independently employed and find that these slow times take too much of a psychological or financial toll on you, then consider taking a break and find a full- or part-time job. Rather than viewing it as a failure or setback, find a job that will provide you with some new skills or opportunities to learn and grow. You might find a job that suits you better than consulting or gives you opportunities to do the things you like without the added stress that self-employment can bring.

As we have noted throughout this book, many consultants work for consulting companies or other organizations where they are still using the skills and knowledge they would use in their own companies. You may find that you can continue to consult in communities while you draw a regular paycheck. Or you might find a part-time job that provides benefits (health insurance, library privileges, or other) and decide to do that while you pursue some independent work as well. Keep in mind that being a successful community consultant is more about working with communities to facilitate their goals than it is about having your own business.

9.7 Key Points

- When deciding whether to respond to an RFP, be thoughtful and strategic. Respond to RFPs that are a good fit, and those that fit well with your larger plans, or the mission of the organization for which you are responding. Be sure to read and follow the instructions carefully. Be complete and concise in your writing and give yourself plenty of time.
- When opportunities arise, be sure you are prepared to respond to them in a competitive manner.
- If you are not funded, ask what you could have done to be more competitive if that is possible. And then, learn from the experience, let it go, and prepare to respond to the next suitable RFP.
- It is not unusual for community consultants who work independently to experience slow times. For most people, starting a consulting practice involves experiencing 'lean' periods.
- Find ways to manage lean times practically and psychologically. Write, learn, get organized and meet with potential clients, past clients, and other colleagues. Ask for support from colleagues and loved ones. If the stress of lean times takes too much of a toll financially and psychologically, then it may be time to consider stepping away, even if it is just for a short break.

10 The Future of Community Consulting

The greatness of a community is most accurately measured by the compassionate actions of its members.

—Coretta Scott King (2000)

If you want to go quickly, go alone. If you want to go far, go together.

—Alleged African proverb (Whitby, 2020)

Chapter 10 presents an overview of the current state of community consulting, the positive aspects, and what we can expect in the future.

Over the past ten years funders, government, and philanthropic organizations have become more aware that to be successful, community members must be engaged in the work being done to change their communities. Health Resources and Services Administration (HRSA) requires its Healthy Start projects to implement the Collective Impact Model. CDC and Substance Abuse and Mental Health Services Administration (SAMHSA) now require community coalitions for some of their funded projects. One specific example is CDC's Racial and Ethnic Approaches to Community Health (REACH) program, which funds community work to reduce health disparities in racial and ethnic communities with the highest risk or rates of chronic disease. REACH grantees engage community members to help design strategies that will be most effective for their communities. Community members also are involved in implementation and evaluation. A central goal is for communities to hire or partner with individuals and organizations that best represent the needs of the community so that programs reflect cultural norms, language, and practices. This recognition of the importance of community engagement is the zeitgeist of our times.

As a result, professionals who are engaged in community-based programming and systems-level change are more often directly engaged with community members and community-based organizations. Holding values that guide us to engage with communities in a way that is genuine, does no harm, and approaches our collaboration in a respectful manner is an important part of facilitating real and effective change. Having the right skills and knowledge can ensure that community members and community-based organizations receive support that is high quality and meets their needs as they have defined them, which will ensure that changes that occur are effective and address the focal issue. In other words, community consulting work can be beneficial and have impact if it is done well. If it is not done well or with the right values and spirit, we continue to perpetuate harm or accomplish nothing.

10.1 Concerns about the Current State of Practice

As noted above, effective practice requires that those who are engaged receive sufficient and appropriate preparation. Too often we have seen consultants and consulting organizations that lack the proper training and competencies to work in communities. Some consultants don't have sufficient experience to navigate community complexity. There are also numerous organizations or consultants who are engaged by organizations to make data-driven decisions but lack knowledge of and experience in the complexity of community interventions. Other organizations and some consultants are masters of image and marketing. As a result, they are focused on *looking good* rather than *doing good*. They lead initiatives that appear to achieve outcomes, while changing little. Programs come and go as funding is available, but social and health disparities persist in the absence of systems-level change.

Education and training programs need to prepare professionals to engage in effective community consulting. Many professions (social work, psychology, public health) provide good disciplinary focused training and skills, but do not specifically prepare students for consultation. Moreover, we would argue that they do not prepare people to work in communities. For example, program evaluation training usually consists of research methods, statistics, and perhaps an intervention design course. There is often a community-based project in which a group of students design an evaluation for a local nonprofit, but this is largely the extent of their community experience. While some of the skills and knowledge needed for community consulting can be taught in classes, most is acquired through mentorship and experience. It is this real-world experience that is an essential skill for someone who is interested in community consulting.

10.2 Positive Aspects of the Current State of Practice

Despite our concerns, we are optimistic about the current state of community consulting. Through our work, we have met and had the opportunity to collaborate with and learn from many highly competent and amazing community consultants. There are several factors that continue to fuel our optimism about this line of work.

First, program evaluation is the core service both of us provide. The field continues to grow and develop. There is an increasing acknowledgment that our methods and practices must be equitable and culturally responsive.

Second, there are more resources available to support community consultants. One of our favorites is the Community Tool Box. This is a free, online resource designed and provided by the Work Group for Community Health and Development at the University of Kansas to provide information and tools for those working in communities. There are over 300 educational modules and other free tools offered in English, Spanish, and Arabic.

Third, there is an increased emphasis by government and other funders on place-based solutions, coalitions and collaboratives, and developing new systems-level solutions to community problems. The result is that there are more opportunities for community consultants to share their expertise in more interesting ways and have greater impact. We both receive many requests from coalitions and collaboratives to facilitate their development, help them to formulate their theory of change, engage in strategic action planning, evaluate their work, and use data to drive their decisions and direction.

Fourth, there are many opportunities to engage in policy and advocacy work. In our work with community-based organizations and coalitions, many of them have no idea where to get started and become overwhelmed when talking about changing policies or engaging in advocacy. Community consultants can help with organizing data, creating fact sheets, preparing information packets, writing letter templates for others to use to contact their legislators, organizing community gatherings, serving as "expert" witnesses at city council hearings, modeling how to conduct a visit with local, state, and federal legislators, helping to secure funding to support advocacy work, and other related activities.

10.3 What Can We Expect in the Future?

Since we started this book five years ago, the world has changed dramatically. More than six million people have died from COVID-19 as the pandemic shut down most of the world. A police officer was captured on video deliberately choking an already subdued George Floyd to death, which led to widespread recognition and acknowledgment of the extent of wrongful shootings of Black Americans at the hands of law enforcement. This, along with the murders of other Black people (Ahmaud Arbery, Breonna Taylor), energized the Black Lives Matter movement attracting people of every race. The "MeToo" movement led to more than 12 million women publicly acknowledging that they had experienced sexual abuse or assault at some time in their lives. And now, as we finish this book, a war rages in Ukraine.

Despite the proliferation of interventions and programs, communities continue to experience problems such as poverty and crime. Health and educational disparities continue, as does racism, sexism, ageism, and other forms of discrimination at the individual and systemic levels. There is still a lot of work to be done and the need for individuals with the requisite skills and experiences is growing. So, what can community consultants expect in the future?

Changing needs, shifting political forces, changing economics, and cultural shifts will continue. Communities will benefit from close community consultant/academic partnerships, each sharing information and resources. Academic partners can use their resources to benefit communities, increase their practical "real world" experience, and create internship opportunities for their students. Community consultants can remain apprised of new theories and models that are developed by academic institutions and serve as a dissemination and community connection resource.

As funders increase their focus on macro-level interventions, support collaborations, and require accountability through evaluation and outcome measurement, there will be more roles for community consultants. Consultants can contribute to the development of prevention and intervention models, facilitate coalition and collaborative formation, and promote racial equity and social justice. Community consultants who engage in evaluation will continue to develop, implement, analyze, report, and help ensure sustainability and utilization of program and systems-level change in order to help resolve existing and persistent social and health disparities.

In each chapter of this book, we have provided what we hope are inspirational quotes. We leave you with this last quote: "There is no power for change greater than a community discovering what it cares about" (Wheatley, 2009).

We believe in the power of community members coming together to identify and address their problems. We believe that local and federal government agencies have a role to play, as does the philanthropic community. Individual programs that target individual people will not close the gap on disparities. We believe we can and must work toward the common good and learn to speak with those with whom we disagree. Maybe then we can find out what we really care about. Let's get started.

Community Consulting Professional Development Planning Tool

Communities and organizations are complex entities. Sometimes the needs and dynamics can challenge even the most seasoned consultant. Because of this, community consulting requires continuous professional development of knowledge, values, and skills.

The purpose of this inventory is to provide a tool for people who are currently working in communities or who are interested in working in communities, to rate themselves on the knowledge, values, and skills needed to effectively work as a community consultant. The assessment will help you identify areas in which you need additional professional development. We recommend that you revisit this tool annually. We include many of the qualities, knowledge, values, and skills important for community consulting and recognize there may be others we have left off.

There are three parts to this assessment. Part I includes personal characteristics and qualities you will need to work in communities. Ask yourself if you possess these personal characteristics and qualities. If you do not, are you willing and able to work to develop them?

Part II includes knowledge domains and values that are needed to work in communities.

Part III is the technical skills that you may or may not need depending upon the focus of your consulting.

As you complete each part it is important to be honest with yourself.

At the end of the self-ratings there is a tool you can use to plan for your professional development.

Instructions for Part I: For each personal quality listed, first circle the word that describes how much each applies to you using the ratings below. If you circle "not at all" or "somewhat", then circle the response regarding whether you are willing and able to develop the quality.

- Not at all – I do not have this at all
- Somewhat – Although this is not typical of me, I can demonstrate it to some extent if I need to
- Mostly – I demonstrate this often, but not always consistently
- Completely – This is typical of me

Personal Qualities and Questions to Ask

Quality	Description	How much this applies to you				Are you willing and able to develop this quality?		
Tolerate ambiguity and uncertainty	Can remain calm and positive during times of uncertainty.	Not at all	Somewhat	Mostly	Completely	No	Maybe	Yes
Appreciate complexity	Can visualize and tend to multiple layers of problems and solutions.	Not at all	Somewhat	Mostly	Completely	No	Maybe	Yes
Patience	Can accept or tolerate delay, trouble or suffering without becoming angry or upset.	Not at all	Somewhat	Mostly	Completely	No	Maybe	Yes
Sociability	Can put people at ease; can comfortably interact across settings and with a wide variety of individuals; can find a way to connect with most individuals.	Not at all	Somewhat	Mostly	Completely	No	Maybe	Yes
Can exercise tactfulness, sensitivity, professionalism	Can demonstrate sensitivity when discussing difficult issues; can express self in ways that reflect positively on self and others regardless of personal feelings; able to remain neutral during conflicts and disagreements.	Not at all	Somewhat	Mostly	Completely	No	Maybe	Yes
Can effectively interact with strong-willed individuals	Can understand that community members and organizations may disagree and can effectively navigate such situations.	Not at all	Somewhat	Mostly	Completely	No	Maybe	Yes
Understand organizational and community context	Can identify and understand community and organizational contextual features.	Not at all	Somewhat	Mostly	Completely	No	Maybe	Yes
Comfort with strong emotions	Can maintain poise and calm demeanor when anger and other strong emotions are expressed	Not at all	Somewhat	Mostly	Completely	No	Maybe	Yes
Can handle norming, forming, and storming	Can maintain a neutral position, facilitate consideration of all perspectives, and help to restore equilibrium when community groups or coalitions are in "storming" phase.	Not at all	Somewhat	Mostly	Completely	No	Maybe	Yes
Politically savvy	Can manage politics and competing agendas in organizations and community	Not at all	Somewhat	Mostly	Completely	No	Maybe	Yes

Personal Qualities and Questions to Ask If You Are Planning Solo Consultation

Susan Wolfe and Associates

Community
EVALUATION SOLUTIONS

Personal Qualities and Questions to Ask

Quality	Description	How much this applies to you				Are you willing and able to develop this quality?		
High tolerance for solitary work	Able to work alone and function without a team; comfortable sending and submitting things even if nobody can review or give feedback	Not at all	Somewhat	Mostly	Completely	No	Maybe	Yes
Self-motivation and self-discipline	Can motivate yourself to get things done no matter how you feel; able to stick to tasks without being distracted; dependable; able to set time and activities boundaries	Not at all	Somewhat	Mostly	Completely	No	Maybe	Yes
Organized	Keep documents and electronic files organized; able to put systems in place for efficiency	Not at all	Somewhat	Mostly	Completely	No	Maybe	Yes
Dedicated workspace	Have a dedicated space set aside to serve as an "office."	Not at all	Somewhat	Mostly	Completely	No	Maybe	Yes
Financial management skills and stability	Enough resources to manage financially for at least six months without work; financially literate; able to understand business finances.	Not at all	Somewhat	Mostly	Completely	No	Maybe	Yes
Time Management	Able to efficiently manage time; never late; do not forget meetings; do not miss deadlines	Not at all	Somewhat	Mostly	Completely	No	Maybe	Yes

Instructions for Part II: For each area of knowledge or value listed, first circle the word that describes how much each applies to you using the ratings below. If you circle "not at all" or "somewhat", then circle the response regarding how willing and able you are to develop that knowledge or value.

- Not at all – I do not have this at all
- Somewhat – Although this is not typical of me, I can demonstrate it to some extent if I need to
- Mostly – I demonstrate this often, but not always consistently
- Completely – This is typical of me

Areas of Knowledge and Values

Knowledge or Value	Description	How much this applies to you				How willing and able you are to develop this quality		
Cultural competence	Able to understand the definition of culture, navigate the effects of social identities; and address privilege and power.	Not at all	Somewhat	Mostly	Completely	Not at all	I may be willing	Definitely willing
Cultural humility	Able to maintain an interpersonal stance that is other-oriented in relation to aspects of cultural identity that are most important to the person.	Not at all	Somewhat	Mostly	Completely	Not at all	I may be willing	Definitely willing

Susan Wolfe
and Associates

Community
EVALUATION SOLUTIONS

Areas of Knowledge and Values

Knowledge or Value	Description	How much this applies to you				How willing and able you are to develop this quality		
Cultural responsiveness	Aware of your own power and privilege to dialog with communities to work to address their needs and willing to make the lifelong commitment to reflect upon and understand unique cultural strengths, challenges, and their impact on community engagement.	Not at all	Somewhat	Mostly	Completely	Not at all	I may be willing	Definitely willing
Anti-racist	Support an antiracist policy through action and able to express antiracist ideas. Understand white supremacy culture.	Not at all	Somewhat	Mostly	Completely	Not at all	I may be willing	Definitely willing
Decolonizing	Able to challenge methods that center European or Western ways of understanding and doing things when developing programs, strategies, and evaluations.	Not at all	Somewhat	Mostly	Completely	Not at all	I may be willing	Definitely willing
Value racial and social justice, equity, and liberation.	Place high value on and promote equity and racial justice consistently in practice. Work toward benefit of community members and serve as a resource.	Not at all	Somewhat	Mostly	Completely	Not at all	I may be willing	Definitely willing
Trauma informed approach	Able to consider potential trauma in your approach to work and take precaution to approach sensitive topics with care. Can incorporate principles of trauma-informed care into work.	Not at all	Somewhat	Mostly	Completely	Not at all	I may be willing	Definitely willing
Ecological or systems perspectives	Can articulate and apply multiple ecological perspectives and levels of analysis in community practice.	Not at all	Somewhat	Mostly	Completely	Not at all	I may be willing	Definitely willing
Empowerment	Can articulate and apply a collective empowerment perspective, to support communities that have been marginalized in their efforts to gain access to resources and participate in community decision making.	Not at all	Somewhat	Mostly	Completely	Not at all	I may be willing	Definitely willing
Community partnership	Able to promote genuine representation and respect for all community members and act to legitimize divergent perspectives on community and social issues.	Not at all	Somewhat	Mostly	Completely	Not at all	I may be willing	Definitely willing
Ethical reflective practice	Can identify ethical issues and address them; articulate how your own values influence your work.	Not at all	Somewhat	Mostly	Completely	Not at all	I may be willing	Definitely willing
Dedication to Continuous Personal and Professional Development	Consistently engage in ongoing personal and professional development to keep existing skills and knowledge strong and current and to develop new skills.	Not at all	Somewhat	Mostly	Completely	Not at all	I may be willing	Definitely willing

Susan Wolfe and Associates

Community
EVALUATION SOLUTIONS

Instructions for Part III: For each skill area, identify whether it is a skill you need or want, or might need or want. For those skills that you need or will need, rate your current level of skill. After you have rated your current level of skill for skills you need or will need, circle the response that best describes how much you need to focus on developing the skill.

- Not at all – I do not need or want these skills at all
- A little – I have a little need for or interest in these skills.
- Somewhat – I sometimes need or want these skills.
- Very much – I very much need or want these skills.

Skills You Might Need or Want

Skill	Description	How much do you need or want this skill?				How much do you need to focus on developing it?		
Community leadership and mentoring	Able to enhance individual and group capacity to effectively lead; assist community members to identify personal strengths and social and structural resources they can further develop and use to enhance empowerment, community engagement, and leadership.	Not at all	A little	Somewhat	Very much	Not at all	Some	It is a priority
Budgeting, financial planning, and organizational management	Able to assess an organization's financial status compared to its goals; to leverage organizational relationships, structures, and functions or program management; to develop and implement programs, policies, and procedures.	Not at all	A little	Somewhat	Very much	Not at all	Some	It is a priority
Program development	Able to assess community issues, strengths, needs and resources; work with community partners to develop theory of change and logic model, formulate program goals and measurable outcomes, design a program to attain goals.	Not at all	A little	Somewhat	Very much	Not at all	Some	It is a priority
Program implementation	Can implement program to attain goals; recruit, train and support program staff, monitor and maintain program fidelity.	Not at all	A little	Somewhat	Very much	Not at all	Some	It is a priority
Program management	Able to manage staff, resources, and activities effectively; monitor finances; report program process and outcomes, partner with community-based organizations and individuals; ensure sustainability through community buy-in, securing funding, and regulatory compliance.	Not at all	A little	Somewhat	Very much	Not at all	Some	It is a priority
Prevention and health promotion.	Can articulate and implement a prevention perspective and implement prevention and health promotion community programs.	Not at all	A little	Somewhat	Very much	Not at all	Some	It is a priority

Susan Wolfe
and Associates

Community
EVALUATION SOLUTIONS

185

Skills You Might Need or Want

Skill	Description	How much do you need or want this skill?				How much do you need to focus on developing it?		
		Not at all	A little	Somewhat	Very much	Not at all	Some	It is a priority
Small and large group processes - facilitation skills	Able to work with small and large group processes to facilitate the capacity of community groups to work together productively.	Not at all	A little	Somewhat	Very much	Not at all	Some	It is a priority
Resource development	Can identify and integrate the use of human, material, and financial resources including community assets and social capital; use effective grant writing and fundraising skills.	Not at all	A little	Somewhat	Very much	Not at all	Some	It is a priority
Consultation and organizational development	Able to facilitate organization's goal attainment capacity growth.	Not at all	A little	Somewhat	Very much	Not at all	Some	It is a priority
Collaboration	Able to help groups with common interests and goals to do together what they cannot do apart.	Not at all	A little	Somewhat	Very much	Not at all	Some	It is a priority
Coalition development	Can facilitate inclusive coalition membership and discussion that represents views of all segments of the community; assist with developing effective structures and processes for community coalitions.	Not at all	A little	Somewhat	Very much	Not at all	Some	It is a priority
Community development	Able to help a community develop a vision and take actions toward becoming a healthy community; work collaboratively with community members to gain power to improve conditions affecting their community.	Not at all	A little	Somewhat	Very much	Not at all	Some	It is a priority
Community organizing	The ability to enter communities and work directly with community members. Includes listening, building relationships, challenging individuals, and clarifying your self-interest.	Not at all	A little	Somewhat	Very much	Not at all	Some	It is a priority
Public policy analysis	Able to translate research findings into useful information to assess impact of policies; able to analyze policies and their outcomes to determine effectiveness	Not at all	A little	Somewhat	Very much	Not at all	Some	It is a priority
Public policy development	Can write policy briefs, present testimony, draft policies, consult with policy makers at local, state/province, and federal levels.	Not at all	A little	Somewhat	Very much	Not at all	Some	It is a priority
Community advocacy	Can build and sustain effective communication and working relationships with policy makers, elected officials, community leaders; facilitate organizing individuals and communities to influence change with effective strategies.	Not at all	A little	Somewhat	Very much	Not at all	Some	It is a priority

Susan Wolfe and Associates

Community
EVALUATION SOLUTIONS

Skills You Might Need or Want								
Skill	Description	How much do you need or want this skill?				How much do you need to focus on developing it?		
		Not at all	A little	Somewhat	Very much	Not at all	Some	It is a priority
Community education and information dissemination	an provide community members information to strengthen their capacity for action; engage diverse groups in dialogue about information; tailor messages and dissemination methods to targeted audiences; promote information spread; develop capacity of individuals and organizations to use information.	Not at all	A little	Somewhat	Very much	Not at all	Some	It is a priority
Participatory community research	Can work with community partners to plan and conduct contextually appropriate research that meets high standards of scientific evidence and to communicate research findings in ways that promote community capacity to use the information.	Not at all	A little	Somewhat	Very much	Not at all	Some	It is a priority
Program and systems evaluation	Able to develop culturally and linguistically competent program evaluation methods appropriate for program context; build organizations' capacity to evaluate and use findings; collect and analyze data and report findings; conduct program evaluations that adhere to professionally accepted standards of practice, including utility, feasibility, propriety, accuracy, and accountability.	Not at all	A little	Somewhat	Very much	Not at all	Some	It is a priority
Communicating and using research and evaluation results	The ability to retrieve, describe, and apply scientific evidence; discuss the limitations of the research; and discuss, critique, and explain the scientific foundations of the field and the lessons learned historically. It also includes being able to translate research results into formats that are easily understood by non-researchers.	Not at all	A little	Somewhat	Very much	Not at all	Some	It is a priority

Susan Wolfe and Associates

Community
EVALUATION SOLUTIONS

Using the Results of this Reflection

Now that you have finished reflecting upon your characteristics, knowledge, values, and skills you can use the information to develop a professional development plan using the table below. Your timeline should cover a three-to-five-year span.

Professional Development Plan for Characteristics		
Characteristic	My development need is . . .	I will develop this characteristic by doing the following . . .	I will do this during this time-period

(Note: the table above spans four columns: Characteristic; My development need is . . . ; I will develop this characteristic by doing the following . . . ; I will do this during this time-period — with empty rows below.)

Professional Development Plan for Knowledge and Values		
Knowledge and Values	My development need is . . .	I will develop this knowledge or these values by doing the following . . .	I will do this during this time-period

Professional Development Plan for Skills		
Skills	My development need is . . .	I will develop these skills by doing the following . . .	I will do this during this time-period

Susan Wolfe and Associates

Community
EVALUATION SOLUTIONS

APPENDIX 2

Resources

Chapter 1

AEA Graduate Education Diversity Internship (GEDI). www.eval.org/gedi (accessed on November 17, 2022).

Barrington, G. V. (2012). *Consulting Start-Up and Management*. Los Angeles, CA: SAGE.

Scott, V. C. and Wolfe, S. M. (Eds.) (2015). *Community Psychology: Foundations for Practice*. Los Angeles, CA: SAGE.

Viola, J. J. and McMahon, S. D. (Eds.) (2010). *Consulting and Evaluation with Nonprofit and Community-Based Organizations*. Sudbury, MA: Jones and Bartlett Publishers.

Chapter 2

The Community Psychologist: This publication by the Society for Community Research and Action includes articles focused on community-based employment across a variety of settings. In addition to articles about different careers in the Community Practitioner column (consulting, foundations, evaluation, education), there are also life histories that describe individuals' career development in Living Community Psychology. www.scra27.org/publications/tcp/ (accessed on November 17, 2022).

The Global Journal of Community Psychology Practice: This online journal presents articles describing the application of competencies across international settings and may be especially interesting for individuals who want to pursue international work. www.gjcpp.org/en/ (accessed on November 17, 2022).

Viola, J. J. and Glantsman, O. (Eds.) (2017). *Diverse Careers in Community Psychology*. New York: Oxford University Press.

Chapter 3

Tolerance for Ambiguity

University of Maryland, College Park. (n.d.). What is your tolerance for ambiguity? www.coursera.org/learn/corporate-entrepreneurs-opportunity/lecture/Sw8B2/what-is-your-tolerance-for-ambiguity (accessed on November 17, 2022).

Appreciation for Complexity

Armson, R. (2011). *Growing Wings on the Way: Systems Thinking for Messy Situations*. Portland, OR: Triarchy Press Ltd.

Meadows, D. (2009). *Thinking in Systems: A Primer*. London and Sterling, VA: Earthscan.

Patience

Lokos, A. (2012). *Patience: The Art of Peaceful Living*. New York: Penguin Random House.

Social Skills

Bradberry, T., Parks, T., and Greaves, J. (2009). *Emotional Intelligence 2.0*. Grand Haven, MI: Brilliance Publishing, Inc.

Tact and Professionalism

Whitmore, J. (2016, April 26). The 5 elements of the consummately tactful professional. *Entrepreneur*. from www.entrepreneur.com/article/274585 (accessed on February 21, 2018).

Understanding Organizational Context

Handy, C. (2005). *Understanding Organizations* (4th ed.). New York: Penguin Global.

Handling Truth

Brandon, J. (2015). How super-confident people react to bad news. Inc. www.inc.com/john-brandon/how-super-confident-people-react-to-bad-news.html (accessed on March 4, 2018).

Comfort with Strong Emotions

Stevahn, L., King, J. A., and King, J. A. (2005). Managing conflict constructively in program evaluation. *Evaluation*, 11(4), 415–427.

Group Dynamics

Tuckman, Bruce W. (1965). Developmental sequence in small groups. *Psychological Bulletin*, 63(6), 384–399.

Political Savvy

Johnson, L. K. (2008, February 27). Sharpen your political competence. *Harvard Business Review*. https://hbr.org/2008/02/sharpen-your-political-compete-1&cm_sp=Article-_-Links-_-Top%20of%20Page%20Recirculation (accessed on November 17, 2022).

Lafair, S. (2015, August 27). 5 ways to become politically savvy at work. Inc. www
.inc.com/sylvia-lafair/5-ways-to-become-politically-savvy-at-work.html (accessed on
March 4, 2018).

Comfort with Being Alone

Brandon, J. (2013, August 23). 6 ways to combat loneliness when you're starting up.
Inc.   www.inc.com/john-brandon/6-ways-to-combat-loneliness-when-you-work-
alone.html (accessed on November 17, 2022).

Cook, G. (2012, January 24). The power of introverts: A manifesto for quiet brilliance.
Scientific American. www.scientificamerican.com/article/the-power-of-introverts/
(accessed on November 17, 2022).

Self-Motivation

Clear, J. (2018). *Atomic Habits: Tiny changes, Remarkable Results. An Easy & Proven
Way to Build Good Habits & Break Bad Ones.* New York: Avery, an imprint of
Penguin Random House.

Cohen, J. (2014, June 18). 5 proven methods for gaining self-discipline. *Forbes.* www
.forbes.com/sites/jennifercohen/2014/06/18/5-proven-methods-for-gaining-self-
discipline/#67d5e1f53c9f (accessed on March 4, 2018).

Gagne, M. and Deci, E. L. (2005). Self-determination theory and work motivation.
Journal of Organizational Behavior, 26, 331–362. https://selfdeterminationtheory.org/
SDT/documents/2005_GagneDeci_JOB_SDTtheory.pdfSelf-Discipline   (accessed
on November 17, 2022).

Patel, D. (2017, February 22). 10 powerful ways to master self-discipline. *Entrepreneur.*
www.entrepreneur.com/article/287005 (accessed on March 4, 2018).

Organizational Skills

Thomas, M. (2015, April 22). Time management training doesn't work. *Harvard
Business Review.* https://hbr.org/2015/04/time-management-training-doesnt-work
(accessed on March 4, 2018).

Walsh, P. (2005). *How to Organize (Just About) Everything: More than 500 Step-by-Step
Instructions for Everything from Organizing Your Closets to Planning a Wedding to
Creating a Flawless Filing System.* New York: Free Press.

Can You Afford to Quit Your Day Job?

Ransom, D. (2013, March 7). Can you afford to quit your day job? *Entrepreneur.* www
.entrepreneur.com/article/225937 (accessed on February 21, 2018).

Chapter 4

Cultural Humility and Anti-Racism

Diangelo, R. (2018). *White Fragility: Why It's So Hard for White People to Talk about
Racism.* Boston, MA: Beacon Press.

Dismantling Racism Works Web Workbook. www.dismantlingracism.org/ (accessed
on November 28, 2022).

Harvard University (n.d.). Project Implicit: Implicit Association Test (IAT). https:// implicit.harvard.edu/implicit/takeatest.html (accessed on November 17, 2022).

Kendi, I. X. (2019). *How to Be an Antiracist*. New York: Random House.

Kite, M. E. and Walser, S. (2018, February). Resources for teaching about prejudice and discrimination. American Psychological Association. www.apa.org/ed/precollege/ ptn/2018/02/prejudice-discrimination.aspx (accessed on November 17, 2022).

Lee, K. (2015). Effecting social change in diverse context: The role of cross-cultural competency. In: V. C. Scott and S. M. Wolfe (Eds.), *Community Psychology: Foundations for Practice (pp. 113–131)*. Thousand Oaks, CA: SAGE.

Learning for Justice. www.learningforjustice.org/ (accessed on November 17, 2022).

Resources for Responsible and Ethical Engagement. Cultural Humility. https:// community.duke.edu/wp-content/uploads/2021/02/Resources-for-Engagement.pdf (accessed on November 17, 2022).

Decoloniality

Kivel, P. (2007). Social service or social change? In: INCITE! (Ed.), *The Revolution Will Not Be Funded: Beyond the Non-profit Industrial Complex*. Durham, NC: Duke University Press.

Smith, L. T. (2021). *Decolonizing Methodologies: Research and Indigenous Peoples* (3rd ed.). New York: Bloomsbury Publishing.

Active Commitment to Improving Public Welfare, Social and Racial Justice, and Equity

Annie E. Casey's Race Equity and Inclusion Action Guide. www.aecf.org/resources/ race-equity-and-inclusion-action-guide/ (accessed on November 17, 2022).

The Community Toolbox Resources for Organizing for Equity and Justice. www .myctb.org/wst/CEJ/Pages/Principle-1.aspx (accessed on November 17, 2022).

Racial Equity Tools. (n.d.). Evaluate. www.racialequitytools.org/evaluate (accessed on November 17, 2022).

W. K. Kellogg Foundation. (2021). Doing evaluation in service of racial equity: Debunk myths. https://wkkf.issuelab.org/resource/doing-evaluation-in-service-of-racial-equity-debunk-myths.html (accessed on February 6, 2022).

W. K. Kellogg Foundation. (2021). Doing evaluation in service of racial equity: Deepen community engagement. https://wkkf.issuelab.org/resource/doing-evaluation-in-service-of-racial-equity-deepen-community-engagement.html (accessed on February 6, 2022).

W. K. Kellogg Foundation. (2021). Doing evaluation in service of racial equity: Diagnose biases and systems. https://wkkf.issuelab.org/resource/doing-evaluation-in-service-of-racial-equity-diagnose-biases-and-systems.html (accessed on February 6, 2022).

Wolff, T., Minkler, M., Wolfe, S. M., Berkowitz, B., Bowen, L., Butterfoss, F., Christens, B., Francisco, V., Himmelman, A., Holt, C., and Lee, K. (2017). Collaborating for equity and justice: Moving beyond collective impact. *Nonprofit Quarterly*, Winter 2016, 42–53.

Ecological Perspectives

Kelly, J. G. (2006). *Becoming Ecological*. New York: Oxford University Press.

Stelzner, S. P. and Wielkiewicz, R. M. (2015). Understanding ecological systems. In: V. C. Scott and S. M. Wolfe (Eds.), *Community Psychology: Foundations for Practice (pp. 63–112)*. Thousand Oaks, CA: SAGE.

Empowerment

Rappaport, J. (1987). Terms of empowerment/exemplars of prevention: Toward a theory for community psychology. *American Journal of Community Psychology*, 15(2), 121–148.

Zimmerman, M. A. (1995). Psychological empowerment: Issues and illustrations. *American Journal of Community Psychology*, 23(5), 581–599.

Community Partnership

Community Science. (n.d.). www.SenseofCommunity.com (accessed on November 17, 2022).

Viola, J. J., Olson, B. D., Reed, S. F., Jimenez, T. R., and Smith, C. M. (2015). Building and strengthening collaborative community partnerships. In: V. Scott and S. M. Wolfe (Eds.), *Community Psychology: Foundations for Practice* (pp. 237–261). Thousand Oaks, CA: SAGE.

Ethical Reflective Practice

Morris, M. (2015). Professional judgment and ethics. In: V. Scott and S. M. Wolfe (Eds.), *Community Psychology: Foundations for Practice* (pp. 132–156). Thousand Oaks, CA: SAGE.

Dedication to Continuous Personal and Professional Development

We feature some national organizations that offer professional development resources. We recommend that you also check for state and local chapters of these organizations and explore the continuing education offerings at your local university and community college.

> The American Evaluation Association. www.eval.org (accessed on November 17, 2022).
>
> The American Public Health Association. www.apha.org (accessed on November 17, 2022).
>
> The Evaluators Institute. https://tei.cgu.edu/ (accessed on November 17, 2022).
>
> The National Association of Social Workers. www.socialworkers.org (accessed on November 17, 2022).
>
> The SCRA Community Psychology Practice Council. www.scra27.org/what-we-do/practice/(accessed on November 17, 2022).

Chapter 5

Leadership and Management

The Community Tool Box, Chapters 13 through 16. Leadership and Management. http://ctb.ku.edu/en/table-of-contents (accessed on November 17, 2022).

The Foundation Center. Leadership and Management. http://foundationcenter.org/improve-your-skills/leadership-and-management (accessed on November 17, 2022).

Trautlein, B. (2013). *Change Intelligence: Use the Power of CQ to Lead Change that Sticks*. Austin, TX: Greenleaf Book Group Press.

Financial Planning and Management

The Community Toolbox, Chapter 43. Managing Finances. http://ctb.ku.edu/en/table-of-contents/finances/managing-finances (accessed on November 17, 2022).

National Council of Nonprofits. Tools and Resources, Financial Management. www.councilofnonprofits.org/tools-resources-categories/financial-management (accessed on November 17, 2022).

Community Program Development and Management

CDC National Center for Chronic Disease Prevention and Health Promotion. www.cdc.gov/chronicdisease/index.htm (accessed on November 17, 2022).

The Community Tool Box, Chapter 19. Choosing and Adapting Community Interventions. http://ctb.ku.edu/en/table-of-contents/analyze/choose-and-adapt-community-interventions (accessed on November 17, 2022).

The Community Tool Box, Chapters 20 through 26. Implementing Promising Community Interventions. http://ctb.ku.edu/en/table-of-contents (accessed on November 17, 2022).

Gargani, J. and Donaldson, S. I. (2015). *Theory-Driven Program Design and Redesign: A Practical Guide to Achieving Social Impact*. Newbury Park, CA: SAGE.

Getting to Outcomes® Improving Community-Based Prevention. www.rand.org/health/projects/getting-to-outcomes.html (accessed on November 17, 2022).

Jenkins, R. A. (2015). Planning, implementing, and developing evidence-based interventions in the context of federally funded programs. In: V. C. Scott and S. M. Wolfe (Eds.), *Community Psychology: Foundations for Practice (pp. 28–49)*. Thousand Oaks, CA: SAGE.

Lien, A. D., Greenleaf, J. P., Lemke, M. K., Hakim, S. M., Swink, N. P., Wright, R., and Meissen, G. (2011). Tearless logic model. *Global Journal of Community Psychology Practice*, 2(2), 1–12. www.gjcpp.org/ (accessed on October 16, 2016).

Wolfe, S. M., Tornatzky, L. G., and Graham, B. C. (2015). Dissemination and sustainability: Changing the world and making it stick. In: V. C. Scott and S. M. Wolfe (Eds.), *Community Psychology: Foundations for Practice (pp. 349–378)*. Thousand Oaks, CA: SAGE.

Community and Organizational Capacity Building

The Community Tool Box, Chapters 8 through 12. Developing a strategic plan and organizational structure. http://ctb.ku.edu/en/table-of-contents (accessed on November 17, 2022).

The Community Tool Box, Chapter 42. Getting grants and financial resources. http://ctb.ku.edu/en/table-of-contents/finances/grants-and-financial-resources (accessed on November 17, 2022).

Evans, S., Raymond, C., and Perkins, D. D. (2015). Organizational and community capacity building. In: V. C. Scott and S. M. Wolfe (Eds.), *Community Psychology: Foundations for Practice (pp. 89–219)*. Thousand Oaks, CA: SAGE.

Francescato, D. and Zani, B. (2013). Community psychology practice competencies in undergraduate and graduate programs in Italy. *Global Journal of Community Psychology Practice*, 4(4), 1–12.

International Society for Organizational Development and Change. https://isodc.org/ (accessed on November 17, 2022).

Office of Minority Health, U.S. Department of Health and Human Services. Assessing your nonprofit organization. https://managementhelp.org/aboutfml/diagnostics .htm#anchor421212 (accessed on November 17, 2022).

Organizational Development Network. www.odnetwork.org/ (accessed on November 17, 2022).

Viola, J. J., Olson, B. D., Reed, S. F., Jimenez, T. R., and Smith, C. M. (2015). Building and strengthening collaborative community partnerships. In: V. C. Scott and S. M. Wolfe (Eds.), *Community Psychology: Foundations for Practice (pp. 237–261)*. Thousand Oaks, CA: SAGE.

Community and Social Change

The Code of Federal Regulations. www.govinfo.gov/help/cfr (accessed on November 17, 2022).

The Congress. Resource to research current and past legislation. www.congress.gov/ (accessed on November 17, 2022).

The Community Tool Box, Chapter 4. Getting issues on the public agenda. http:// ctb.ku.edu/en/table-of-contents/assessment/getting-issues-on-the-public-agenda (accessed on November 17, 2022).

The Community Tool Box, Chapter 6. Communications to promote interest. http:// ctb.ku.edu/en/table-of-contents/participation/promoting-interest (accessed on November 17, 2022).

The Community Tool Box, Chapter 7. Encouraging involvement in community work. http://ctb.ku.edu/en/table-of-contents/participation/encouraging-involvement (accessed on November 17, 2022).

The Community Tool Box, Chapters 30 through 35. Organizing for effective advocacy. http://ctb.ku.edu/en/table-of-contents (accessed on November 17, 2022).

Jason, L. A., Beasley, C. R., and Hunter, B. A. (2015). Advocacy and social justice. In: V. C. Scott and S. M. Wolfe (Eds.), *Community Psychology: Foundations for Practice (pp. 262–289)*. Thousand Oaks, CA: SAGE.

Speer, P. W., and Christens, B. D. (2015). Community Organizing. In: V. C. Scott and S. M. Wolfe (Eds.), *Community Psychology: Foundations for Practice (pp. 220–236)*. Thousand Oaks, CA: SAGE.

Tom Wolff & Associates, Creating Collaborative Solutions. www.tomwolff.com/ (accessed on November 17, 2022).

Community Research

Ann K. Emery Newsletters and Blogs about data visualization. https://depictdatastudio .com/ (accessed on November 17, 2022).

The Community Tool Box, Chapter 3. Assessing community needs and resources. http://ctb.ku.edu/en/table-of-contents/assessment/assessing-community-needs-and-resources (accessed on November 17, 2022).

The Community Tool Box, Chapters 36 through 39. Evaluating community programs and initiatives. http://ctb.ku.edu/en/table-of-contents (accessed on November 17, 2022).

Davidson, E. J. (2012). *Actionable Evaluation Basics: Getting Succinct Answers to the Most Important Questions*. New York: Create Space Independent Publishing.

Fetterman, D. M., Kaftarian, S. J., and Wandersman, A. (2015). *Empowerment Evaluation: Knowledge and Tools for Self-Assessment, Evaluation Capacity Building, and Accountability* (2nd ed.). Thousand Oaks, CA: SAGE.

Jason, L. A. and Glenwick, D. S. (2016). *Handbook of Methodological Approaches to Community-Based Research*. New York: Oxford University Press.

Office of Minority Health, U.S. Department of Health and Human Services. (2010). Evaluation Planning Guidelines for Grant Applicants. https://minorityhealth.hhs.gov/Assets/pdf/Checked/1/Evaluation_Planning_Guidelines.pdf (accessed on November 17, 2022).

Patton, M. Q. (2008). *Utilization Focused Evaluation*. Thousand Oaks, CA: SAGE.

Patton, M. Q. (2018). *Principles Focused Evaluation: The Guide*. New York: Guilford Press.

Stephanie Evergreen Blog about Data Visualization. www.stephanieevergreen.com (accessed on November 17, 2022).

Watson-Thompson, J., Collie-Akers, V., Woods, N. K., Anderson-Carpenter, K. D., Jones, M. D., and Taylor, E. L. (2015). Participatory approaches for conducting community needs and resources assessments. In: V. C. Scott and S. M. Wolfe (Eds.), *Community Psychology: Foundations for Practice (pp. 157–188)*. Thousand Oaks, CA: SAGE.

Chapter 6

Barrington, G. V. (2012). *Consulting Start-Up and Management*. Los Angeles, CA: SAGE.

Community Evaluation Solutions Blog. www.communityevaluationsolutions.com/blog (accessed on November 17, 2022).

Community Possibilities Podcast. www.communityevaluationsolutions.com/podcast (accessed on November 17, 2022).

Glass Door. www.glassdoor.com (accessed on November 17, 2022).

Internal Revenue Service (IRS). This is a useful resource on information about taxes. www.irs.gov/ (accessed on November 17, 2022).

MBO Partners. Website to help calculate an hourly rate. www.mbopartners.com/bill-rate-calculator/income (accessed on November 17, 2022).

Small Business Administration. Instructions to prepare a business plan. www.sba.gov/starting-business/write-your-business-plan (accessed on November 17, 2022).

Starting a Small Business Partnership. Everything you need to know. www.fundera.com/blog/small-business-partnership (accessed on November 17, 2022).

Susan Wolfe and Associates Blog. https://susanwolfeandassociates.com/blog (accessed on November 17, 2022).

United States Patent and Trademark Office. Search trademark database. www.uspto.gov/trademarks/search (accessed on November 17, 2022).

Chapter 7

Rothman, J. (2003, January 1). Collaborating with other consultants. www.jrothman.com/articles/2003/01/collaborating-with-other-consultants/ (accessed on March 16, 2018).

Chapter 8

Butterfoss, F. (2013). *Ignite! Getting Your Community Coalition "Fired Up" for Change*. Bloomington, IN: Authorhouse.

Mattessich, P. W. (2003). *The Manager's Guide to Program Evaluation: Planning, Contracting, and Managing for Useful Results*. St. Paul, MN: Fieldstone Alliance.

Wolff, T. (2010). *The Power of Collaborative Solutions: Six Principles and Effective Tools for Building Health Communities*. San Francisco, CA: Jossey-Bass.

Chapter 9

Information about applying for grants and locating grant opportunities. www.grants.gov/ (accessed on November 17, 2022).

Glossary

This glossary of terms provides definitions for key terms used throughout this book. The definitions we provide are consistent with our use of these terms and may not include wider and more generalized definitions.

8(a) firm. A small business owned and operated by socially and economically disadvantaged citizens that has been accepted into the 8(a) Business Development Program.

Ableism. Discrimination in favor of able-bodied people.

Advocacy. The act or process of supporting a cause or proposal (Merriam-Webster, n.d.a).

Ageism. Prejudice or discrimination on the grounds of a person's age.

Ambiguity. The state of being uncertain (Cambridge Business English Dictionary, n.d.).

Anti-racist. One who is supporting an anti-racist policy through their actions or expressing an anti-racism idea (Kendi, 2019).

Applied anthropology. Using anthropological methods and ideas to solve real-world problems (American Anthropological Association, n.d.).

Applied social psychology. The practical application of social psychology, the exploration of interpersonal and group relationships on human behavior (American Psychological Association, n.d.b).

Applied sociology. Practitioners who use sociological theories and methods outside of academic settings with the aim to produce positive social change through active intervention (Bruhn, 1999).

Automobile insurance. A contract between an individual and an insurance company in which the individual agrees to pay premiums in exchange for protection against financial losses stemming from an accident or other damage to the vehicle.

Billable hours. Hours worked that can be charged to a client.

Blog. A website that is regularly updated, typically run by an individual or small group, and written in an informal or conversational style. It generally contains personal reflections and comments.

Board of directors. An executive committee that jointly oversees a for-profit or non-profit organization.

Branding. A marketing concept that consists of a process of creating a strong, positive perception of a company, its products, or its services.

Business liability insurance. Insurance that protects against accusations that your business caused damages, injuries, or losses.

Business owner policy. An insurance policy that combines business property and business liability insurance into one insurance policy.

Business plan. A document that sets out a business's future objectives and the strategies to achieve them.

By-laws. A set of rules established by an organization to regulate itself.

Capacity building. Whatever is needed to bring an organization or community to the next level of operational, programmatic, financial, organizational, or community maturity. The goal is to advance its mission more effectively and efficiently (Council of Nonprofits, n.d.).

C corporation. A legal entity owned by its shareholders.

Certified Public Accountant (CPA). An accounting professional who has met state licensing requirements to earn this designation through education, experience, and passing the CPA exam.

Change Intelligence. The awareness of one's own change leader style and the ability to adapt one's style to be optimally effective across a variety of people and situations.

Coalition. Partnerships of the many sectors of a community which gather collaboratively to solve the community's problems and guide the community's future (Wolff, n.d.).

Coalition development. Facilitating inclusive coalition membership and discussion that represents views of all segments of the community, assisting with developing effective structures and processes for community coalitions, collaboratives, affiliates, or networks.

Collaboration. A relationship in which each organization shares risks, responsibilities, and rewards to help its partners become the best that they can be (Himmelman, 1992). On the individual level it refers to the action of working with someone to produce or create something.

Colonialism. The colonial legacy that refers to the existence of historical colonial powers that magnify, transform, or constrain existing power relations and continue cycles of subjugation and disenfranchisement of people impacted by the colonial legacy (Chandanabhumma & Narasimhan, 2020).

Colorism. A practice of discrimination by which those with lighter skin are treated more favorably than those with darker skin. (Nittle, 2021).

Community. A unified body of individuals, such as: (1) people with common interests living in a particular area; (b) a group of people with common characteristics or interests living together within a larger society; (c) a body of persons of common and especially professional interests scattered through a larger society; (d) a body of persons or nations having a common history or common social, economic, and political interests; (e) a group linked by a common policy; (f) an interacting population of various kinds of individuals in a common location; or (g) a state, commonwealth (Merriam Webster Dictionary, n.d.b).

Community advocacy. Building and sustaining effective communication and working relationships with policy makers, elected officials, and community leaders with the purpose of facilitating the organization of individuals and communities to influence change with effective strategies.

Community-based organization (CBO). A public or private nonprofit organization of demonstrated effectiveness that: (A) is representative of a community or significant segments of a community; and (B) provides educational or related services to individuals in the community (20 USC § 7801(5)).

Community collaborative. See coalition.

Community consultant. Someone who enters a temporary relationship with a group of individuals to share knowledge, skills, and tools to build the group's capacity to reach a goal.

Community development. A skill to help a community develop a vision and take actions toward becoming a healthy community.

Community engagement. Actions or initiatives that seek to involve the community to achieve long-term and sustainable outcomes, processes, relationships, discourse, decision-making, or implementation (Penn State Department of Agricultural Economic, Sociology, and Education, n.d.).

Community leadership. The ability to enhance the capacity of individuals and groups to lead effectively, through a collaborative process of engaging, energizing, and mobilizing those individuals and groups regarding an issue of shared importance (Dalton & Wolfe, 2012).

Community organizing. The process of building power through involving a constituency in identifying problems they share and the solutions to those problems that they desire; identifying the people and structures that can make those solutions possible; enlisting those targets in the effort through negotiation and using confrontation and pressure when needed; and building an institution that is democratically controlled by that constituency that can develop the capacity to take on further problems and that embodies the will and the power of that constituency (Beckwith & Lopez, n.d.).

Community partnership. Purposeful, lasting, mutually beneficial relationships between community members or organizations and external stakeholders to work together on behalf of the community.

Community psychology. The subdiscipline of psychology that is concerned with understanding people in context of their communities, the prevention of the problems of living, the celebration of human diversity, and the pursuit of social justice through social action (Nelson & Prilleltensky, 2010).

Community psychology practice. Practice that aims to strengthen the capacity of communities to meet the needs of constituents and help them to realize their dreams to promote well-being, social justice, economic equity, and self-determination through systems, organizational, and/or individual change (Julian, 2006).

Conflict resolution. The informal or formal process that two or more parties use to find a peaceful solution to a dispute (Harvard Law School Program on Negotiation Daily Blog, 2021).

Consultant. An individual or group that enters a temporary relationship to assist a person, group, organization, or community wanting to build their capacity, accomplish a task, or achieve a goal (Lukas, 2001).

Cooperation. Networking, coordination, and sharing resources for a common purpose (Himmelman, 2001).

Coordination. Information exchange and activities with mutual benefit and no actual sharing of resources (Himmelman, 2001).

Corporation. A legal entity with a specific purpose, established by one or more individuals that is separate from its owners.

Cost-plus pricing. A pricing strategy where a markup percentage is added to the actual costs of providing a product or service.

Critical community psychology. In solidarity and close partnership with groups – oppressed through violence, exploitation, marginalization, powerlessness, or cultural imperialism – critical community psychology seeks to draw attention to the socially divisive and ecologically destructive broader patterns and structures – such as capitalism, neoliberal globalization, patriarchy, colonialism, hegemony, and racism – that condition the scope of social problems and engage in collective action to dismantle oppressive social arrangements (Evans, Duckett, Lawthom, & Kivell, 2017).

Cultural competence. Understanding the definition of culture; navigating the effects of social identities; and addressing privilege and power. The ability to interact, function, and work effectively among people who may not share your demographic attributes, language, beliefs, history, and experiences (Lee, 2015).

Cultural humility. The ability to maintain an interpersonal stance that is other-oriented (or open to the other) in relation to aspects of cultural identity that are most important to the person (Hook, Davis, Owen, Worthington, & Utsey, 2013).

Cultural responsiveness. Recognition of our personal and professional biases and awareness of our power and privilege to dialog with communities to work to address their needs.

Decoloniality. Meaningful and active resistance to forces of colonialism that perpetuate subjugation and exploitation of minds.

Deliverables. The products that will be provided during and at the end of a project.

Ecological perspective. The ability to articulate and apply multiple levels of analysis in community practice.

Empowerment. A process by which people gain control over their lives, democratic participation in the life of their community, and a critical understanding of their environment (Perkins & Zimmerman, 1995).

Epidemiologist. An individual who uses epidemiologic methods to find the causes of health outcomes and diseases in populations.

Epidemiology. This is the study of the distribution and determinants of health-related states and events in specified populations, and the application of this study to the control of health problems (Centers for Disease Control and Prevention, 2016).

Equity. The state, quality, or ideal of being just, impartial, and fair. Equity involves trying to understand and give people what they need to enjoy full, healthy lives (Annie E. Casey Foundation, 2021).

Errors and omissions insurance. A type of insurance that protects service businesses from errors and/or omissions made by a business owner, employee, or contractor working on behalf of the company.

Ethical practice. A process of continual ethical improvement; identifying ethical issues in your practice and responsibly addressing them.

Evaluation. Evaluation is a systematic process to determine merit, worth, value, or significance (American Evaluation Association, n.d.).

External consultant. A consultant who provides services to an organization or community on a contractual basis and who is not considered an employee or ongoing staff member.

Facilitation. Planning and managing a process that helps a group to achieve its goals.

Financial planning. The ability to assess an organization's current financial status compared to its financial goals.

Fixed-fee contract. A contract where the fee does not change no matter how many hours are dedicated to the project.

For-profit. An entity whose primary goal is to earn income.

Foundation. A nonprofit organization that supports charitable activities to serve the common good.

Funding Opportunity Announcement (FOA). A document U.S. federal agencies use to announce the availability of grant funds to the public.

Generalist. A person or business who has knowledge and skills or provides services in several different fields or activities.

General partnership. A business arrangement whereby all profits, losses, and management duties are normally divided equally among partners.

Getting to Outcomes™ model. A model for program development and implementation that provides a concrete step-by-step process to ensure all aspects of program design are attended to (Chinman, Imm, & Wandersman, 2004).

Global initiative. Policies and programs that inspire, fund, and act on a global basis as part of a social responsibility agenda.

Group process. How members of an organization work together to get things done, including the interpersonal dynamics.

Health equity. Everyone has a fair opportunity to be as healthy as possible.

Historically Underutilized Business (HUB). Any business formed to make a profit in which at least 51 percent of the ownership is held by one or more persons who are educationally or economically disadvantaged because of their identification with one of the following groups: African Americans, Hispanic Americans, Asian Pacific Americans, Native Americans, or American women of any ethnicity.

Independent consulting. Individually providing services on a contract basis.

Information dissemination. Providing community members with information to inform and strengthen their capacity for action. It includes tailoring messages and methods to targeted audiences, promoting information spread, and developing the capacity of individuals and organizations to use the information.

Informational interview. A meeting to learn about the real-life professional experience of someone working in a field or a company that interests you.

Informed consent. A process whereby a researcher or evaluator explains the purpose of the research, including the participant's role, how things will work, and any potential consequences or benefits.

Interdisciplinary. Involving two or more academic disciplines or areas of knowledge.

Intergenerational trauma. The transmission of the oppressive or traumatic effects of a historical event to younger generations.

Internal consultant. A consultant who provides consulting services to an organization as an employee or staff member.

Internship. A professional learning experience that offers meaningful, practical work-related experience to a student in their field of study or career interest.

Intervention. Acting on something to affect its outcome.

Joint venture. A general business partnership typically in place for a limited time or for a single project.

Leadership humility. A style of leadership whereby the leader exhibits self-awareness, appreciation of others' strengths and contributions, and openness to new ideas and feedback regarding their performance.

Liberation. The act of setting someone free from imprisonment, slavery, or oppression or providing freedom from limits on thoughts and behaviors.

Limited liability company (LLC). A pass-through structure used by many small businesses whereby owners get most of the personal asset protection of a corporation and are taxed similarly to sole proprietorships or partnerships.

Limited partnership. A business arrangement that allows partners to have limited liability and limited input into management decisions, dependent on each partner's investment percentage.

Local government. The entity with authority to determine and execute measures within an area smaller than a whole state. Examples would include cities, townships, and counties.

Logic model. A picture of how a program is intended to work. It identifies the program's main process and outcome components and how they should relate to one another (Centers for Disease Control and Prevention, n.d.).

Mastermind groups. Groups of peers who meet to give one another advice and support.

Mentor. An individual who provides support, guidance, and advice to another person.

Mentoring. The ability to assist community members in identifying community strengths and social and structural resources that they can develop further and use to enhance empowerment, community engagement, and leadership (Dalton & Wolfe, 2012).

Needs and resources assessment. A comprehensive analysis that examines the historical and existing context, conditions, assets, and capacity of the community to respond to a community issue (Watson-Thompson, Collie-Akers, Woods, Anderson-Carpenter, Jones, & Taylor, 2015).

Networking. Gathering for the purpose of meeting one another (Himmelman, 2001).

Nongovernmental organization (NGO). A voluntary group of individuals or organizations not affiliated with government that is formed to provide services or to advocate for a public policy.

Nonprofit. An organization where no part of the organization's net earnings can be used for the benefit of any private shareholder or individual.

Organizational development. An effort focused on improving an organization's capability through alignment of strategy, structure, people, rewards, metrics, and management processes.

Organizational management. Leveraging organizational relationships, structures, and functions to develop and implement programs, policies, and procedures.

Participatory approach. Substantively involving stakeholders, particularly those affected by the focal issue, in the project planning and evaluation processes including involvement in design, data collection, analysis, reporting, and management of a project and the evaluation (Better Evaluation, n.d.).

Participatory community research. Applying basic research skills to help communities identify their needs and build their capacity to engage in research.

Partnership. Dynamic and reciprocal relationships of two or more people or organizations with a shared set of goals that are developed to find mutual and practical solutions. Can also be seen as a network of constructive working relationships with clients, communities, organizations, and professional colleagues across diverse sectors and academic frames of reference (Viola, Olson, Reed, Jimenez, & Smith, 2015).

Philanthropy. An organization distributing or supported by funds set aside for humanitarian purposes (Merriam-Webster, n.d.c).

Policy. A set of general guidelines that outline an organization's or government entity's plan for managing specific issues.

Policy development. Writing policy briefs, presenting testimony, drafting policies, consulting with policy makers at local, state/province, and federal levels.

Population medicine. A series of activities, taken by one healthcare system alone or with partners in different sectors, to promote total population health beyond individual needs.

Prevention. Intervening before a problem occurs (primary), screening to identify problems in the earliest stages before the onset of signs and symptoms (secondary), or managing problems or diseases post-diagnosis to stop their progression (tertiary).

Prevention and health promotion. A set of skills to articulate a prevention-oriented intervention perspective, understand the different types of prevention (primary, secondary, tertiary), and have some knowledge of the prevention literature relevant to your areas of interest.

Primary prevention. Intervention before health effects or other negative consequences occur.

Professional development. Continuing education and career training after an individual has completed formal education or entered the workforce to develop new skills and keep existing skills current.

Professional liability insurance. Insurance designed to protect professionals against negligence and other claims initiated by their clients.

Program development. The ability to assess community issues, strengths, needs, and resources; work with community partners to develop a theory of change and logic model; formulate program goals and measurable outcomes; and design a program to attain the goals.

Program evaluation. A systematic method of collecting, analyzing, and using information to answer questions about projects, policies, and programs.

Program implementation. The act of administering a program to attain goals; recruit, train, and support program staff; monitor and maintain program fidelity.

Program management. Managing program staff, resources, and activities effectively; monitoring finances; reporting program process and outcomes; partnering with community-based organizations and individuals; ensuring sustainability through community buy-in, securing funding, and regulatory compliance.

Property insurance. A series of insurance policies that offer either property protection to cover loss or damage due to theft, fire, flood, or other reason; liability coverage for accidents and injuries that occur on the insured property.

Public administration. A branch of political science dealing primarily with the structure and workings of agencies charged with the administration of government functions (Merriam-Webster, n.d.d).

Public health. The science of protecting and improving the health of people and their communities. This work is achieved by promoting healthy lifestyles, researching disease and injury prevention, and detecting, preventing, and responding to infectious disease (CDC Foundation, n.d.).

Public policy analysis. Translating research findings into useful information to assess impact of policies; analyzing policies and their outcomes to determine their effectiveness.

Qualitative methods. Methods that produce descriptive (non-numerical) data, such as observations of behavior or personal accounts of experiences. The goal is to examine how individuals can perceive the world from different vantage points. Techniques include content analysis of narratives, in-depth interviews, focus groups, participant observation, and case studies (American Psychological Association, n.d.a).

Racial equity. A process of eliminating racial disparities to improve outcomes for everyone.

Racial justice. The systematic fair treatment of people of all races, resulting in equitable opportunities and outcomes for all.

Racism and racist. Prejudice, discrimination, or antagonism directed against a person or people based on their membership in a particular racial or ethnic group. It includes beliefs that different races possess distinct characteristics, abilities, or qualities as to distinguish them as inferior or superior to one another. Racist refers to those actions that represent or reinforce racism.

Request for applications. A formal statement that invites applications in a well-defined area to accomplish specific program objectives.

Request for proposals. A business document that announces a project, describes it, and solicits bids from qualified contractors to complete it.

Request for quotes. A solicitation for goods or services whereby an organization invites vendors to submit price quotes and bid on the job.

Resource development. Identifying and integrating the use of human and material resources, including community assets and social capital (Dalton & Wolfe, 2012).

Root cause analysis. An approach to identify the underlying causes of a problem to identify the most effective solutions.

S corporation. A corporation created through an IRS election whereby the corporation files a tax return, but the profits or losses pass through to the shareholder's income tax returns.

Scope creep. When a consultant provides services that are outside of those specified in the contract.

Scope of work (SOW). A formal agreement on work to be performed on a project.

Search engine optimization (SEO). The process of driving website traffic usually through unpaid means. SEO aims to improve your website's position in search results.

Secondary prevention. Screening to identify diseases or problems in the earliest stages before the onset of signs and symptoms.

Self-employment tax. Taxes consisting of Social Security and Medicare taxes imposed primarily on individuals who work for themselves.

Sociable. Friendly or agreeable in company; companionable; characterized by agreeable companionship (Dictionary.com, n.d.).

Social change. Changes in human interactions, relationships, cultural norms, behavior patterns, policies, and practices that transform cultural and social institutions.

Social entrepreneurship. The process and practice of identifying a group that has been marginalized, developing a solution, or finding an opportunity and bringing it forth, and facilitating the solution becoming the new status quo.

Social justice. A fair and mutual obligation in society, meaning that we are responsible for one another, and that we should ensure that all have equal chances to succeed in life (Children's Rights Education, n.d.).

Social media. Websites and applications that enable users to create and share content or participate in social networking.

Social work. A practice-based profession and academic discipline that promotes social change and development, social cohesion, and the empowerment and liberation of people. Principles of social justice, human rights, collective responsibility, and respect for diversities are central to social work (International Federation of Social Workers, n.d.).

Sole proprietorship. An unincorporated business owned and run by a single individual.

Specialist. A professional or business who concentrates primarily on a particular subject, activity, or service; a person who is highly skilled in a specific and restricted field.

Stakeholder. An individual or group with an interest in a decision or activity of an organization.

Strategic planning. An organization's process to define its strategy and direction and make decisions about allocating resources to pursue them.

Subcontractor. An individual or business who signs a contract to perform part or all of the obligations of another individual or business's contract.

Systems. A set of things that are interconnected in such a way that they produce their own pattern of behavior over time (Meadows, 2008, p. 2).

Systems approach. An approach that applies scientific insights to understand the elements that influence outcomes; models the relationships between the elements; and alters design, processes, or policies based on the knowledge to produce better results.

Systems-level change. Change that requires adjustments or transformations in the policies, practices, power dynamics, social norms, or mindsets that underlie the societal issue at stake. It often involves the collaboration of a diverse set of players and can take place on a local, national, or global level (Catalyst 2030, 2021).

Systems map. The creation of visual depictions of a system, such as its relationships and feedback loops, actors, and trends (Gray, Tyson, & Bloch, 2020).

Tact. A keen sense of what to do or say to maintain good relations with others or avoid offense (Merriam Webster, n.d.e).

Tearless Logic Model. A logic model development process that is easy to use with non-evaluators (Lien et al., 2011).

Tertiary prevention. Efforts aiming to reduce the effects of a disease or problem after it has been established in an individual or community.

Theory of change. A comprehensive description and illustration of how and why a desired change is expected to happen in a particular context (Center for Theory of Change, 2021).

Theory driven program design. The systematic application of social science research procedures and/or an explicit theoretical model that includes articulation of the causal link between the intervention and outcomes to conceptualize, design, implement, and evaluate a social intervention program.

Time and materials contracts. Contracts that pay you by the hour plus project related expenses.

Trauma. An emotional response to a terrible event or exposure to a series of events that are emotionally disturbing or life-threatening.

Trauma-informed approach. Practices that promote a culture of safety, empowerment, and healing.

Utilization focused evaluation. An evaluation approach based on the principle that an evaluation should be judged on its usefulness to its intended users. Evaluations should be planned and conducted in ways that enhance the likely use of the process and findings to inform decisions and improve performance.

Value-based pricing. A strategy of setting the price of a consultancy primarily based on a client's perceived value of a product or service.

Values. An individual or organization's principles or standards of behavior.

W2 employee. A W2 is a tax form on which businesses report annual compensation paid to an employee and the payroll taxes that are withheld from the compensation. Employees who receive a W2 are paid through an employer's payroll and have taxes withheld from their paychecks.

White fragility. A state in which even a minimum amount of racial stress becomes intolerable, triggering a range of defensive moves which function to reinstate white racial equilibrium (DiAngelo, 2011).

White privilege. The implicit societal advantages afforded to white people relative to those who experience racism (racismnoway.com.au).

White supremacy. The belief system that white people should have dominance over people of other backgrounds; that white people have their own "culture" that is superior to others; and that white people are genetically superior to others.

Women-Owned Small Business. A business that is at least 51 percent owned and controlled by one or more women, each with $6 million or less in personal assets.

Worker's compensation insurance. Insurance that provides medical expenses, lost wages, and rehabilitation costs for employees who suffer work-related injuries or illnesses.

References

American Anthropological Association. (n.d.). Applied and practicing anthropology. www.americananthro.org/AdvanceYourCareer/Content.aspx?ItemNumber=2150 (accessed on December 13, 2021).

American Evaluation Association. (n.d.). What is evaluation? www.eval.org/Portals/0/What%20is%20evaluation%20Document.pdf (accessed on December 14, 2021).

American Evaluation Association. (2022). AEA Graduate Education Diversity Internship (GEDI). www.eval.org/gedi (accessed on November 16, 2022).

American Evaluation Association. (2018). The 2018 AEA evaluator competencies. www.eval.org/Portals/0/Docs/AEA%20Evaluator%20Competencies.pdf (accessed on May 12, 2022).

American Evaluation Association. (2011, April). The American Evaluation Association (AEA) public statement on cultural competence in evaluation. www.eval.org/Portals/0/Docs/aea.cultural.competence.statement.pdf (accessed on May 12, 2022).

American Psychological Association. (n.d.a). Qualitative research. *APA Dictionary of Psychology*. https://dictionary.apa.org/qualitative-research (accessed on December 14, 2021).

American Psychological Association. (n.d.b). Social psychology applied. www.apa.org/education-career/guide/subfields/social (accessed on December 13, 2021).

American Psychological Association. (2016). APA Health Equity Ambassadors Program. www.apa.org/pi/health-equity/ambassadors (accessed on November 16, 2022).

Angelique, H. and Kyle, L. (2002). Monterey declaration of critical community psychology. *The Community Psychologist*, 35(1), 35–36.

Annie E. Casey Foundation. (2021, April 14). Equity vs. equality and other racial justice definitions. www.aecf.org/blog/racial-justice-definitions (accessed on December 14, 2021).

Armstead, T. L. (2017). Federal careers for applied community psychologists: Transitioning into a public health agency. In: J. J. Viola and O. Glantsman (Eds.), *Diverse Careers in Community Psychology* (pp. 20–27). New York: Oxford University Press.

Arnstein, S. R. (1969). A ladder of citizen participation. *Journal of the American Institute of Planners*, 35(4), 216–224.

Asare, J. G. (2021, January 14). 4 myths about white supremacy that allow it to continue. *Forbes*. www.forbes.com/sites/janicegassam/2021/01/14/4-myths-about-white-supremacy-that-allow-it-to-continue/?sh=601df2f17aac (accessed on February 5, 2022).

Axelrod, D. (n.d.). DiscoverQuotes.com. https://discoverquotes.com/david-axelrod/
quote3421379/ (accessed on August 31, 2022).

Barrington, G. V. (2012). *Consulting Start-Up and Management*. Los Angeles, CA:
SAGE Publications.

Beattie, A. (2020). The power of branding. Investopedia. www.investopedia.com/
articles/financial-theory/11/branding-ultimate-economic-moat.asp (accessed on May
16, 2022).

Beckwith, D. and Lopez, C. (n.d.). Community organizing: People power from the
grassroots. https://comm-org.wisc.edu/papers97/beckwith.htm (accessed on May 10,
2022).

Better Evaluation. (n.d.). Participatory evaluation. www.betterevaluation.org/plan/
approach/participatory_evaluation (accessed on December 14, 2021).

Blasberg, D. (2011, April 13). Lady Gaga: The interview. *Harper's Bazaar*. www
.harpersbazaar.com/celebrity/latest/news/a713/lady-gaga-interview/ (accessed on
August 31, 2022).

Bloodworth, M. (2017). Practicing community psychology in a small evaluation
and consulting firm. In: J. J. Viola and O. Glantsman (Eds.), *Diverse Careers in
Community Psychology* (pp. 147–156). New York: Oxford University Press.

Bronfenbrenner, U. (1974). Developmental research, public policy, and the ecology of
childhood. *Child Development*, 45(1), 1–5.

Brown, M. (2020, April). Becoming a trauma-informed evaluator. Online workshop
presented for the American Evaluation Association eStudy series. www.pathlms
.com/aea/courses/15601 (accessed on November 16, 2022).

Bruhn, J. G. (1999). Introductory statement: Philosophy and future direction.
Sociological Practice, 1(1), 1–2.

Busque, L. (2012, December 5). Plays well with others: Brand partnerships and your
business. *Huffpost*. www.huffpost.com/entry/plays-well-with-others-br_b_2238835
(accessed on August 31, 2022).

Butterfoss, F. (2013). *Ignite! Getting Your Community Coalition "Fired Up" for Change*.
Bloomington, IN: Authorhouse.

Butterfoss, F. and Kegler, M. (2009). The community coalition action theory. In:
R. J. DiClemente, R. A. Crosby, and M. C. Kegler (Eds.), *Emerging Theories in
Health Promotion Practice and Research: Strategies for Improving Public Health*
(pp. 237–276). San Francisco, CA: Jossey-Bass.

Cambridge Business English Dictionary. (n.d.). Ambiguity. https://dictionary
.cambridge.org/us/dictionary/english/ambiguity (accessed on May 12, 2022).

Catalyst 2030. (2021). About systems change. https://catalyst2030.net/what-is-systems-
change/#:~:text=Systemic%20change%20is%20generally%20understood,
local%2C%20national%20or%20global%20level (accessed on May 12, 2022).

CDC Foundation. (n.d.). What is public health? www.cdcfoundation.org/what-public-
health (accessed on December 14, 2021).

Centers for Disease Control and Prevention. (n.d.). Identifying the components of
a logic model. www.cdc.gov/std/program/pupestd/components%20of%20a%20
logic%20model.pdf (accessed on May 12, 2022).

Centers for Disease Control and Prevention. (2016). What is epidemiology? www.cdc
.gov/careerpaths/k12teacherroadmap/epidemiology.html (accessed on January 3,
2022).

Center for Theory of Change. (2021). What is theory of change? www.theoryofchange
.org/what-is-theory-of-change/ (accessed on May 12, 2022).

Chandanabhumma, P. P. and Narasimhan, S. (2020). Towards health equity and social justice: An applied framework of decolonization in health promotion. *Health Promotion International*, 35 (4), 831–840.

Children's Rights Education. (n.d.). Focus 2.2 – Analysis: Social justice. http://childrensrightseducation.com/22-social-justice.html (accessed on December 14, 2021).

Chinman, M., Imm, P., and Wandersman, A. (2004). Getting to Outcomes 2004. Rand Corporation. www.rand.org/pubs/technical_reports/TR101.html (accessed on November 16, 2022).

Clark, N. (2019). Building a culturally responsive independent consulting practice. In: N. Martinez-Rubin, A. A. Germuth, and M. L. Feldmann (Eds.), *Independent Evaluation Consulting: Approaches and Practices from a Growing Field. New Directions for Evaluation*, 164, 81–88.

Clayton, R. R., Cattarello, A. M., and Johnstone, B. M. (1996). The effectiveness of drug abuse resistance education (Project DARE): 5-year follow-up results. *Preventive Medicine*, 25(3), 307–318.

Collins, C. (2018). What is white privilege, really? *Teaching Tolerance Magazine*, 60, 39–41.

The Council on Linkages Between Academia and Public Health Practice. (2021). Core competencies for public health professionals. www.phf.org/resourcestools/pages/core_public_health_competencies.aspx (accessed on May 12, 2021).

Council of Nonprofits. (n.d.). What is capacity building? www.councilofnonprofits.org/tools-resources/what-capacity-building (accessed on January 3, 2022).

Dalton, J. and Wolfe, S. M. (2012). Joint column: Education connection and the community practitioner. *The Community Psychologist*, 45(4), 7–14.

Davidson, E. J. (2013). *Actionable Evaluation Basics: Getting Succinct Answers to the Most Important Questions*. New York: Create Space Independent Publishing.

DiAngelo, R. (2011). White fragility. *International Journal of Critical Pedagogy*, 3(3), 54–70.

Dictionary.com (n.d.). Sociable. www.dictionary.com/browse/sociable (accessed on May 12, 2022).

Effendi, S. (1938, December 25). *The Advent of Divine Justice*. www.bahai.org/library/authoritative-texts/shoghi-effendi/advent-divine-justice/advent-divine-justice.pdf?35f67691 (accessed on August 31, 2022).

Evaluation Toolbox. (2016). What is evaluation. Community Sustainability Engagement Evaluation Toolbox. http://evaluationtoolbox.net.au/index.php?option=com_content&view=article&id=11&Itemid=17 (accessed on November 16, 2022).

Evans, S., Raymond, C., and Perkins, D. D. (2015). Organizational and community capacity building. In: V. C. Scott and S. M. Wolfe (Eds.), *Community Psychology: Foundations for Practice* (pp. 189–219). Thousand Oaks, CA: SAGE Publications.

Evans, S. D., Duckett, P., Lawthom, R., and Kivell, N. (2017). Positioning the critical in community psychology. In: M. A. Bond, I. Serrano-Garcia, and C. B. Keys (Eds.), *APA Handbook of Community Psychology: Vol. 1. Theoretical Foundations, Core Concepts, and Emerging Challenges* (pp. 107–128). Washington, DC: American Psychological Association.

Foster-Fishman, P., Berkowitz, D., Jacobson, S., and Allen, N. (2001). Building collaborative capacity in community coalitions: A review and integrative framework. *American Journal of Community Psychology*, 29(2), 241–261.

Francescato, D. and Zani, B. (2013). Community psychology practice competencies in undergraduate and graduate programs in Italy. *Global Journal of Community Psychology Practice*, 4(4), 1–12.

Garate, T. (2017). Accidental community psychologist: From the classroom to the state capitol. In: J. J. Viola and O. Glantsman (Eds.), *Diverse Careers in Community Psychology* (pp. 50–60). New York: Oxford University Press.

Gargani, J. and Donaldson, S. I. (2015). *Theory-Driven Program Design and Redesign: A Practical Guide to Achieving Social Impact*. Newbury Park, CA: SAGE Publications.

Goldstein, M. and Daviau, J. (2017). Nonprofit support: Can you profit from working with nonprofits? In: J. J. Viola and O. Glantsman (Eds.), *Diverse Careers in Community Psychology* (pp. 157–168). New York: Oxford University Press.

Gray, D. (2010). *Start & Run a Consulting Business* (9th ed.). Bellingham, WA: Self-Counsel Press.

Gray, E., Tyson, M., and Bloch, C. (2020). Systems mapping: A vital ingredient for successful partnerships. https://rmi.org/systems-mapping-a-vital-ingredient-for-successful-partnerships/ (accessed on May 12, 2022).

Grimm, E. (2021). Establishing and honoring boundaries while consulting. AEA365 Blog. https://aea365.org/blog/establishing-and-honoring-boundaries-while-consulting-by-elizabeth-grim/ (accessed on May 22, 2022).

Harvard Law School Program on Negotiation Daily Blog (2021, December 28). What is conflict resolution and how does it work? www.pon.harvard.edu/daily/conflict-resolution/what-is-conflict-resolution-and-how-does-it-work/ (accessed on January 3, 2022).

Harvey, R. and Mihaylov, N. L. (2017). Doing community psychology internationally: Lessons learned in the field. In: J. J. Viola and O. Glantsman (Eds.), *Diverse Careers in Community Psychology* (pp. 270–293). New York: Oxford University Press.

Heywood, J. (2008). A dialogue conteinyng the nomber in effect of all the prouerbes in the englishe tongue compacte in a matter concernyng two maner of mariages, made and set foorth by John Heywood. Oxford Text Archive. http://hdl.handle.net/20.500.12024/A03168 (accessed on November 16, 2022).

Himmelman, A. (1992). *Communities Working Collaboratively for a Change*. Minneapolis, MN: The Himmelman Consulting Group.

Himmelman, A. (2001). On coalitions and the transformation of power relations: Collaborative betterment and collaborative empowerment. *American Journal of Community Psychology*, 29(2), 277–285.

Hook, J. N., Davis, D. E., Owen, J., Worthington, E. L., and Utsey, S. O. (2013). Cultural humility: Measuring openness to culturally diverse clients. *Journal of Counseling Psychology*, 60(3), 353–366.

hooks, bell (2003). *Teaching Community: A Pedagogy of Hope*. New York: Routledge.

Hutchinson, K. (2019). *Evaluation Failures: 22 Tales of Mistakes Made and Lessons Learned*. Thousand Oaks, CA: SAGE Publications.

Internal Revenue Service. (2022). Topic no. 762 independent contractor vs. employee. www.irs.gov/taxtopics/tc762 (accessed on February 28, 2022).

International Federation of Social Workers. (n.d.). Global definition of the social work profession. www.ifsw.org/what-is-social-work/global-definition-of-social-work// (accessed on November 28, 2022).

Ishikawa, K. (1990). *Introduction to Quality Control*. Translated by J. H. Loftus. Berlin: Springer Dordrecht.

Jarvis, P. (2019). *Company of One: Why Staying Small Is the Next Big Thing for Business*. Boston, MA: Mariner Books.

Jenkins, R. A. (2017). Federal careers for applied community psychologists: Pathways and roles. In: J. J. Viola and O. Glantsman (Eds.), *Diverse Careers in Community Psychology* (pp. 28–49). New York: Oxford University Press.

Jones, K. and Okun, T. (2001). *Dismantling Racism: Workbook for Social Change Groups*. www.dismantlingracism.org (accessed on November 28, 2022).

Julian, D. (2006). Defining community psychology practice: Meeting the needs and realizing the dreams of the community. *The Community Psychologist*, 39(4), 66–69.

Kelly, J. G. (1966). Ecological constraints on mental health services. *American Psychologist*, 21(6), 535–539.

Kendi, I. (2019). *How to Be an Antiracist*. London: Bodley Head.

King, C. S. (2000, February 15). *Address at Georgia State University*. https://en.wikiquote.org/wiki/Coretta_Scott_King (accessed on November 16, 2022).

Kivel, P. (2007). Social service or social change? In: INCITE! (Ed.), *The Revolution Will Not Be Funded: Beyond the Non-profit Industrial Complex* (pp. 129–150). Durham, NC: Duke University Press.

Koyenikan, I. (2016). *Wealth for All: Living a Life of Success at the Edge of Your Ability*. Fuzuay-Varina, NC: Grandeur Touch, LLC.

Lash, J. P. (1980). *Helen and Teacher: The Story of Helen Keller and Anne Sullivan Macy* (p. 489). New York: Delacorte Press.

Lee, K. (2015). Effecting social change in diverse context: The role of cross-cultural competency. In: V. C. Scott and S. M. Wolfe (Eds.), *Community Psychology: Foundations for Practice* (pp. 113–131). Thousand Oaks, CA: SAGE Publications.

Levin, G. (2017). Living community psychology: Kyrah K. Brown, Ph.D. The Community Psychologist, 50(2). https://scra27.org/publications/tcp/tcp-past-issues/tcpspring2017/living-community-psychology/ (accessed on November 28, 2022).

Lewin, K. (1936). *Principles of Topological Psychology*. New York: McGraw-Hill.

Lien, A. D., Greenleaf, J. P., Lemke, M. K., Hakim, S. M., Swink, N. P., Wright, R., and Meissen, G. (2011). Tearless logic model. *Global Journal of Community Psychology Practice*, 2(2), 1–12. www.gjcpp.org/ (accessed on October 16, 2016).

Lukas, C. (2001). *Consulting with Nonprofits: A Practitioner's Guide*. St. Paul, MN: Amherst H. Wilder Foundation.

Lyons, M. and Harrington, M. J. (2006). Entrepreneurial consulting: Some structural and personal learnings. *New Directions for Evaluation*, 111, 51–56.

Majer, J. M. (2017). Community colleges: A place for community psychology in action. In: J. J. Viola and O. Glantsman (Eds.), *Diverse Careers in Community Psychology* (pp. 189–204). New York: Oxford University Press.

Martin, A. J. (2017). Five years as a "hired gun": Working in for-profit evaluation consulting. In: J. J. Viola and O. Glantsman (Eds.), *Diverse Careers in Community Psychology* (pp. 129–146). New York: Oxford University Press.

Martin, R. L. and Osberg, S. (2007). Social entrepreneurship: The case for definition. *Stanford Social Innovation Review*. http://ssir.org/articles/entry/social_entrepreneurship_the_case_for_definition (accessed on June 26, 2016).

The Martin Luther King, Jr. Center [@TheKingCenter]. (2021, September 6). No work is insignificant. All labor that uplifts humanity has dignity and importance and should be undertaken with painstaking excellence. #MLK #LaborDay. [Tweet] Twitter. https://twitter.com/thekingcenter/status/1434889693800370184?lang=en (accessed on November 16, 2022).

Mattessich, P. W. (2003). *The Manager's Guide to Program Evaluation: Planning, Contracting, and Managing for Useful Results*. St. Paul, MN: Fieldstone Alliance.

McNamara, G. (2015, February 11). Access for all? Teach for America founder Wendy Kopp '89 on diversity, equity and education. John H. Pace Jr. '39 Center for Civic Engagement, Princeton University. https://pace.princeton.edu/news/2015/access-all-teach-america-founder-wendy-kopp-89-diversity-equity-and-education-0 (accessed on August 31, 2022).

Meadows, D. H. (2008). *Thinking in Systems: A Primer*. White River Junction, VT: Chelsea Green Publishing.

Merriam-Webster. (n.d.a). Advocacy. www.merriam-webster.com/dictionary/advocacy (accessed on May 10, 2022).

Merriam-Webster. (n.d.b). Community. www.merriam-webster.com/dictionary/community (accessed on May 10, 2022).

Merriam-Webster. (n.d.c). Philanthropy. www.merriam-webster.com/dictionary/philanthropy (accessed on May 10, 2022).

Merriam-Webster. (n.d.d). Public administration. www.merriam-webster.com/dictionary/public%20administration (accessed on May 10, 2022).

Merriam-Webster. (n.d.e). Tact. www.merriam-webster.com/dictionary/tact (accessed on May 10, 2022).

Meyer, J. (2017). The world of foundations: An ideal setting for a community psychologist. In: J. J. Viola and O. Glantsman (Eds.), *Diverse Careers in Community Psychology* (pp. 69–77). New York: Oxford University Press.

Milne, A. A. (n.d.). *Quotes*. Goodreads. www.goodreads.com/author/quotes/81466.A_A_Milne?page=3 (accessed on August 31, 2022).

National Association of Social Workers. (2015). Standards and indicators for cultural competence in social work practice. www.socialworkers.org/LinkClick.aspx?fileticket=7dVckZAYUmk%3d&portalid=0 (accessed on May 22, 2022).

Neigher, W. D., Lounsbury, D. W., and Lee, R. E. (2010). Community psychology practice in health care. *The Community Psychologist*, 43(3), 10–12.

Nelson, G. and Prilleltensky, I. (2010). *Community Psychology in Pursuit of Liberation and Well-being*. New York: Palgrave Macmillan.

Network of Schools of Public Policy, Affairs, and Administration. (n.d.). Standard 5: Matching operations – Student learning. www.naspaa.org/accreditation/standards-and-guidance/standard-standard-guidance/standard-5-matching-operations (accessed on May 12, 2022).

Nittle, N. K. (2021, February 28). The roots of colorism, or skin tone discrimination: This bias was born in the practice of human enslavement. ThoughtCo. www.thoughtco.com/what-is-colorism-2834952 (accessed on November 16, 2022).

Patton, M. Q. (2008). *Utilization Focused Evaluation*. Thousand Oaks, CA: SAGE Publications.

Penn State Department of Agricultural Economics, Sociology, and Education. (n.d.). What is community engagement? https://aese.psu.edu/research/centers/cecd/engagement-toolbox/engagement/what-is-community-engagement (accessed on January 3, 2022).

Perkins, D. D. and Zimmerman, M. A. (1995). Empowerment theory, research, and application. *American Journal of Community Psychology*, 23 (5), 569–579.

Smedley, B. D. and Syme, S. L. (Eds.) (2000). *Promoting Health: Intervention Strategies from Social and Behavioral Research*. Washington, DC: National Academies Press.

Smith, L. T. (2021). *Decolonizing Methodologies: Research and Indigenous Peoples* (3rd ed.). New York: Bloomsbury Publishing.

Solarz, A. (2013). Independent consulting: One practitioner's journey. *The Community Psychologist*, 46(3), 13–14.

Speer, P. W. and Christens, B. D. (2015). Community organizing. In: V. C. Scott and S. M. Wolfe (Eds.), *Community Psychology: Foundations for Practice* (pp. 220–236). Thousand Oaks, CA: SAGE Publications.

St. Francis. (n.d.). *The Peace Prayer of St. Francis.* www.journeywithjesus.net/poemsandprayers/554-saint-francis-of-assisi (accessed on August 31, 2022).

SUCCESS Staff. (2011, July 22). Patrick Lencioni's simple naked truth. SUCCESS. www.success.com/patrick-lencionis-simple-naked-truth/ (accessed on August 31, 2022).

Tanyu, M. (2017). Practicing community psychology in a large nonprofit research and evaluation organization. In: J. J. Viola and O. Glantsman (Eds.), *Diverse Careers in Community Psychology* (pp. 115–128). New York: Oxford University Press.

Tervalon, M. and Murray-García, J. (1998). Cultural humility versus cultural competence: A critical distinction in defining physician training outcomes in multicultural education. *Journal of Health Care for the Poor and Underserved*, 9(2), 117–125.

Texas Comptroller of Public Accounts. (n.d.). HUB certification process. https://comptroller.texas.gov/purchasing/vendor/hub/certification-process.php (accessed on May 24, 2022).

Trautlein, B. (2013). *Change Intelligence: Use the Power of CQ to Lead Change That Sticks.* Austin, TX: Greenleaf Book Group Press.

Tuckman, Bruce W. (1965). Developmental sequence in small groups. *Psychological Bulletin*, 63(6), 384–399.

United States Conference of Catholic Bishops. (2002). *Charter for the Protection of Children and Young People.* www.usccb.org/issues-and-action/child-and-youth-protection/charter.cfm (accessed on November 16, 2022).

Viola, J. J. and McMahon, S. D. (2010). *Consulting and Evaluation with Community-based Organizations: Tools and Strategies to Start & Build a Practice.* Boston, MA: Jones & Bartlett Publishers.

Viola, J. J., Olson, B. D., Reed, S. F., Jimenez, T. R., and Smith, C. M. (2015). Building and strengthening collaborative community partnerships. In: V. C. Scott and S. M. Wolfe (Eds.), *Community Psychology: Foundations for Practice* (pp. 237–261). Thousand Oaks, CA: SAGE Publications.

Watson-Thompson, J., Collie-Akers, V., Woods, N. K., Anderson-Carpenter, K. D., Jones, M. D., and Taylor, E. L. (2015). Participatory approaches for conducting community needs and resources assessments. In: V. C. Scott and S. M. Wolfe (Eds.), *Community Psychology: Foundations for Practice* (pp. 157–188). Thousand Oaks, CA: SAGE Publications.

Wheatley, M. J. (2009). *Turning to One Another.* San Francisco, CA: Berrett-Koehler Publishers.

Whitby, A. (2020, December 25). Who first said: If you want to go fast, go alone; if you want to go far, go together? https://andrewwhitby.com/2020/12/25/if-you-want-to-go-fast/ (accessed on August 31, 2022).

Whitman, W. (1860). Song of the broad-axe. *Leaves of Grass.* Boston, MA: Thayer and Eldridge.

Wolfe, S. (2017). Going solo: Community psychology as a small business. In: J. J. Viola and O. Glantsman (Eds.), *Diverse Careers in Community Psychology* (pp. 169–182). New York: Oxford University Press.

Wolfe, S. M., Long, P. D., and Brown, K. K. (2020). Using a principles-focused evaluation approach to evaluate coalitions and collaboratives working toward equity and social justice. In: S. M. Wolfe, A. Price, and K. K. Brown (Eds.), *Evaluating Community Coalitions and Collaboratives. New Directions for Evaluation* (165), 45–65.

Wolff, T. (n.d.). What coalitions are not: Coalition building tips. AHEC/Community Partners. www.tomwolff.com/resources/cb_what_not.pdf (accessed on November 16, 2022).

Wolff, T. (2010). *The Power of Collaborative Solutions: Six Principles and Effective Tools for Building Health Communities*. San Francisco, CA: Jossey-Bass.

Index

Ingram Content Group UK Ltd.
Milton Keynes UK
UKHW032249140323
418596UK00025B/305